COPING WITH VULNERABILITY

The Achievement of John Osborne

Herbert Goldstone
The University of Connecticut

UNIVERSITY
PRESS OF
AMERICA

Library of Congress Cataloging in Publication Data

Goldstone, Herbert.
   Coping with vulnerability.

   Bibliography: p.
   1. Osborne, John, 1929-   --Criticism and interpreta-
tion. I. Title.
PR6065.S18Z67 1982   822'.914   81-40912
ISBN 0-8191-2617-9
ISBN 0-8191-2618-7 (pbk.)

DEDICATION

For my mother,

Rose

ACKNOWLEDGEMENTS

First and foremost, I want to thank the Research Foundation of the University of Connecticut, and in particular the Director, Associate Dean Dr. Hugh Clark, for their encouragement and general support all the way through from beginning to end.

I also want to thank Ms. Jean Ouellette for typing several versions of this manuscript starting from scrawling longhand, and Ms. Jean Hankins for typing the final copy.

I am indebted to the press officers and staffs of the Royal Court Theatre and the National Theatre in London and the Greenwich Theatre, Greenwich, England, for access to press clippings of valuable reviews of productions of John Osborne's plays.

Permission to quote from John Osborne's works, exclusive of Look Back in Anger and A Better Class of Person (Volume I of his autobiography), comes from Faber and Faber Ltd., London. Permission for Look Back in Anger comes from S. G. Phillips, Inc., New York, New York, copyright 1957, and for A Better Class of Person from E. P. Dutton, Inc., New York, New York, copyright 1981.

CONTENTS

INTRODUCTION

i

I am writing about John Osborne, over twenty-five
years after his first success *Look Back in Anger*,
because, more than any other single playwright, he is
most responsible for the great reinvigoration of British
drama that has occurred since the 1950's--possibly the
most important development in British literature since
the end of World War II. Beginning with that play, the
dramatization of the tormented life of an articulate,
sensitive, working class intellectual, both isolated
from and yet concerned about his society, Osborne has
gone on to write some sixteen other plays, not to mention a translation, adaptations, television scripts,
and movie scenarios, that in subject matter and form
have significantly enlarged the range of experience of
the modern theatre. He has written revues, "well made
plays," and Brechtian epic theatre--to mention just a
few forms; he has written about historical figures, such
as Martin Luther, Col. Redl of the Austrian army, and
Coriolanus, and a variety of contemporary characters
with different problems; he can be very funny and very
serious and combine the two interestingly; he has
written some of the great acting parts in the British
theatre; and he has enriched dramatic language, particularly as a means of presenting the fascinating, painful, yet at times humorous, and intensely self aware
efforts on the part of his expressive main characters to
live with their complex selves, the people they need and
care about, and their society with which they are often
at odds and yet in which they are deeply involved.

At the heart of such efforts on the part of the main
characters is their passionate and articulate interaction with those they care about in their personal
lives and with the larger outside world that brings
out into the open in escalating tensions so many of
the strong pressures they are confronting.

As a result, Osborne's plays, however varied their
format, the particular issues of most concern, and the
range of emotions generated, make themselves readily
accessible to audiences and readers. Yet their very
accessibility has seemed to encourage gross oversim-
plifications and misconceptions about the nature and
quality of Osborne's achievement to date.

The most obvious oversimplification is to label most, if not all, Osborne heroes as being angry. At first glance this may not seem important but, as J. W. Lambert points out in a review of Osborne's most recent play, this is not so. The reason is that such criticism only reveals half of Osborne's vision--the contempt that is present. However, it ignores the other half, which is the undeniable emphasis on love, friendship, and kindness that has pervaded his work from the beginning.[1] Moreover, even when Osborne characters are angry, they differ considerably. For example, three of Osborne's most recent main characters, Pamela, the talented actress heroine of Time Present, Frederica, the beautiful, intellectual daughter of Wyatt Gilman, the celebrity-writer major male character of West of Suez, and Sally Prosser, the novelist second wife of film director, Ben Prosser, the major male character of Osborne's most recent play, Watch It Come Down, are angry--if that can encompass being abrasive and outspoken. Yet whether this justifies lumping them all together merely as three Osborne bitchy females, as did one reviewer, is another matter.[2] Pamela's abrasiveness and outspokenness reveal themselves most characteristically in the vigorous way she expounds to friends (who ask her) her opinions of others in the theatre. She makes no bones how many of them are mediocrities who have fooled critics, but she also expresses some admiration for them. Through hyperbole, she is trying to show her highly ambivalent reactions as well as to express her pleasure in having an audience that appreciates her energy and awareness. Frederica's abrasiveness and outspokenness reveal themselves primarily by her terse, ironical comments and probing questions designed to force those she cares about most to be more honest with themselves and others. She does so not only because she feels that they are hurting themselves but others (including herself) by undermining some of their feelings of trust. Sally's abrasiveness and outspokenness come out most strongly in free wheeling put downs directed mainly against her husband whom she holds responsible for almost all that frustrates her--and that comprises a lot.

Clearly these women differ a great deal. Yet common to all of them and what helps provide focus and depth to Osborne's characterization is their desire to love and be loved and yet their self doubts which aggravate such desires. In turn, this underlying similarity, together with the differences I've emphasized, adds complexity to his portrayal of each.

2

Even worse than oversimplification of Osborne's characters, is a serious misconception of their real natures that turns on the meaning of <u>self concerned</u>. In this regard I am referring to a tendency to dismiss many of his characters as narrow and egotistical because they care about themselves a lot.[3] However, as Willard Gaylin points out, we can't care a lot about others unless we care a lot about ourselves.[4] When we look at Osborne's characters from this perspective and observe what they care about themselves, we get a very different impression of them, one that helps us see the large, vital human context in which Osborne views them and his strong concerns about them.

To begin with, (1) they care about participating in many facets of life in their society. Yet they also feel strongly that real injustices exist in this society that make them critical of many of its values. (2) They have a sense of themselves as different or non-conformist in some respects and they value such feelings. (3) They care about setting high standards for themselves, especially in areas of achievement, and try to live up to these, particularly because of pride and conscience. (4) They value being highly self aware and honest and yet recognize how difficult such efforts can be, even with people who are understanding and sympathetic. (5) But most of all, they care a great deal about their feelings which vary greatly in range and depth and reveal themselves most noticeably in their interaction with others. Consequently, they greatly value relationships of friendship, loyalty, and love for through the right feedback they not only feel a heightened sense of their own worth and the life around them, but they hopefully might stimulate such reactions in others.

Clearly what these characters care about is considerable and reflects their awareness of many of the great potentialities that can be realized in human beings' lives. In doing so, they reveal a vitally important concern Osborne has about his characters that helps us understand the depth and complexity of his view of life. That concern is one that he shares with many modern dramatists, namely with the problem of self-realization or what we currently speak of as identity. By this, I mean at least two things, both interrelated: <u>self awareness</u>, or individuals' efforts to understand <u>their own</u> natures in their many ramifications, and <u>self-fulfillment</u>, or their efforts to come to terms <u>with their</u> natures through the dynamics of their interplay with those forces and persons who

3

most strongly affect them. As Erik Erikson, who has
contributed some of the most important pioneering
research in this area has observed, "If the dominant
problem of Freud's age was confronting our feelings of
sexuality, that for our period centers on identity."[5]
Even if we might feel that Erikson is overstating his
point, there is no doubt, merely judging from the
wealth of literature on the subject, that the problem
has received a great deal of attention in recent years.
Moreover, some compelling reasons exist as to why this
should be so. In particular, I would emphasize the
heightened pressures upon people because of rapid
changes of many kinds (as in science and technology)
and the resulting increasing complexity of many
aspects of their lives; the weakening of older, established institutions, such as church and family that in
the past have provided sources of values and stability;
the liberating effects of changing attitudes, as in
sexuality, but which also have created value conflicts;
threats to community, intimacy, and sense of self
because of the increasing depersonalization of many
areas of life; and the stifling of opportunities for
individual growth and the possibilities of a better
life, especially for the underprivileged, because of
various forms of oppression.

What is distinctive about Osborne's exploration of
this problem and makes it so pertinent is the rich
human perspective in which he views it and the dramatic contexts in which he places it because of his
strong convictions about human beings and society and
the many conflicts these engender. He creates this
perspective by focussing on the main characters who
are, as is apparent in my discussion of the wide range
of their concerns for themselves and others, acutely
aware of so many of the potentialities for such realization but, as will be evident, also aware of the pain
and difficulties that result because of what I would
call their heightened sensitivity or vulnerability.
Nevertheless, the pain and difficulties can also impel
such people to struggle to realize as much as they can
of what they most value in themselves, those they care
about, and the life around them.

As for the dramatic context, it is one in which
the main characters and others are living at close
quarters and concerned with their intimate lives and
yet simultaneously reacting to other forces that are
crucially affecting them, whether openly or internally.
These forces include the impact of a larger world outside, both that of their peer group and society, which

4

provides opportunities for realization but also creates
tensions; aspects of their past life, particularly key
relationships or crucial memories which surface as
they do in Ibsen (but in different ways); and aspects
of the recent or historical past which may still significantly affect some of their attitudes and
behavior as well as those of their society. As for
the dramatic structure, it may be an occasion, serious
or even slight, which (just by the very meeting of
people) may provide a catalyst to bring out into the
open the various feelings and attitudes I have mentioned. As a result, through a series of reversals
and discoveries, widely ranging conversations that
touch on many exposed nerve ends, or the shifting consciousness of the main characters reacting to what is
affecting them, a kind of pressure cooker force is
generated that can't be contained. Or instead of an
occasion there may be some crisis or near crisis, such
as marital tension or the impending death of a loved
one, that generates the pressure. Still a third possibility may be a crucial formative event in a person's
early career, the dynamics of which (as well as those
of other experiences), significantly affect other
phases in his life as it unfolds at different stages.
As a result, any Osborne play, however narrow its setting or slight its action, may create an atmosphere in
which, to quote Donne's poem, "one little room becomes
an everywhere." As to the nature and quality of the
explosions generated in this room, these will become
more evident when we explore some of the reasons why
the characters are so vulnerable.

    To begin with, the list of concerns or cares I've
emphasized is so impressive and exacting--living up to
high standards, acting out of a good conscience, being
deeply self honest and consistently self aware, daring
to be different, and deeply involving themselves in
many caring relationships of depth--that just to realize some of them under optimal conditions would be
demanding. For example, wanting to have a good conscience could be almost a life time's effort in
itself since a person could discover that he has a
confused conscience, an overly demanding one, or just
a minimal one. Furthermore, even under optimal conditions, some of these cares and concerns could conflict
with one another. For example, valuing high achievements might mean trying to become successful in one's
society. However, if a person has a critical view of
many aspects of his society and values himself as
being different or non-conformist, he can experience
strong conflicts. These conflicts, in turn, can

become more acute because of the character's self awareness and the need to be honest, not to mention a demanding conscience that insists upon weighing carefully the merits of conflicting demands. Conversely, not living up to high standards can generate comparable, but different, conflicts--and so on.

If, in the second place, some of these feelings of caring derive from earlier experiences that reflect considerable frustration and unhappiness, then the need to satisfy them may be all the greater. Yet by the same token the capacity for doing so may be severely limited. For example, if some of the feelings of differentness have resulted from considerable isolation, one consequence for such a person might have been that he didn't receive much love and therefore needs this all the more. As Gaylin also points out, "To care adequately for ourselves, we need others to care for us."[6] Consequently, under such conditions a person could feel differentness so acutely that he might experience what Eric Fromm describes as a "sense of separateness" that could be devastating. As Fromm has remarked in The Art of Loving, "The awareness of separateness without reunion by love is the source of shame. It is at the same time the source of guilt and anxiety."[7] It is also significant to point out that feelings of guilt and shame could make a conscience demanding in a punitive way and so create other areas of conflict. Or, to take still another example, if feelings of differentness are associated with those of inferiority as a member of a lower social class, then the difficulties of having an adequate sense of self worth become all the greater. Consequently, differentness can seem to be such a burden that a person may try to compensate by trying hard to conform in some areas of society. Yet doing this may militate against other values he esteems.

If, in the third place, one reason to set high standards results from a need to prove oneself in order to deserve love rather than feel it unconditionally, then these expectations can seriously affect a person's sense of self worth or his need to care adequately for himself. Since one of the strongest traits of an Osborne character is a capacity to love others and be loyal to them, then the effort to live up to standards of loved ones becomes all the greater. Yet again the capacity for feeling worthy to do so may become less, especially if the character's values differ from those of loved ones.

6

In the fourth place, the main character's acute sensitivity to others' feelings, which makes feedback so stimulating and the giving and receiving of love so enriching, can also greatly accentuate his sensitivity in a number of ways. If, for example, his doubts about self worth also comprise guilt or shame feelings from earlier experiences, then he may feel all the more intensely the need for feedback. Yet he may feel so apprehensive about his worthiness to receive such feedback that this causes him both to seek it and yet distrust it. As a result, he may strike out in self destructive behavior which, in turn, can hurt those whom he needs above all to understand and support him. Besides, persons so sensitive to others' feelings, as Osborne's characters are, may pick up from the latter many of their feelings and internalize them. If, for example, the latter also feel guilt, not to mention other emotions, as so many of them do in Osborne's plays, such feelings may so affect those of the main character, already burdened with conflicts from earlier experiences, that he will feel these all the more acutely in a present relationship. As a result, he may experience feedback that can make already painful feelings of low self worth and guilt almost unbearable. In this context and others, we could do well to remember R. D. Laing's observations in The Politics of Experience that the way others experience us significantly affects the way we experience ourselves.[8] For characters so responsive as Osborne's are to feedback, such experiencing can accentuate vulnerability in many areas.

Just from the few examples of vulnerability I've cited, it is apparent how closely related, pervasive, and painful such feelings can be within a person. Consequently, we might at this point conclude how despairing the results might be. Yet need this really be the case? To be able to confront so many aspects of one's life forcefully and to feel the impact so acutely can also reveal strength, resilience, understanding, and determination. Moreover, if one also has, as most of these characters do even at their lowest point, energy and a sense of humor, then the outcome can reveal sources of hope.

Obviously, just from this brief discussion, some compelling reasons exist for writing about Osborne's work. Yet at least one other reason I haven't mentioned exists. That is, that all of the books written about his plays to date were completed in 1969 or shortly thereafter. Consequently, they have little, if

7

anything, to say about his most recent works. Nevertheless, Osborne has written three plays, in particular, that have received highly mixed reviews and certainly need more sustained attention than they have received to date. These are West of Suez, a play about an aging writer and his four daughters spending Christmas reunion at a West Indian villa belonging to one of them; A Sense of Detachment, a free wheeling, Hellzapoppin' revue that spoofs social mores and facile role playing; and most recently Watch It Come Down, a play about the failure of a marriage and of a commune supposedly based on mutual need. Mary Holland in reviewing West of Suez felt that she was seeing the play only because she had been sent to do so and out of loyalty to Osborne's earlier work.[10] On the other hand, Helen Dawson spoke of the play very favorably as "brave and loving and providing an impressive evening in the theatre."[11] In reviewing A Sense of Detachment, Benedict Nightingale spoke of the "Disintegration of John Osborne."[12] In contrast, Michael Billington described the play as inventive ans masterful, an original work.[13]

To come nearer to home, almost all of the reviews of Osborne's newest play, Watch It Come Down, have been unfavorable and markedly so. J. W. Lambert begins one of the few moderately favorable reviews by acknowledging that the faults of the play are too obvious to mention.[14] One such is high flown language.[15] For example, Ben Prosser (Sally's husband) eulogizes a dead writer homosexual friend of his (modelled on Lytton Strachey) in these words: "But he didn't trim, he didn't deceive himself, he preserved his precious English personality and grinned at everyone--". Here the alliteration and phrasing create a combination that is ornate and stilted. But, since Ben is being portrayed as both a sentimentalist and snob, such language might be appropriate here.

Moreover, even if we should still prefer earlier Osborne to his later work, we may appreciate the former all the more pointedly when we realize how consistent and yet varied his work has been from the beginning.

Clearly, Osborne's concerns, as I've been describing them, have great relevance for us today, aware as we are of how much the pressures and insecurities he describes pervade many areas of our lives. Osborne helps make us understand how much we can hurt ourselves and one another, particularly when we live in societies that do considerable damage to our potential for caring.

This awareness of where we may be hurting most at a particular time in the present may explain what Frank Marcus had in mind at the end of his review of Watch It Come Down. After acknowledging many reservations, he concluded that, nonetheless, the play may be important because Osborne again, as in the past, may be taking our current moral temperature accurately.[16]

But equally important, Osborne also shows us how much we can do to find sources of strength arising out of these needs, particularly if we remain vital, honest, judiciously self aware, able to trust ourselves and others, and willing to assume as much responsibility for our lives as we can.

While almost all Osborne plays have the kind of format I've described so that they might seem to lend themselves to some kind of common approach or grouping, they differ significantly because each presents its particular areas of vulnerability, its distinctive characters and society, and its own dramatic shape, emotional tones, and even language. For all these reasons, it is best to explore each play separately in depth and in a way appropriate to each. This is what I propose to do by focussing on the plays I consider Osborne's best to date: Epitaph for George Dillon, Look Back in Anger, The Entertainer, Luther, Inadmissible Evidence, A Patriot For Me, A Bond Honoured, Time Present, The Hotel in Amsterdam, West of Suez, A Sense of Detachment, and Watch It Come Down. In some cases this means that I have relied more on certain aspects of the play than others, and that proportionately I have gone into more detail in discussing Osborne's three most recent plays, not necessarily because they are his best but because they depend on many rapidly shifting contrasts of varying dimensions that don't easily lend themselves to compression or selectivity.

However, before exploring each play separately, I want to point out some details of Osborne's life as we know of them, some of his values as a writer that emerge from his occasional journalistic pieces and interviews he has granted over the years, and some features of the post World War II England that affect his work, for these help us better understand some of the features I have been stressing about his plays.

ii

So far as Osborne's life is concerned, we are particularly fortunate now, because in addition to interviews and occasional pieces that have come out since 1956, there has just appeared Volume I of his auto-biography, <u>A Better Class of Person</u>,[17] which in roughly chronological form presents the first twenty-six years of his life up through the acceptance by George Devine and the English Stage Company of <u>Look Back in Anger</u>. <u>A Better Class of Person</u> is important not only because of what it reveals about some of the major forces that have shaped Osborne's life, but also as a literary work in its own right for its sharply focussed detail, its striking contrasts in tone, especially from wry humor to stabbing pain, and its compelling, if also disquieting, insights into human nature.

John Osborne was born on December 12, 1929, in Fulham, London, where he spent the first five years of his life before his family moved out to more suburban Stoneleigh, near where his father's parents lived. His mother, Nellie Beatrice Grove, came from an upper working class background, her father having been a fairly prominent publican, and Mrs. Osborne herself has worked most of her life as a bar maid. Osborne's father, Thomas, came from a family of impoverished gen-tility, his father having lost his jewelry business because he spent too much of his time playing cricket. During the years that Osborne knew the latter, he was little more than a flunkey, since he kept busy doing errands for his wife, and he subsisted on pittances she gave him from money she earned in alternate years by taking care of the son of her nephew, a civil servant in Africa who was able to have his wife but not child stay with him every other year. Osborne's father from early life on was sickly. When he was sixteen, he won first prize in a contest, the award for which was a free trip to South Africa. Despite strong family objec-tions, young Osborne accepted the prize. Unfortunately he suffered such a severe asthma attack en route that at Gibraltar he had to be removed from the boat, hos-pitalized, and then sent back by train to England, all at his family's expense. Mr. Osborne's mother not only never forgave her son for incurring such expenses but badgered him so much that he agreed to will over to her his estate, such as it was, to repay the debt. Osborne saw little of his father during his youth since the latter was away much of the time convalescing from tuberculosis. Moreover, even when Mr. Osborne was able to work at his job as an advertising copy writer, he wasn't around the house a lot since he and his wife apparently didn't get along too well and so for con-siderable periods of time remained unofficially separated. When Osborne was eleven, his father died.

10

At this point I should add that Osborne had a sister a
year younger than himself who died, also of tuberculosis, when she was two.

Because of the details I've mentioned, Osborne not
only grew up as an only child but a heavily burdened
one. He accompanied his father on visits to the latter's parents where he had to listen to reproaches
heaped upon his father because of what happened at
Gibraltar. In addition, Osborne had to serve as a
sounding board for his mother as she poured out many of
her complaints about her life.

Not only did Osborne witness a lot of illness, he
also experienced a great deal himself, as well as
other sources of pain. Since early childhood, he was
sickly and scrawny and had a long siege of rheumatic
fever which necessitated his lying on his back for
almost a year and then recuperating for two years in a
grubby public convalescent home. In addition, Osborne
frequently had to change schools since his mother constantly kept moving from one apartment to another
because she was perennially dissatisfied with every
place to which she insisted on moving. One consequence
was that Osborne, as a newcomer, was forced into
fights which he always lost. Nor was being beaten up
the only painful consequence of Osborne's relations
with people his own age. During these years he had
just two friends his own age, and one of them, a girl
named Joan Buffen, treated him, as I want to show
later, with great disdain.

As for Osborne's schooling itself, it was desultory
since, except for one brief period he spent at a third
rate public school, St. Michael's, to which he was sent
as a follow up from his convalescence from rheumatic
fever, his teachers paid him little attention and were
boring to listen to. Although Osborne did receive
some encouragement from the headmaster at St. Michael's
and did well on some preparatory examinations, he was
expelled for hitting the headmaster when the latter
slapped him hard and unexpectedly in public. Embarrassing as the dismissal was, it did provide Osborne with
the opportunity for a freer, more varied life than he
had previously known.

Even though Osborne had few vocational skills, he
was able on his return home to get a job for some trade
journals as a reporter. Here he made friends with one
of the journal editors, a Canadian named Arnold Running,
who liked Osborne and encouraged him to write. At the

same time Osborne decided to do something to overcome his feelings of social backwardness and began taking dancing lessons. Not only did he discover that he was a good dancer but that he had made quite an impression on an attractive, sincere young woman in the neighborhood, Renee Shippard, who was also taking lessons. Before Osborne quite knew what has happening, he found himself encouraged by Renee's parents to become engaged. However, almost as quickly, he became aware of how narrow and stifling such a projected life as a lower middle class suburbanite could be. Besides the entrapment of marriage, Osborne also felt that he was, like so many other young men of his age, doomed to two years of military service as a draftee. However, much to his surprise, Osborne discovered that his physical disabilities, for which he was not responsible, disqualified him once and for all from military service of any kind. Therefore he was free to begin establishing a life of his own away from Renee, even if this meant hurting her and her parents. At this point Osborne had some more luck because his dancing teacher praised him for what she regarded as his innate acting talent and encouraged him to join a local amateur theatre company. On the strength of this experience and his obvious desire to take more control of his life, Osborne got a job as Assistant Stage Manager with a touring theatrical company. Not only did the position give Osborne experience in assuming varied responsibilities, but it provided him with an excuse to use as a basis for terminating his engagement to Renee (in a letter which he describes as "long winded, dishonest, and evasive, larded with banalities about Life, Art, and God"). Nevertheless, the letter achieved its purpose, and Osborne was free to devote himself to the theatre and a more diversified and exciting personal life. Professionally, from this point on, except for brief periods of unemployment or temporary jobs, Osborne spent the years up to the writing of Look Back in Anger working in a variety of companies as Assistant Stage Manager, getting some acting experience and, most important, writing in collaboration plays of varying quality.

His first such effort was a play entitled The Devil Inside Him, which he did with Stella Linden, an attractive, sexually overpowering actress in one of the companies in which he worked and with whom he was having an affair that at least for a while did wonders for his ego (until Stella terminated it, as she warned that she would, when it began interfering with her career and personal life). As for the play itself, it was based

12

on a melodramatic script Osborne had begun about a romantic young Welshman, and it was eventually put on for one performance at Huddersfield. Whatever originality the play might have had, despite its obvious crudeness, was eliminated by Stella's ruthless play doctoring based on her rigid and simplistic ideas of commercial audience expectations.

Much more important artistically were two plays that Osborne did in 1954-55 with Anthony Creighton (with whom he was involved in a repertory company at Hayling Island in 1950 and with whom he became friendly). The first, entitled Personal Enemy, derived from Osborne's interest in Senator Joseph McCarthy's anti-Communist witch hunting which was then at its height. Osborne, aided by Creighton who supplied a melodramatic plot framework of a thriller, wrote dialogue apparently based on actual testimony that showed how destructive such tactics could be. Although Osborne was unsuccessful in getting the American actor Sam Wanamaker (who was then appearing in London and was one of the targets for McCarthy's attacks) to put on the play because the latter feared that British audiences wouldn't tolerate its anti-American politics, he did have the satisfaction of knowing that Wanamaker was impressed by the work. The other was Epitaph for George Dillon which derived from an experience that happened to Creighton (while he was working as a bill collector) when two middle aged women took a strongly maternal interest in his career. For now it is enough to say that Osborne found this collaboration in Epitaph for George Dillon more satisfying than either of the others because he could concentrate even more on what he liked best, character development and confrontation, while Creighton willingly restricted himself to exposition and minor plot details. Just as important, Osborne could control the pace of the writing, and he had the satisfaction of knowing that Creighton, unlike Sheila, accepted his standards.

So far as Osborne's personal life with women is concerned, just the brief description of his affair with Stella shows how much more exciting it was than that with Renee. However, in addition, Osborne had two other involvement with actresses. The first was with Sheila, a romantic and expressive actress younger than Stella, who resisted all of Osborne's attempts to seduce her by exhibiting hysterical symptoms at just the right time.

The second, which was much deeper and more painful, was Osborne's marriage to Pamela Lane, a young actress whom he met when both were members of a repertory company in Pamela's home town of Bridgwater. While all of the women with whom Osborne was involved impressed him from the beginning, none affected him as strongly as did Pamela. From the moment that he first saw her when they were playing minor parts in one of the company's productions, Osborne was so stricken that he felt virtually helpless. In part he felt drawn to her as a fellow rebel since she had cut her hair to the bone to show her defiance of her local public that expected her to live up to their conventional expectations of how an actress should look and act. In part she made such an impression because of her large green eyes which, as he remarks, " . . . must mock or plead affection, preferably both at least." Still another reason may have been Osborne's misunderstanding of Pamela's temperament. "Pamela's emotional equivocation," he observes, "seemed so unstudied that I regarded it as ineffable passion." If all the foregoing reasons weren't enough, the strong opposition to his involvement that came from local residents and Pamela's family (who hired a private detective to watch his movements) made Osborne all the more determined to have Pamela as his own. He proposed; she accepted, as he states, "warmly and casually"; and despite opposition and intrigue that almost seemed like comic opera, they were married.

As for their married life, which was spent mainly in and around London where both continued their careers, what stood out was its continuing precariousness and their growing estrangement. In part, such consequences were difficult to avoid because they were forced to remain apart from each other so much. Yet to a greater extent these consequences resulted because Osborne discovered how increasingly lonely and insecure he felt while Pamela was away, and yet how easily she accepted such separations, especially as she was getting better parts and improving her acting noticeably.

It is true that Osborne sensed that they were drifting further and further apart. Yet he continued to resist such awareness, all the more so when Pamela managed to get her company, then playing in Derby, to hire him, and he, upon arriving, noticed how well she was looking. However, when they were finally alone, she let the truth out as she told him "uncomplainingly that she found marriage and a career difficult."

14

Osborne was so stunned by what he regarded as her hackneyed and superficial answer that he couldn't reply. "Sweet reason," he remarks, "was unanswerable, demoralizing as it did unconfident reason or passion." Under these circumstances, he couldn't feel any malice on either side. "Almost soothingly," he concludes, "she had wiped our slate out." It is true that they remained together for a while at Derby, and Osborne continued to hope, despite his learning that Pamela had been unfaithful to him earlier and was going on holiday with someone else, that she might come back. However, for all practical purposes, their relationship ended that first night in Derby.

What seems almost like a footnote, I might add, is Osborne's brief notation, some twenty pages later in A Better Class of Person and one year later chronologically, that he wrote Look Back in Anger in just over a month. Yet this very terseness might indicate how far he had progressed in coming to terms with the experience, since some of it, as he freely admits (especially Pamela's coolness and parental opposition), underlies Look Back in Anger.

iii

Just from these details I've emphasized, at least three strong impressions emerge. The first is how much of Osborne's life before he became famous involved the theatre. In particular, he consistently saw the differences between mediocrity or hackneyed commercialism, such as that of Stella and others, and honest efforts to have standards and a voice of one's own, even if these were not recognized immediately. Yet even Osborne's disdain for mediocrity didn't keep him from appreciating good acting wherever he found it and of entertainment as a source of energy, joy, and shared human experience.

The second, as the accounts of illness and schooling for example show, is how much pain Osborne experienced. Yet the details I've mentioned represent just the tip of the iceberg. The feelings, attitudes, and behavior of his family, as well as the social environment in which he grew up, created, if possible, even more anguish.

To begin with, Osborne received very little attention from the people around him. At the end of the first chapter of his autobiography, he observes, "Throughout my childhood no adult addressed a question

15

to me . . . " even though a few pages later, he notes,
" . . . but then I was the only one who seemed to listen to anybody. They didn't talk to each other so much
as barrack themselves." What is more, the kind of
attention Osborne did receive from adults often constituted outright rejection. For example, immediately
after stating that no adult addressed a question to him,
Osborne goes on to say:

> When I was at boarding school, when I went
> out to work, until the day she died when I
> was thirty, my father's mother never once
> asked me anything about myself. I think she
> had a glancing fondness for me. If I volun-
> teered information, she would smile a thin
> winter of contempt and say nothing. Or change
> the subject firmly. To how well my cousin
> Tony was doing at Sandhurst. How her niece
> Jill was engaged to such a nice young man.
> Who had been to Blundells School and had a
> very high position in Lloyds Bank in Lombard
> Street. I was convinced that her dismissive
> smile was aimed only to chill my father's
> coffin yet again.

Yet painful as the foregoing, as well as other
comparable incidents must have been, it doesn't compare to the impact that resulted because of the kind
of attention that he did receive from his mother
(about whom I also want to say more later). For now
it is enough to call attention to what Osborne continually calls the "Black looks" that she gave him
for almost anything that he did. Even as an adult, he
could expect them as soon as he came in the door. To
make matters worse, after his father's death, his
mother not only would give him one of her Black looks
but also would let him know that his behavior was also
affronting his father's memory, even though the opposite was probably true, since, after his father's
death, he frequently made choices by ascertaining what
he thought his father would do in such a situation.

Just as members of Osborne's family could hurt him
emotionally, so could people on the outside, especially
those who came from a higher class or fancied themselves, to paraphrase the title of his autobiography,
'a better class of person.' A very good example of
such social cruelty would be some of the treatment
Osborne received from Joan Buffen (a young girl I've
already referred to), with whom at the age of nine he
became friendly. It is true that Joan, to whom he was

16

was attracted because she was vigorous and daring, did initiate him into some mysteries of sex and invited him to her home a number of times. Nevertheless, Osborne felt feeply hurt when Joan's cousin (who went to one of the right schools) appeared for a visit. Although Joan still saw Osborne during this time, it was clear to him where her preference lay and how deeply inferior he came to feel:

> I began to see that my longing for any scrap of affection, friendliness or even tolerance would come to nothing. The crumbs would diminish and be given with less and less grace until they were withdrawn altogether. I was a makeshift, and a poor and fleeting one at that. When her cousin left, I would be reprieved. For a day or two she would smile on my enthusiasm until her patience broke again. Seeing my misery only urged her on to throw me back to whence I came, like an amusing mongrel who quickly proves his dull breeding, untrained, untrainable, and ultimately unrewarding.

To add to Osborne's pain, he had to listen to his mother telling him regularly that such treatment was what he should expect in life. "My mother," he points out, "always made it clear that my place in the world was unlikely to differ from her own. There was no reason why Mrs. Buffen or her daughter should care to speak to me. I had nothing to offer the Buffens, therefore why should they bother to acknowledge my existence . . . "

Besides feeling the pain of inferiority (accentuated, I might add, by his awareness of how undesirable he was because of his "weak body, blemished skin, ugly limbs, teeth, and dandruff"), Osborne had to spend many years around people, mostly his family, who led joyless, narrow lives. For one thing, almost all of them filled their days with petty routine. His mother spent every Friday cleaning so angrily and noisily that his father preferred remaining at his parents' home during this time, despite the rebukes he would experience there. As for Grandmother Osborne, every afternoon she ate chocolates, read one newspaper and a novel by Warwick Deeping, and then dozed off, although stoutly denying that this was taking place; as for Grandfather Osborne, all that he did was to take a nap until tea time. Although these and other examples I could mention seem harmless enough, yet the tragedy is, as

17

Osborne points out, that such routine repressed whatever vitality and sexuality they may have felt: "Grandfather Osborne, poor neutered old dog, was to die in 1941, going without his oats for thirty eight years. I thought of them in their feather bed, of the old man lying upstairs alone every afternoon, Annie [his wife] downstairs reading the South Wales Argus. What were his thoughts. Denied affection, sex, respect, even the work he shunned . . . "

Considering how empty these people's lives were, it isn't surprising that they should be bitter, unhappy, and resigned. Whatever the reason may be, such feelings became most articulate and disquieting at Christmas time in what turned out to be the most important and yet distressing ritual of all, the annual family row when all the accumulated bitterness of so many years would, as Osborne put it, "claim its victims long before the Christmas wrappings had been thrown away." It is true that the rows differed in some ways. That of the Grove family was more violent and often used religion for its fuel. In comparison, that of the Osborne family was more subtle and enduring in its effects. Nevertheless, as Osborne makes clear in one of the most powerful descriptions in the book, profound disappointment dominated both:

> Disappointment was oxygen to them. Their motto might have been ante coitum triste est. The Grove despond was all chaos, shouting and tearful rebukes. Their battle cries were: 'You've always had it easy.'...'You didn't have to go out to work like I did when I was twelve.'...'You were always Dad's favourite.' ...'What about you and Mum then?'...'I've worked hard for everything I've ever had.' The Osborne slough was full of sly casual strokes, all the more wounding to my mother because no one said openly what they meant, not about money and certainly not about property, but about emotional privilege, social advantage, hypocrisy and religiosity against ordinary plain dealing. The Osbornes appeared to preserve calm while being more succinct and specific. Their bitterness and sense of having been cheated from birth were certainly deeper. If my mother tried to wade in to an Osborne Row she was soon made speechless by the cold stare of Grandma and the passing looks of amusement between her and Nancy as my mother mangled the language and

mispronounced words and became confused at
their silences. 'Did you see that?' she'd
say afterwards. 'They were passing looks.'
She would flush through her flaking Tokalon
powder, bite her nails and turn to my father
for support, which seldom came.

For Boxing Day, Grandma Osborne had per-
fected a pumpkin trick which turned all the
cold Christmas pudding and mince pies suddenly
into funeral baked meats. She did it almost
on the stroke of five and in one wand-like
incantation. Lying back in the Hymnal position, she would close her eyes, smile her
thin gruel of a smile and say, 'Ah, well,
there's another Christmas over.' I dreaded
the supreme satisfaction with which she laid
the body of Christmas spirit to rest. In
this one phrase she crushed the festive
flower and the jubilant heart. On New Year's
Eve she used less relish in confirming that
there was little reason to feel good about the
year passing and certainly less about the
coming one.

Undeniably such infighting could well provide
Osborne with rich dramatic material, but at what a
human cost so far as it could affect belief in trust,
goodness, and the joy of life!

Yet even more distressing than the fall out connected with the family row was that which resulted from
the feelings about love that dominated Osborne's
mother (and to a lesser extent members of her family).
While Osborne points out many examples of this attitude
perhaps none is more revealing and devastating than
the very first mention he makes of it, namely when he
comments about the reasons that his mother's family
strongly disapproved of Auntie Winnie, one of Grandmother Grove's sisters:

. . . Her affectionate nature didn't seem to
be returned by her sisters who dismissed her
with, 'Poor old Auntie Winn, she'll never
leave that place.' No one made any effort to
see that she might. They were all pushy in
their way, tolerating one another peevishly
rather than having any actual exchange of
feelings. If one of them died, fell ill or
short of money it was something to be talked
about rather than experienced in common. It
was as if they felt obliged to live within

the literal confines of their emotional circumstances. The outlet for friendship or
conviviality was narrow in spite of the
drunken commiseration, endless ports and
pints of beer and gin and Its. This may in
part explain my mother's stillborn spon-
taneity and consistent calculation that affection had only to be bought or repaid in the
commonest coinage. 'He doesn't owe you anything,' or 'You don't owe him anything.'
'What's she ever done for you?' These were
the entries that cooked the emotional and
filial books. They were chill words, flaunt-
ing their loveless, inexorable impotence.

It would be difficult to imagine a harsher, more
despairing description of cold heartedness than "flaunt-
ing their loveless, inexorable impotence," unless it
would be a later passage which comes after the comment
I've already quoted about Mrs. Osborne's insistence
that because her son had nothing to offer people like
the Buffens, he could hardly expect them, as indicated,
to acknowledge his existence. Immediately afterwards,
Osborne goes on to say, "It was consistent with her
[his mother's] view of affection or friendship as a
system of rewards, blackmail, calculation, and aggran-
dizement in which people would only come off best or
worst. Nothing ever strikes me with such despair and
disbelief as the truly cold heart. It disarms utterly
and never ceases to do so. I wish it were otherwise."
Although Osborne in the first passage quoted recognizes why his mother and people like her react as they
do, he still tries to shield himself from the impact
of such behavior. However, such efforts on his part
became increasingly difficult, as two other examples
pointedly show.

The first centers on his mother's behavior at the
time of his father's death and its effect on Osborne
who was then eleven. Despite his mother's insistence that Osborne should stay with her when it became
obvious that his father's death was imminent, Mr.
Osborne's doctor mercifully arranged that Osborne
should stay with friends who lived nearby. However,
immediately after her husband's death, Mrs. Osborne
insisted again that her son should return at once.
Although Mrs. Osborne was prevailed upon to let her
son stay away one more day, as soon as he returned she
took him to view his father in the coffin. Osborne
describes this scene, like that of the family row, in
stark detail:

. . . The smell in the room was strong and strange and, in his shroud, he was unrecognizable. As I looked down at him, she said, 'Of course, this room's got to be fumigated, you know that, don't you. Fumigated.' Frumigated was how she pronounced it. With my father's body lying in the bedroom across the landing, I had been obliged to share my briefing room with my mother, who spent hour upon hour reading last Sunday's News of the World, the bright light overhead, rustling the pages in my ear and sighing heavily. For the first time I felt the fatality of hatred.

It is no wonder that from this point on Osborne could never again refer to his mother as "Mum" or "Mummy," as he used to, all the more so since she apparently had no idea as to why the change occurred.

The second example is one of a number of entries from Osborne's diary (dated 1955) that he includes in the text of A Better Class of Person. After he notes what must have been a standard response that his mother made about theatre acquaintances that he brought home ("I'll say that for him--he's never been ashamed of me. He's always let me meet his friends-- and they're all theatrical people, a good class all of them, they speak nicely") there follows this entry: "I am ashamed of her as part of myself that can't be cast off, my own conflict, the disease which I suffer and have inherited, what I am and never could be whole. My disease, an invitation to my sick room." Despite all of Osborne's efforts to the contrary, such as the quotations I've cited about the effort to deny the impact of cold heartedness, he feels that his mother has profoundly, if not irrevocably, affected his life because, to restate Willard Gaylin's observation to which I've already referred, the way that others care about us affects the way we care about ourselves. Clearly Osborne's journal entry expresses profound disappointment that verges on self punishment.

Although he may regard such feelings of self punishment as unfair, unlike members of his family for whom disappointment was oxygen, Osborne realizes that he has so deeply internalized feelings he is describing that they are uniquely his. However, unlike members of his family on Christmas day, he can't escape by projecting them onto others. This awareness leads to the third strong impression that emerges from reading A Better Class of Person--the necessity to assume full

21

responsibility for one's life and to cope with all its
limiting conditions as hopefully as one can, however
difficult, complex, and even misunderstood such efforts
may be.

In this regard the one person in Osborne's family
who honestly made such efforts, restricted as they
were, was his father. This constitutes a strong
reason why Osborne admired the latter so much. Significantly, the very first episode Osborne recalls in
A Better Class of Person is that of his father waving
goodbye to his mother and himself from the window of a
train that was taking him to a sanitarium from which
all three knew that he was unlikely to return. Nevertheless, his father leaned out the window, smiled, gave
Osborne a ten shilling note, and said, "Take your
mother to the pictures, son, and then go to Lyons
Corner House."

An incident such as this helps make clearer
Osborne's comments that he made in an interview with
John Freeman in a volume called The Playwrights Speak
(edited by Walter Wager). In the interview Osborne
acknowledged that while his father always seemed to be
in the control of other people, he was "a man of
tremendous strength, tremendous integrity."[18] As for
other incidents that would also corroborate Osborne's
admiration of his father, I would mention these: 1) He
was honest and thoughtful in expressing his feelings
for others. For example, while in the sanitarium Mr.
Osborne wrote only brief post cards to his son, as well
as including post scripts to his wife. He did so
obviously not to upset them but also to avoid writing
the proper but dishonest letters that a dutiful father
might be expected to send home. 2) He made some efforts
to modify the conditions of his life as shown by the
unofficial separations from his wife. Yet he continued
to show a sense of responsibility towards his wife and
his son. 3) Unlike other family members, Mr. Osborne
interested himself in a larger world outside as shown
by his extensive reading, his appreciation of song and
social companionship, and his insistence on formulating
his own careful opinions about religion, politics, and
the character of those around him. 4) He was, as the
train episode shows, affectionate and cheerful in his
relationship with his son, and to the extent that this
was possible, with his wife and parents.

As for Osborne's own behavior, A Better Class of
Person clearly shows how much it resembles that of his
father. 1) Osborne did try to enjoy his life, even in

22

his isolated, painful childhood, as shown in his frank
appreciation of whatever happy times he experienced.
2) He was honest, as shown in his admission of the way
he treated Renee, his fiancee. 3) His careful efforts
to understand others' motives and to that extent limit
their responsibility for their effect on him, as shown
in his insights into his mother's and grandparents'
behavior and the absorbing attention he showed to the
lives of those around him. 4) His devotion to his
father, especially the way he remained close to the
latter and spent many hours reading to him before his
death, and his appreciation of those few people who
treated him kindly and encouraged him.

At the same time Osborne seemed better able than
his father, even before the success of Look Back in
Anger, to bounce back as shown in his reaction to the
break up with Pamela. Perhaps one reason that Osborne
could do so was that he profited from his father's
example. But, in addition, Osborne may have done so
because, from a very early age, as we have seen, he was
so much on his own that he became tougher and more
resilient than perhaps he realized.

iv

Finally, I would emphasize a fourth impression that
emerges, partly from Osborne's autobiography, but even
more so from early occasional pieces and interviews,
and that is a strong social conscience. Actually, in
pointing out Osborne's awareness of class snobbery I've
revealed part of this concern. Yet, in addition, I
would point out Osborne's comments on the convalescent
home to which he was sent to recuperate from rheumatic
fever, particularly the dismal surroundings and the
insensitive responses of staff members to the shame
and embarrassment felt by some of the boys.

However, other works provide stronger evidence of
Osborne's social concern. In "They Call It Cricket,"
Osborne's contribution to a collection of essays
(Declaration, edited Tom Maschler) by "angry young
writers," he insisted that it wasn't his job as a
writer to propose solutions to problems.[19] Nevertheless, his angry tone and the precise questions that he
raised about specific problems indicate that he was
more of an activist than he admitted. For example,
Osborne proposed that writers should ask questions
about the kinds of housing and education that people
should have, the kind of political leaders they need,
and the intellectual and cultural environment required

23

to develop as freer, happier human beings.[20]

Even stronger evidence of Osborne's concern and his belief that a writer, although not active in specific political action or programs will try to affect what happens, reveals itself in his well known, if greatly misunderstood, "A Letter to My Fellow Countrymen" (1957).[21] Osborne wrote this because he greatly admired Bertrand Russell's efforts to make the British people aware of the disastrous consequences of British nuclear policy as it was then being formulated by Harold Macmillan and Hugh Gaitskill, then leaders of, respectively, the Conservative and Labour Parties, without any real effort to involve the British people, or even Parliament, in the decision making process. If anything, the leaders were avoiding doing just that. Since Osborne felt that Russell wasn't reaching either the public or the leaders directly, he decided that he would deliberately adopt a tone of cold hatred towards the leaders to provoke them to answer in such a way as to expose their real purposes to the public and therefore arouse the latter to mobilize opposition. Unfortunately, Osborne's efforts backfired so that many people thought that he was just expressing spiteful personal hostility rather than outraged general concern.[22] That "A Letter" didn't succeed doesn't invalidate Osborne's efforts to stir people up politically, the counterpart to what is still his best known statement about his purpose as a writer, namely his assertion in "They Call It Cricket," "I want to give my audiences lessons in feeling."

Nevertheless, the most powerful early statement of Osborne's social awareness is this comment in the Preface to the Evans Acting Edition of Look Back in Anger: "People who believe that the setting of Look Back in Anger is unutterably squalid are simply unaware of the facts of life, that there is a housing shortage, that a great many houses are not only old, dirty, and hideous, but are unaware of the ugliness of their own surroundings, ugliness they have helped create themselves."[23]

Yet precisely because of the force of this criticism, it is difficult not to feel in reading later comments, such as those Osborne made in a two-part interview with Kenneth Tynan in The Observer (June 30 and July 7, 1968), that his position had changed, at least for a while. The most obvious thing to say, and to some extent Osborne himself would agree, is that at this time he became somewhat conservative in his poli-

tics and social attitudes. Not only did he admit to
Tynan that he "got the hell out of the working class"
but that he looks critically on working class political action.[24] "The trouble is," he told Tynan, "that
history has rather pulled the carpet out from under
[the working class as a political force]. The Labour
Party has appealed to cupidity and the appeal has been
answered by technology." Nor does Osborne just limit
his attacks to the working class, for he also looks
critically at the student radicals of the Sorbonne
(who were then, as we know, pressing for major changes
in many areas of French life). While he frankly
admits that, if the student radicals came to power,
they would threaten his security, he also expresses
strong reservations about their ideology. "But a lot
of left wing feeling," he insists, "strikes me nowadays
as mashed potato radicalism. It hasn't been felt
through and worked through. I find it easy and superficial and tiresome."[25]

On the other hand, much more recent evidence suggests that Osborne may be reverting back to his earlier
more anti-establishment position. In an interview on
his fiftieth birthday, he had these strong words to say
about present day England. "I'm not so much angry as
passionate. I am passionate about the way this country
has changed since I wrote that play Look Back in Anger.
We used to be the gentlest nation on earth. Now we've
become brutal, aggressive, and competitive. People do
not care about each other."[26] Certainly in this comment Osborne expresses stronger, more open concern for
a better life for people than seems evident in the
Tynan interviews. Still this concern seems less
sharply focussed on particular social and economic
problems than was true of the earlier statements that
I've quoted.

v

That Osborne should express a strong concern for a
more humane and just society is understandable. Just
the most cursory glance at some of the underlying
social, political, and economic problems confronting
Great Britain since 1945 makes clear how necessary
such concern is, for, although much has changed for the
better, real grounds for dissatisfaction still exist.

It is true that even the most reactionary Tory
government won't dare touch the National Health Program
that provides almost totally free medical care to
anyone in the United Kingdom or denationalize more than

a few industries that have been put in the public sector. Moreover, some class barriers have been weakened, as shown in the adoption of the comprehensive school, to begin to replace the public (or what we would call private) school system and the increasing democratization of the arts, as Osborne's own career attests. Furthermore, many social attitudes, particularly those involving sex and divorce, have become much more liberal, and efforts are being made to update some features of the judicial system.

Nevertheless, real grounds for enduring dissatisfaction remain. To cite just a few of these, I would emphasize the following: 1) the loss of national self esteem and sense of identity that resulted from the long overdue liquidation of the Empire and the failure of any real national sense of community to emerge to compensate. 2) The continuing technological obsolescence, managerial incompetence, and low worker productivity that still keep British industry in a disadvantageous position in comparison to that of Japan and some of the western European countries. 3) The continuing existence of strong class barriers in many areas. 4) The rise of Fascist groups such as the National Front and the noticeable increase in racism, as shown most recently in violent clashes in the summer of 1981 between whites and non-whites in Brixton and other areas of London. 5) The continued violence and political and social oppression in Northern Ireland that have taken such a toll in human lives. 6) Pervasive hardcore poverty and marginal subsistence as shown most dramatically in the current unemployment figures of 11.7 percent (as of January 1982) that represent the highest since the 1930's.

II

EPITAPH FOR GEORGE DILLON

Although <u>Epitaph for George Dillon</u> is one of two
plays Osborne wrote in collaboration with Anthony
Creighton, it is the only one which he will include
in his canon. For this reason alone it merits consideration. But two other good reasons exist for
considering the play as an Osborne work. 1) The main
character, George Dillon, is an authentic Osborne
hero, a creative, expressive, and hypersensitive person at odds with and yet wantonly dependent on his
environment. 2) Most of Act II, which involves a
confrontation and would-be love scene between George
and a forty-year old divorcee, in which each expresses
strongly ambivalent feelings towards the other, has,
as Kenneth Tynan justly observes, the tension and
articulateness characteristic of Osborne's best
dialogue.[27]

Very briefly, <u>Epitaph for George Dillon</u> portrays
how a facile writer-actor lets himself fall into a
trap he can't escape or chooses not to escape--or even
both. Down on his luck, George Dillon accepts the
invitation of Mrs. Elliot, one of the women in the
office (where until recently he worked) that he stay
with her family until he finds himself. Mrs. Elliot
extends the invitation because she is generous and
because George reminds her of her son Raymond, a boy
with some artistic aspirations who was killed in World
War II. A bustling, warm hearted person, Mrs. Elliot
never questions her actions because she accepts all
the standard values, or, as George calls them, cliches.
She goes to church regularly, believes that young
people marry for love rather than sex and/or money,
and that faith will win out. As for Percy, her husband, he is a picayunish, querulous person to whom she
barely speaks, and her two daughters, Josie and Nora,
are dull and lightheaded. The household also includes
her younger sister, Ruth, a divorcee, who has been
living with the Elliots for the past nine years.
Although bright and interesting, Ruth has become so
disillusioned in her politics and personal life that
she can't face living by herself. On the other hand,
Ruth feels uncomfortable and embarrassed because of
being so dependent--feelings which add to Mrs. Elliot's
difficulties.

As for George's reasons for coming, two seem

apparent, at least initially. 1) He can't resist exploiting people and 2) It appears he can't resist having an audience. For example, when George receives a one minute walk-on part in a television show, he celebrates the occasion as though he were a star performer. He telephones ahead beforehand, brings home a bottle of wine, and assigns everyone a role:

> Now let the wine flow on this day of days. And what a day it's been. Do you know, one agent I went to see this morning looked me up and down in this duffelcoat and said: 'No, we ain't got no <u>Biblical</u> parts today.' Must have thought I looked like John the Baptist. Perhaps if I go in a kilt, he'll offer me a gangster part.

> Glasses, Mrs. E. Bring out the golden goblets. That's right. For in spite of George continually being told he's too young, too old, too short--in spite of his wig, glass eye, false teeth, and wooden leg, George has got himself a job. (<u>He hands wine to MRS. ELLIOT</u>.)

That George also wants to exploit his "family" seems evident from the plot action. At first George almost has an affair with Ruth since each finds the other interesting. However, Ruth backs away because, though she won't admit it, George reminds her too much of her own self and her doubts. George then turns to Josie, Mrs. Elliot's younger daughter, who from the beginning has found him fascinating because he differs so much from the ordinary run of her boyfriends. In successive complications that sound like a combination of <u>Camille</u> and soap opera, George gets Josie pregnant, has a siege of tuberculosis, and turns out to be married. At the same time, however, thanks to the practical suggestions of a hard-headed producer, he revises a play so that it becomes a real box office success. Meanwhile, George recovers from his illness and reveals that he and his wife (ironically a successful actress herself) parted years ago but simply have never bothered to get a divorce. Free now to marry Josie, George can now become one of the family; in fact, he becomes its central figure. As the play ends, he dances with Mrs. Elliot, whom he calls "Mum."

On the surface George has become successful beyond his wildest dreams. As Mr. Elliot remarks, who would

have believed that George, whom he regarded as a para-
site, would "make it." But George's success is
illusory for the world in which he "makes it," as
well as that of his play, seems right out of a soap
opera. Yet these very details point to ambivalences
in George's character and situation which make him an
interesting, authentic Osborne hero.

The heroine of George's play is a girl in distress,
a prostitute who becomes pregnant, or "in the family
way." But thanks to the third-act reformation of the
hero, she becomes an honest woman. Nor is the play
successful in the West End or outside of London.
Rather, it goes on tour in Wales where it does a land
office business. Besides, the Elliots themselves
resemble soap opera characters. Nora, the older sister, resembles a type character from television of the
1950's, that of the cheerful bachelor girl. Rejected
twice at the altar, she now spends her time watching
television, going on weekend bus tours with other
such bachelor girls, and imbibing her mother's cheery
philosophy. Mrs. Elliot herself represents another
soap opera character, that of the middle class "mum."
As the stage directions about her tell us, she is a
"sincere, emotionally restrained little woman in her
early fifties, who firmly believes that every cloud
has a silver lining."

Most damning of all, as George himself realizes
with a bitter laugh, his own real life situation dup-
licates the plot of his play. Like his own hero,
George himself "gets the heroine," Josie, "in the
family way" and he, too, conforms to middle class
morality when he agrees to marry her.

In short, it would seem that instead of succeeding,
George has prostituted whatever real talent he possesses. Just before preparing to marry Josie, who,
true to soap opera conventions, has apparently told
her mother how much she loves George, when in reality
she is too indifferent to love anybody, George dramatizes his plight to Ruth in this Epitaph:

> No wait. Shall I recite my epitaph to you?
> Yes, do recite your epitaph to me. 'Here
> lies the body of George Dillon, aged thirty-
> four--or thereabouts--who thought, who hoped,
> he was that mysterious, ridiculous being
> called an artist. He never allowed himself
> one day of peace. He worshipped the physical
> things of this world, and was betrayed by his

own body. He loved also the things of the
mind, but his own brain was a cripple from the
waist down. He achieved nothing he set out to
do. He made no one happy, no one looked up
with excitement when he entered the room. He
was always troubled with wind round his heart,
but he loved no one successfully. He was a
bit of a bore, and, frankly, rather useless.
But the germs loved him. (He doesn't see RUTH
as she goes out and up the stairs.) Even his
sentimental epitaph is probably a pastiche of
someone or other, but he doesn't quite know
who. And, in the end, it doesn't really
matter!

Not only is the Epitaph, as George points out, an imi-
tation, but the tone, especially at the beginning, is
melodramatic, which is just about right for an audience
like the Elliots.

But notice the Epitaph again. At the same time
that it is overdone, it is in its way honest. George
didn't have to admit the source or make himself out
to be his worst enemy. To the Elliots, at least, he
was far from boring. From the day he arrived he made
their life, which they suspected was dull, lively and
dramatic. Even his celebration of his one-minute
walk-on part was amusing and harmless. Nor is there
any reason to doubt some of his earlier statements
that he had had some limited success as an actor. His
play in its original form, before the producer arrived
on the scene, did get performed at an experimental
theatre. And, so far as Josie is concerned, George
has transformed her life. A girl who candidly admits
she enjoys clothes and comfort but is too lazy to exert
herself for anything, Josie becomes successful beyond
her wildest dreams. Moreover, since the Elliots knew
that George was already married, he could have used
that as an excuse not to marry Josie. Nor would Mrs.
Elliot have condemned him, for, when she heard that
George was married, she refused to pass judgment on
him. As she insists to her husband Percy, who has
been waiting for just such an opportunity to expose
George, "But there's a lot you don't know about George.
George will come out tops in the end--you wait."

Mrs. Elliot is right--but for the wrong reasons.
Yet these reasons make the play, despite some crude
writing and plotting, especially in Act III, grimly
amusing and disquieting. For all of his melodramatic
language and gestures in his Epitaph, and in part

30

because of them, George seems destined to be unhappy, confused, and desperate, mostly because he tries to be honest with himself.

Ironically enough, an unctuous minister friend of Mrs. Elliot, Mr. Colwyn-Stuart, who seems to be a parody of Billy Graham, cruelly reveals George's plight. When George, in an argument about religious faith, insists that he can believe only in objective evidence, the minister suddenly sees how unsure of himself George really is:

> GEOFFREY: You see, I come into contact with a great many artistic people. What do you believe in? Yourself?
> GEORGE: Right. (Adding in vocal parenthesis) He said, striking attitude of genius.
> GEOFFREY: You have faith. You have faith in yourself--in your talent. Am I right?
> GEORGE: Well?
> GEOFFREY: Your talent, George. You believe in that with all your heart. And your evidence? Where is that, George? Can you show it to me?
> (Pause. They all look at him.)
> RUTH: Touche.
> (GEORGE is still for a moment. Then he laughs.)

Undeniably, Colwyn-Stuart has found George's Achilles heel, for immediately afterwards, when George and Ruth are alone, George admits how shaken he is. Encouraged because Ruth seems sympathetic, more intelligent than the rest of the family, and a kindred spirit with her own doubts, George begins to admit his deep personal uncertainties. Yet precisely because Ruth feels such doubts herself but can't admit them, she ridicules George. However, instead of retreating or playing verbal games with Ruth, George persists because he values candor and cares for Ruth:

> RUTH: Perhaps you have got talent, George. I don't know. Who can tell? Even the experts can't always recognize it when they see it. You may even be great. But don't make a disease out of it. You're sick with it.
> GEORGE: It's a disease some of us long to have.
> RUTH: I know that. I met it once before.
> GEORGE: Then you must know it's incurable.

RUTH: Galloping--like a consumption.
GEORGE (sharply): What did that mean?
RUTH: Nothing.
GEORGE: But do you know what is worse? Far, far worse?
RUTH: No, Brother Bones, tell me what is worse.
GEORGE: What is worse is having the same symptoms as talent, the pain, the ugly swellings, the lot--but never knowing whether or not the diagnosis is correct. Do you think there may be some kind of euthanasia for that? Could you kill it by burying yourself here--for good?
RUTH: Why do you ask me?
GEORGE: Would the warm, generous, honest-to-goodness animal lying at your side every night, with its honest-to-goodness love-- would it make you forget?
RUTH: All you're saying is that it's a hard world to live in if you're a poet--particularly if it should happen that you're not a very good poet.
GEORGE: Unquote.
RUTH: Unquote. Life is hard, George. Anyone who thinks it isn't is either very young or a fool. And you're not either. Perhaps even bad artists have their place in the scheme of things . . .

I quote this long exchange for two reasons. The first is that it reveals how taut and incisive the writing is. In less than forty lines George has expressed his most painful weaknesses and Ruth has triumphantly seized upon them. The second is that the passage reveals how much George does suffer. Though he is living off the Elliotts, he is very unhappy about it. Moreover, if Ruth realizes how much George drives himself, we, too, can believe that he is burning himself out. And for what? He has no proof that he has much talent, and even the roles he plays, as he admits earlier to Ruth, are those of heavies.

Why then does he act as he does? One answer seems to be that he has a demanding conscience. Because he is undeniably sensitive, or, as he says, has the same symptoms as talent he feels that he has to try hard. But more than that, when he talks about play acting, he means that he doesn't know his real feelings and desires. At the very moment he responds so sensitively because he has the right audience, he seems to

be standing apart from himself, unable to believe what
he is doing. Yet only in these moments when he responds so sensitively can George begin to believe he can
honestly feel and therefore be a person. Because Ruth
is too unsure of herself, she not only retreats but
through ridicule discredits both George's feelings and
her own. No wonder when Josie comes in, ready to go
dancing with George, that he goes all out for a triumph. Otherwise he would be even more tormented and
unsure of his feelings than he is. First, he dances
with Josie and flatters her with pseudo-intellectual
seductive arguments. Then, he pulls out all the stops
by asking her to come to his room to see his etchings!

However, what seems like a triumph turns out, as I
indicated, to be a fiasco since Josie, aided by her
mother who sincerely believes the latter's protestations that she loves George, uses her pregnancy
literally to trap George. Besides, Ruth, the one person who tries to understand George, leaves him in the
lurch. Although George declaims his Epitaph to Ruth,
she leaves before he finishes. The bitterest blow is
that he has lost her even as an audience.

No wonder, then, that at the end, as George dances
with Mrs. Elliot and calls her "Mum," he has, as the
stage directions reveal, "a mechanical smile fixed on
his face." Although living at the Elliots may not be
death, at best it is a half-life and a pitiful one,
particularly since Mrs. Elliot sincerely hopes for
the best for George and Josie. Outwardly George may
be, like Jacques Brell, alive and well, but inwardly
he must feel even more frightened and confused than
before, especially since he has no one, not even a hostile Ruth to whom he can relate, if only for a few
moments. The saddest thing of all is that he knows
exactly where he stands and feels so helpless. On the
other hand, George does receive attention and love,
both of which he desperately needs as he knows very
well. Miserable as George's life is, at least for the
first time he has some security, and he has enough concern for survival to appreciate some of his needs.
Therefore, if anything, George might really be too
hard on himself.

Epitaph for George Dillon is a poignant and bitterly
amusing play about small people in a small world. Mrs.
Elliot is generous and lively but also banal and sentimental. When George comes to the house, she shows

him a picture of her son Raymond:

> MRS. E.: (<u>very simply</u>.) He was a lovely boy.
> Clever, like you, artistic, too, but some-
> how he didn't seem to have that drive, that
> sort of initiative. Well, he didn't really
> have much chance to get on. But <u>you</u> will,
> George, I'm sure. With all your talent,
> you just can't go wrong. You're always
> planning things--and all the things you've
> already done too. You've got your acting
> and your plays and I don't know what,
> haven't you?

Yet at the same time Mrs. Elliot treats Percy, her husband, differently. "As far as I'm concerned," she
tells him, "you're just the lodger here."

Josie may seem like a mere caricature, but she also
has animal vitality and cunning. For almost ten
minutes at the beginning of Act I she does nothing but
sprawl on a couch, flip through a magazine, and listen
half-heartedly to a record. Moreover, she has been
doing this for almost the whole day, just waiting for
a pair of hip hugging slacks to be delivered. Yet
even while sprawling, she enjoys admiring her body.
Then, when she gets the slacks, she stands before the
mirror, lovingly rubbing her fingers over her thighs
and legs. What Josie wants may be limited, but she
knows just what it is and how to get it.

George comes across very well as being perpetually
miscast. He tries too hard to be a tragic heavy to
avoid being embarrassed at his success and yet is somewhat proud of it. At the same time, as his long scene
with Ruth reveals, he just can't convince himself that
he can be a person, let alone a decent one, though his
later actions belie this.

I mention "smallness" not to put the play down, but
to give it just praise. On the one hand, some critics
exaggerate the play's merits because, as Simon Trussler
justly observes, they want to show that Osborne really
writes better when he doesn't limit himself to one
dominant character.[28] On the other hand, Trussler
himself exaggerates the play's defects to demonstrate
how much better Osborne learned his craft in later
plays. Admittedly, Act III is thin, perhaps crude, in
the encounter between George and the hack producer.
Moreover, George's illness and his success smack too
much of contrivance, and Ruth is never developed

beyond Act II. Nevertheless, especially in a good production, the very fact that the characters almost seem like the figures on a television screen yet only a bit larger, captures something authentic about many ordinary people's lives. That is, that they are just half lives, whether they are those of the Elliots or of George himself. But even half-lives have painful realities of their own, and those who lead them have a right to survive. At the end, George may, as Trussler observes, be anesthetizing himself.[29] Yet Trussler doesn't recognize that George knows himself well enough to realize that he might not even be able to maintain a half life in the world outside the Elliots because he has such an unabashed need for security and acceptance which at least Mrs. Elliot can give him and without which he could continue to accentuate his doubts that he really exists, or again, to paraphrase Trussler, that he may be acting the part of an actor. However interesting a Pirandello role can be, as George well knows, it can be self destructive for a person as insecure and honest as George turns out to be.

III

LOOK BACK IN ANGER

Look Back in Anger, as we might well think every
one knows by now, concerns itself with the increasingly
destructive consequences of an unhappy marriage between
Jimmy Porter, a young working class intellectual with
some of the attributes of Marchbanks, Stanley Kowalski,
and Rupert Birkin, and Alison Redfern, a beautiful, sensitive girl who has left the apparent security of her
upper middle class family to live with Jimmy in Bohemian
poverty but emotional intensity. Despite the efforts
of Cliff, a good friend of Jimmy's who shares the apartment with them and serves as a buffer between the two,
conditions seem to get worse, particularly when Alison
discovers that she is pregnant and fears that she can't
disclose this to Jimmy who will feel that she has
betrayed him by having let this happen. Although the
unexpected arrival of Helena, a good friend of Alison's
who also comes from a proper upper middle class family,
temporarily brings some relief for Alison, her presence
makes things even worse. The reason is that Jimmy
regards Helena as an even greater threat to his marriage because of her background and possible influence
on Alison. Nor is he wrong, because Helena, out of
sympathy for Alison who is unhappy but also, as it
turns out, for her own motives (which she may not have
recognized) arranges to have Alison's family come and
take her home, a move to which Alison presents no opposition. Then with Alison gone, Helena, who apparently
was much more attracted to Jimmy than she recognized,
has an affair with Jimmy. He, for his part, responds
because he needs someone to turn to. Although this
affair seems to be working out, it doesn't last since
Alison unexpectedly turns up. She does so because she
is so traumatized by having lost her baby in childbirth
and the apparent security this represented that she
found herself driven to return to Jimmy as her last
resort.

To anyone who saw Look Back in Anger in 1956 or
1957, it may seem pointless to try to discuss the play
now. It still isn't possible to forget the shabby
attic apartment in which Jimmy, Alison, and Cliff, who
seems a third 'member of the wedding,' are rooted, or
the terrible monotony of their life in the Midlands in
which reading the Sunday papers provides the sole diver-
sion of the week. Nor is it possible to forget the
weariness of Alison enduring the abuse that Jimmy
heaped upon her, seemingly without reason and without

end, as he kept attacking Alison, her family, the English establishment, and apparently every value of bourgeois society. At the same time there was the sheer delight in just listening to Jimmy's speech cadences because of their images, passion, and devastating wit.

And then there were the articles and reviews which stressed how Jimmy Porter, a young working-class intellectual who is disgusted with his society, became a culture hero, an angry young man who would change society if he knew what he wanted or if he felt he had any chance to succeed. There was also the historic importance of the play in reinvigorating English drama by encouraging bright young people, especially from the working class, to turn to the theatre for their creative fulfillment. On the other hand, there were articles which alleged how confused the play was, for just what was Jimmy so angry about? Was he, for example, really a homosexual but dared not admit it?[30]

Yet, in reality, there is more to say as well as a considerable amount to unsay, especially since we can look back more than twenty-five years later and, in addition, re-experience the play on the basis of at least three revivals, that of 1969 at the Royal Court (directed by Anthony Page), the Young Vic in 1972 at the National Theatre, and the 1980 production in New York (not to mention summer theatre and other productions which keep turning up). Admittedly, much of what has been said about the play remains true: the Midlands setting is bleak, the language is still arresting, Alison does suffer, and Jimmy does excoriate Alison's family and the English literary establishment. Yet the play really is more modest than it seemed in 1956.

I say this because it is now much clearer than it was then that Jimmy isn't a great archetypal hero, a rebel without a cause, as was supposedly revealed in a speech that was widely quoted when the play was first put on. I refer to this complaint which Jimmy makes to Cliff while the former is living with Helena:

> . . . I suppose people of our generation aren't able to die for good causes any longer. We had all that done for us, in the thirties and the forties, when we were still kids. (In his familiar, semi-serious mood.) There aren't any good, brave causes left. If the big bang does come, and we all get killed off, it won't be in aid of the old-fashioned, grand design.

38

It'll just be for the Brave New nothing-very-
much-thank-you. About as pointless and
inglorious as stepping in front of a bus . . .

Certainly these lines do sound like an expression
of regret that no powerful ideological commitments
exist any longer and therefore life at present seems
futile. However, these lines actually are part of a
larger speech that significantly changes their meaning.
This longer speech comes after one in which Cliff has
told Jimmy that he was leaving because he [Cliff] felt
uncomfortable about Jimmy's affair with Helena. In
reply, Jimmy admits that, even though Cliff is worth a
dozen Helenas to him, he still will remain with her,
because, as he says, "of something I want from that
girl downstairs [Helena], something I know in my heart
she's incapable of giving." After Cliff agrees, Jimmy
goes on to elaborate:

Why, why, why, do we let these women bleed us
to death? Have you ever had a letter and on
it is franked, "Please Give Your Blood
Generously." Well, the Postmaster does that
on behalf of all the women of the world.

Then, after the long excerpt I've quoted earlier, Jimmy
concludes with these words. "No, there's nothing left
for it, me boy, but to let yourself be butchered by
the women."

In the full context, Jimmy is admitting, ruefully
and facetiously, how much he and all men need women
and therefore how vulnerable they are. If, as a
result, the speech has a narrower focus, it may, as I
hope to show, illuminate Jimmy's difficulties more
pointedly.

Looking at the play in revivals, and, just as important, reading Osborne's stage directions very carefully, we see, to begin with, that Jimmy at least some
of the time can be more likeable and engaging than he
was when originally played by Kenneth Haigh. Victor
Henry (who played Jimmy at the end of the 1969 revival)
delivered some of Jimmy's great punch lines, not as
though they embodied only metaphysical despair and
indignation but also as efforts to express energy and,
most of all, to shock people. At times Jimmy reminds
us of Jack Tanner, who can mount such offensives
because he concentrates all his energy on talking
rather than acting and because, for all of his wit and
apparent cynicism, he is really an innocent who

believes that people should act out of high principle.
However, the most significant resemblance to Jack is
that both characters really are very insecure with
women; in fact, their bluster and bravado represent a
defense against the latter whom they both need but fear
as well. Jack senses that somehow his life is incom-
plete without Ann and then drives madly towards the
Pyrenees to try to escape her. Jimmy's life centers
on Alison, then Helena, and then, of course, Alison
again after she returns and acknowledges that now that
she has lost her baby she shares his feeling of what
it means to feel helpless.

    At this point, though, the similarities end, for
Jimmy needs women more than Jack does and his defenses
are less formidable. As Alison puts it, when she
explains to Helena how pathetic yet appealing Jimmy was
in courting her: "Jimmy went into battle with his axe
swinging round his head--frail, and so full of fire.
I had never seen anything like it. The old story of
the knight in shining armour--except that his armour
didn't really shine very much." "Frail and so full of
fire"--how aptly these words describe Jimmy and his
dilemma.

    One reason he is so frail is that he feels insecure
because he married a girl from a higher social class.
Certainly, this may help explain Jimmy's consistent,
virulent attacks on Alison's mother and his scorn for
her brother, a member of Parliament, both of whom are
very proud of their class and take it for granted that
it embodies all the virtues. For a person as sensitive
as Jimmy, this kind of opposition can be devastating,
even though neither character ever appears in the play.
At one point, for example, Jimmy excoriates Alison's
brother Nigel for his stodgy conservatism:

        Besides, he's a patriot and an Englishman, and
        he doesn't like the idea that he may have been
        selling out his countrymen all these years, so
        what does he do? The only thing he can do--
        seek sanctuary in his own stupidity. The only
        way to keep things as much like they always
        have been as possible, is to make any alter-
        native too much for your poor, tiny brain to
        grasp. It takes some doing nowadays. It
        really does. But they knew all about character
        building at Nigel's school, and he'll make it
        all right. Don't you worry, he'll make it.
        And, what's more, he'll do it better than any-
        body else!

Although Jimmy seems to exult in his efforts, when we look at the stage directions we realize how insecure he actually feels: "Jimmy is rather shakily triumphant. He cannot allow himself to look at either of them to catch their response to his rhetoric, so he moves across the window, to recover himself, and look out."

However, Jimmy is frail for other reasons. One is that, as he vividly describes to Helena in the longest speech of the play (but one also meant as a plea for understanding by Alison), he was the one member of his family most intimately involved in the death of his father, an experience which has profoundly affected his entire life:

> But, you see, I was the only one who cared. (Turns to the window.) His family were embarrassed by the whole business. Embarrassed and irritated. (Looking out.) As for my mother, all she could think about was the fact that she had allied herself to a man who seemed to be on the wrong side in all things. My mother was all for being associated with minorities, provided they were the smart, fashionable ones. (He moves up C. again.) We all of us waited for him to die. The family sent him a cheque every month, and hoped he'd get on with it quietly, without too much vulgar fuss. My mother looked after him without complaining, and that was about all. Perhaps she pitied him. I suppose she was capable of that. (With a kind of appeal in his voice.) But I was the only one who cared! (He moves L. behind the armchair.) Every time I sat on the edge of his bed, to listen to him talking or reading to me, I had to fight back my tears. At the end of twelve months, I was a veteran. (He leans forward on the back of the armchair.) All that that feverish failure of a man had to listen to him was a small, frightened boy. I spent hour upon hour in that tiny bedroom. He would talk to me for hours, pouring out all that was left of his life to one, lonely, bewildered little boy, who could barely understand half of what he said. All he could feel was the despair and the bitterness, the sweet, sickly smell of a dying man. (He moves around the chair.) You see, I learnt at an early age what it was to be angry--angry and helpless. And I can never forget it. (Sits.) I knew more about--love....betrayal....and death,

> when I was ten years old than you will probably
> ever know all your life. <u>(They all sit</u>
> <u>silently. Presently, HELENA rises.)</u>

I quote this speech in its entirety for it is one
of the most crucial in the play. Although it begins
as a put down of Helena whom Jimmy (as indicated) with
good reason regards as a rival for Alison's allegiances,
it quickly becomes painfully serious. The reason is
that in it Jimmy describes how profoundly his exposure
to suffering at an early age has affected his loyalties
and his sense of self. On the one hand, Jimmy feels
proud that he assumed such responsibility as he did
for his father. Yet, on the other, he feels that this
suffering placed a tremendous burden on him for at least
two reasons. In the first place, Jimmy was so young,
alone, and needed by his father that he felt, however
much he tried, that he couldn't help the latter enough.
Moreover, although Jimmy doesn't say it, perhaps he
has continued to feel that way for years afterwards,
even to this moment. In the second place, Jimmy's
difficulties were compounded because his mother didn't
believe in his father's commitment to the Spanish Civil
War. Consequently, in supporting his father, Jimmy
felt a strong conflict of loyalties so far as his
mother and his family were concerned. Since Jimmy's
mother's family and that of Alison shared many of the
same values, the latter's opposition to Jimmy's marriage (expressed forcefully by Alison's mother) could
have reinforced the original conflict and, therefore,
made all the greater the need for Alison to compensate
by identifying with Jimmy. However, not only didn't
Alison do this, but she kept writing to her family and
not mentioning Jimmy at all. It is no wonder then that
Jimmy kept attacking her for being disloyal.

A third reason for Jimmy's frailty, and related to
his involvement with his father, is that he sets very
high standards for himself but then discovers how painful are the consequences. One such manifestation, as
Alison describes to her father, is what she calls his
"emotional puritanism." Whereas Alison's father might
think that someone as anti-establishment as Jimmy
would believe in pre-marital sex, the truth was that he
refused to have intercourse with her before they were
married. By making such a demand, Jimmy was setting up
a higher standard of romantic love than did others.
Admittedly, one result was to enhance the value and
pleasure he experiences in sex, as he makes clear when
he tells Alison how much he looks forward to making
love to her now that they have become reconciled after

a quarrel in which he deliberately hurt her physically:

> There's hardly a moment when I'm not--watching
> and wanting you. I've got to hit out somehow.
> Nearly four years of being in the same room
> with you, night and day, and I still can't stop
> my sweat breaking out when I see you doing--
> something as ordinary as leaning over an iron-
> ing board. (She strokes his head, not sure of
> herself yet, sighing.) Trouble is--Trouble is
> you get used to people. Even their triviali-
> ties become indispensable to you. Indispen-
> sable, and a little mysterious. . .

However, another consequence is to make Jimmy feel vulnerable because he does value such experiences so much.
This explains why he angrily tells Alison later that,
after having sex with her, he could almost feel that
she was devouring him:

> Do you know I have never known the great
> pleasure of lovemaking when I didn't desire it
> myself. Oh, it's not that she hasn't her own
> kind of passion. She has the passion of a
> python. She just devours me whole every time,
> as if I were some over-large rabbit. That's
> me. That bulge around her navel--if you're
> wondering what it is--it's me. Me, buried
> alive down there, and going mad, smothered in
> that peaceful looking coil. Not a sound, not
> a flicker from her--she doesn't even rumble a
> little. You'd think that this indigestible
> mess would stir up some kind of tremor in
> those distended, overfed tripes--but not her!

Another manifestation of Jimmy's insistence on high
standards reveals itself in his strong feeling for
allegiances or personal loyalties to people he cares
about. These include old girl friends, Cliff, Hugh
Tanner, another working class friend (in whose apartment Jimmy and Alison spent the first night of their
honeymoon), and most of all, Hugh's mother who helped
set Jimmy up in a sweet stall he now operates with
Cliff. Jimmy values these people so much because of
what they have done for him that he feels he must give
his all to them, particularly when, like his father,
they have only him to turn to. But, just for this very
reason, Jimmy also feels that he can't on his own do
justice to such an obligation.

This feeling becomes evident in one of the most

moving scenes in the play, and one which, significantly, occurs immediately after the long account of his father's death. I refer to the scene in which Jimmy learns (through a phone call) that Hugh's mother is dying and that he is the only one she can turn to for support. While Hugh's mother clearly trusts Jimmy and would feel reassured by his mere presence, Jimmy feels such a burden placed upon him, or such a need to live up to high standards, that he can't conceive of going alone. "You're coming with me," he implores Alison, "aren't you? She (he shrugs) hasn't got anyone else now. I need you to come with me." Although Alison hesitates for a moment, she leaves for church with Helena (as she had arranged to do so earlier, despite his plea to her to remain loyal to him). It is true that Jimmy may be expecting too much from Alison, but what is more important is that (as the very last stage direction of the scene clearly shows), he undervalues himself and accordingly punishes himself. "Jimmy falls forward onto the bed, his face buried in the covers."

On the other hand, because Jimmy does feel so frail he has a strong desire to retaliate against those he feels responsible for hurting him, particularly Alison. For such retaliation, his chief weapon is his anger, or to paraphrase Alison, his fire. Since so much has been written about Jimmy's anger, we might wonder what there is to add. However, there are at least two things I would emphasize.

The first is that Jimmy can be very cruel and unremittingly so. As the stage directions reveal, he rehearses many of his attacks. For example, after being ignored by Cliff (who knows Jimmy's ways very well) he asks the latter what seems like a harmless question--whether or not he [Cliff] knows the meaning of pusillanimous. Without thinking, Cliff answers no. As a result, Jimmy seizes the opportunity to read the dictionary definition of the word and then to denounce Alison at length for having such a trait. However, most important, Jimmy seems to know intuitively where to hurt the most. After learning that Helena is coming, Jimmy turns on Alison and utters this terrible curse:

> Oh, my dear wife, you've got so much to learn. I only hope you learn it one day. If only something--something would happen to you, and wake you out of your beauty sleep! (Coming in close to her.) If you could could [sic] have a child, and it would die. Let it grow, let a recognisable human face emerge from that

little mass of indiarubber and wrinkles. (<u>She retreats away from him</u>.) Please--if only I could watch you face that. I wonder if you might even become a recognisable human being yourself. But I doubt it.

Since just a few minutes earlier, Alison had (unknown to Jimmy) confessed to Cliff that she was pregnant but feared to tell Jimmy because he would feel she was betraying him, his curse, as the stage directions make clear, has a devastating impact on Alison.

Yet if Jimmy hurts Alison a great deal, it is important to realize that he hurts himself as well. For one thing, he seems compelled to invite retaliation by testing Alison to see if she will reject him--or at least punish him in some way. This fear seems to account for what seems like some of his most outlandish attacks, namely those on Alison's mother since the latter isn't even present. However, they may represent a desperate need on Jimmy's part to see how far Alison will go in retaliation.

For another--and this is more important--Jimmy can't sustain his anger, particularly when it seems most intense. Even in the scene in which Jimmy has invoked his terrible curse on Alison and her baby, he seems to be in considerable pain, for the stage directions reveal that "...<u>He stands rather helplessly on his own</u>."

However, the scene that shows most forcefully how vulnerable Jimmy's anger makes him is one that occurs at the end of Act II when Jimmy returns from Hugh's mother's funeral. He arrives to discover that Alison has just gone home with her father and left him a note rather than tell him directly, that Cliff is nowhere in sight (because he couldn't face Jimmy's reaction to this news), and that Helena is still present, even though she was supposed to have left some time ago. Worse yet, when Jimmy reads the note, he discovers that it is filled with cliches, and he has to listen to Helena lecture him that Alison is going to have a baby and he isn't responding properly. "Well," she demands, "Doesn't that mean anything, even to you?" Enraged, he edges closer to her and taunts her to slap him in what seems like a real show of strength:

> . . . Listen, if you'll stop breathing your female wisdom all over me, I'll tell you something: I don't care. (<u>Beginning quietly</u>.) I

45

don't care if she's going to have a baby. I
don't care if it has two heads! (He knows her
fingers are itching.) Do I disgust you? Well,
go on--slap my face. But remember what I told
you before, will you? For eleven hours, I
have been watching someone I love very much
going through the sordid process of dying. She
was alone, and I was the only one with her.
And when I have to walk behind that coffin on
Thursday, I'll be on my own again. Because
that bitch won't even send her a bunch of
flowers--I know. She made the great mistake
of all her kind. She thought that because
Hugh's mother was a deprived and ignorant old
woman, who said all the wrong things in all the
wrong places, she couldn't be taken seriously.
And you think I should be overcome with awe
because that cruel, stupid girl is going to
have a baby! (Anguish in his voice.) I can't
believe it. I can't. (Grabbing her shoulders.)
Well, the performance is over. Now leave me
alone, and get out, you evil-minded little
virgin.

But again the stage directions show us something quite
different: "She slaps his face savagely. An expression
of horror and disbelief floods his face. But it drains
away and all that is left is pain. His hand goes up to
his head, and a muffled cry of despair escapes him . . ."
That, immediately after this, Helena kisses him passionately and draws him down to her may seem to contradict what I've been saying. Actually it doesn't
because Helena is revealing how much Jimmy's sensitivity has affected her.

Yet there is still another side of Jimmy, or source
of his 'fire,' and that is his delight in controversy
and excitement. Some of the time when he declaims most
fervently about the need for vitality in modern life
and sounds like a radical out to change society, he
really just wants someone to challenge him. One reason
his relationship with Helena has some credibility is
that she does answer him back and yet not reject him.
As a result, Jimmy, at least for a while, does enjoy
his relationship with her. Yet how long Jimmy might
have sustained that relationship may be another matter,
nor am I suggesting that all that was necessary for
Alison to have done to save their marriage was to
engage in good-natured banter with Jimmy. Although
this certainly would have helped, it ignores what is
most important in this discussion about Jimmy, as well

46

as brings us to a third meaning of "so full of fire."
That is, a strong urge to center his life on a woman
whom he loves as an individual in her own right and
because, like Maud Gonne for Yeats, she embodies many
of the conflicts Jimmy has experienced and the energies
he values. To a certain extent, Jimmy's belief in
allegiances, especially as Alison explains it to Helena,
underlies Jimmy's feelings:

> It isn't easy to explain. It's what he would
> call a question of allegiances, and he expects
> you to be pretty literal about them. Not only
> about himself and all the things he believes
> in, his present and his future, but his past as
> well. All the people he admires and loves,
> and has loved. The friends he used to know,
> people I've never even known--and probably
> wouldn't have liked. His father, who died
> years ago. Even the other women he's loved.
> Do you understand?

As Alison describes Jimmy's beliefs, he could sound very
much like one of E. M. Forster's main characters for
whom personal relations involving love and/or friendship represent the most important values in his life.
However, other statements that Alison makes, not to
mention some by Jimmy himself, reveal something else.
When Alison learns that Helena is leaving Jimmy, she
begs the latter to stay because she realizes how much
of what Jimmy wants centers on a special kind of
relationship with a woman:

> "He wants something quite different from us.
> What it is exactly I don't know--a kind of
> cross between a mother and a Greek courtesan,
> a hench-woman, a mixture of Cleopatra and
> Boswell. But give him a little longer. . ."

Although Alison expresses some uncertainty and confusion, she senses that Jimmy wants to be involved with
clever, spirited, and highly impressionable women. Or,
as Jimmy himself describes to Alison and Cliff, his
former girl friend, Madeline (who was years older than
himself), "She had more animation in her little finger
than you two put together," and "Her curiosity about
things, and about people was staggering. It wasn't
just a naive nosiness. With her, it was simply the
delight of being awake, and watching." Granted that
Jimmy may be exaggerating to let Alison know how indifferent to him he felt that she has become, still he is
emphasizing how much he values openness and vitality.

Such a testimonial may seem a far cry from Jimmy's proud assertion to Alison and Helena, when (as indicated) he is describing the significance of his father's death. "I knew more about love . . . betrayal . . . and death, when I was ten years old than you will probably ever know all your life." Yet what is common to both is a heightened awareness of many contradictory facets of life and a passionate desire to reconcile them. As Jimmy tries to point out to Alison after she has returned, isn't it possible to be both impressionable and strong, especially if you share your life with someone who complements those feelings in you:

> Was I really wrong to believe that there's a--
> a kind of--burning virility of mind and spirit
> that looks for something as powerful as itself?
> The heaviest, strongest creatures in this world
> seem to be the loneliest. Like the old bear,
> following his own breath in the dark forest.
> There's no warm pack, no herd to comfort him.
> That voice that cries out doesn't <u>have</u> to be
> a weakling's does it? <u>He moves in a little</u>.
> Do you remember that first night I saw you at
> that grisly party? You didn't really notice
> me, but I was watching you all the evening.
> You seemed to have a wonderful relaxation of
> spirit. I knew that was what I wanted. You've
> got to be really brawny to have that kind of
> strength--the strength to relax. It was only
> after we were married that I discovered that
> it wasn't relaxation at all. In order to
> relax, you've first got to sweat your guts
> out. And, as far as you were concerned, you'd
> never had a hair out of place, or a bead of
> sweat anywhere . . .

From my discussion so far, it would seem that most of the interest in such a relationship exists on Jimmy's part because he so clearly expects a lot from women and needs them a great deal. Yet for these reasons, as well as the fact that he also has a lot to give, he does have a considerable impact on both Helena and Alison. This impact, in turn, draws Jimmy to both of them all the more.

So far as Helena is concerned, he appeals to her strong maternal instinct to want to protect him. On the one hand, that he has such a need becomes most evident when he was demoralized both by the death of Hugh's mother and the pain of Alison's leaving him. On the other hand, Jimmy is also a refreshing

48

liberation for Helena, at least temporarily, because through her affair with him, she can escape from the confines of her own proper middle-class world and yet still enjoy the benefits of its security. But when Alison returns after the loss of her baby, Helena begins to feel the conflicts she has been evading. Unable to confront them, but also deeply moved by Alison's plight, she quickly decides that she must terminate the affair and acts accordingly. Yet, if in doing so she clearly disappoints Jimmy, she has helped him begin to accept himself more and trust women more. Even when on Alison's return, Jimmy denounces Helena for not being able to confront the pain and conflict that are unavoidable in love, his tone is much less harsh than it had been earlier in the play. And with reason, I should add, since on two occasions Helena had told him unmistakably that she loved him.

But it is Alison who plays a much more important role in Jimmy's life because she inspires his greatest hopes, as well as, unfortunately, much of the time his greatest disappointments.

For her Jimmy represents, as she tells her father, a challenge which she as a woman couldn't resist. Much as she admired her parents and appreciated the security of her background, she was also intelligent and perhaps embarrassed enough because of her dependency to feel the need to oppose them. And through Jimmy she certainly could for he represented a new way of life to her. In addition, her mother's fanatical resistance to her marriage (which even took the form of having private detectives follow Jimmy) further justi- fied her devotion to Jimmy. But, as a proper girl, Alison also retained what she regarded as her loyal- ties to her parents so that (as indicated) once she married Jimmy she kept writing to them, even though she knew how much this angered and demoralized Jimmy. At the same time, Alison had her own pride which was per- haps as strong as Jimmy's. As she admits to Cliff, she knew that when Jimmy attacked her mother and herself he was pleading with her to reassure him. Nevertheless, she just remained quiet and resigned, determined to bear her pain. In doing so, she was making all the greater his need to vindicate his belief in his loyal- ties and values that centered on women and yet making this need all the more difficult to realize.

Worse still, although Alison herself doesn't realize this, in acting as she did she wasn't even retaining her family's loyalties or allegiances. In marrying

Jimmy, she had already chosen his allegiances in place
of theirs. Consequently, anything short of terminating
her relationship to Jimmy wouldn't change that decision. On the other hand, since she knew how Jimmy
felt about her family, her continuing to write home
represented a refusal to commit herself to the way of
life she had already chosen. In his kindly fashion,
Alison's father tells her that the two people most
responsible for the failure of her marriage are not, as
she might think, Jimmy and her mother. Rather, they
are the two of them because they are both fence sitters
who try to evade commitments. Osborne himself, I might
add, has much harsher words to say about Alison. In
the Preface to the Evans Acting Edition of the play, he
remarks that she has absolutely no allegiances to anything, neither her family nor Jimmy.31 Although he
doesn't elaborate, it is fair to say that one inference
we can draw from such a strong comment is that, however
much we sympathize with her because of the abuse she
receives from Jimmy, we have to realize that she contributes significantly to what happens. For by insulating herself and acting as she does like a martyr,
she not only is making Jimmy feel rejected and therefore driven to torment both of them, but she is trying
to evade taking responsibility for her life and looking for a false security. This explains why she was so
shattered by the loss of her child that, as she makes
clear to Jimmy on her return, she now wants to experience only helplessness and pain:

> Don't you understand? It's gone! It's gone!
> That--that helpless human being inside my body.
> I thought it was so safe, and secure in there.
> Nothing could take it from me. It was mine,
> my responsibility. But it's lost. She slides
> down against the leg of the table to the floor.
> All I wanted was to die. I never knew what it
> was like. I didn't know it could be like
> that. I was in pain, and all I could think of
> was you, and what I'd lost. (Scarcely able to
> speak.) I thought: if only--if only he could
> see me now, so stupid, and ugly and ridiculous.
> That is what he's been longing for me to feel.
> This is what he wants to splash about in! I'm
> in the fire, and I'm burning, and all I want
> is to die! It's cost him his child, and any
> others I might have had! But what does it
> matter--this is what he wanted from me! She
> raises her face to him. Don't you see. I'm
> in the mud at last. I'm grovelling! I'm
> crawling Oh, God--

Alison's admission of her helplessness echoes that
of Jimmy earlier in the play, most notably his 'horror
and despair' when (as indicated) Helena slapped him
because he didn't correctly respond as a proper, concerned husband to the news of his wife's pregnancy.
In so reacting, Alison is confirming the authenticity
of the helplessness which Jimmy had experienced and
which he felt driven to defend so strongly. At the
same time, she is also giving him the opportunity to
exult in watching her experience the most terrible pain
he had wished on her when he felt abandoned by her
because of Helena's presence. In what was certainly
one of his cruelest speeches, he said he wanted to see
her grovel, "I want to stand up in your tears, and
splash about in them, and sing. I want to be there
when you grovel. I want to be there, I want to watch
it, I want the front seat." Yet he doesn't exult, and
with good reason, because her suffering creates a real
dilemma for him. In the first place, just before
Alison's return he had finally been able to admit to
Helena how much he needed the support of a woman who
loved him. Moreover, Helena had pledged him that
support. However, with Alison collapsed at his feet,
Jimmy can't expect any such support. In the second
place, in hearing Alison express such a low sense of
her self worth and want to make herself suffer, Jimmy
could feel again, as he did earlier with his father,
that he is responsible for what has happened and
therefore has another intolerable burden to assume.
For these reasons it wouldn't be surprising that Jimmy
may wish to escape, if possible. And, at first glance,
this may seem just what he is trying to do. For he
responds to her by resorting to a childish game called
bears and squirrels that the two of them played when
they couldn't bear the complexity and pain of their
life together:

> We'll be together in our bear's cave, and our
> squirrel's drey, and we'll live on honey, and
> nuts--lots and lots of nuts. And we'll sing
> songs about ourselves--about warm trees and
> snug caves, and lying in the sun. And you'll
> keep those big eyes on my fur, and help me
> keep my claws in order, because I'm a bit of
> a soppy, scruffy sort of a bear. And I'll
> see that you keep that sleek, bushy tail
> glistening as it should, because you're a very
> beautiful squirrel, but you're none too bright
> either, so we've got to be careful. There are
> cruel steel traps lying about everywhere, just
> waiting for rather mad, slightly satanic, and

very timid little animals. Right? . . .

But, if we look more carefully at the passage, particularly by noting the stage directions as well, we
see that Jimmy isn't escaping at all. Instead, in the
most literal way he is assuming his burden as he picks
Alison up, holds her in his arms, and begins to
reassure her verbally with these words, "Don't, Please
don't...I can't...You're all right now. Please...I...
I...not any more." Then, by resorting to their game of
bears and squirrels, he is really enabling her to
accept herself as she is without blame and yet without
false hope. Moreover, in doing so, he is asserting his
own strength but without embarrassing her by accentuating the contrast to her behavior in these words.
" . . . because I'm a bit of a soppy, scruffy sort of
bear . . " At the same time he is also recognising
their situation realistically by his humorous warning,
"There are cruel steel traps lying about everywhere,
just waiting for rather mad, slightly satanic, and very
timid little animals. Right?" Nor is he torturing the
two of them by making this burden seem intolerable.

At the end of the play Osborne isn't insisting that
it is much better to feel self-punitive and helpless
rather than guilt free and strong. Rather, he is
expressing how regrettable it is that people should
have to feel as angry, helpless, and disappointed as
Jimmy does throughout much of the play; as beaten as
Alison does at the end; or even as prone to retreat so
quickly to a safe world of black and white morality as
Helena does when (before leaving) she announces to
Jimmy and Alison, "He Jimmy wants one world and I
want another, and lying in that bed won't ever change
it. I believe in good and evil and I don't have to
apologize for that."

However, Osborne is also pointing out that if people
can begin to admit to their deepest feelings--painful,
confusing, and self punitive as they may be, and be
honest with themselves and one another and at the same
time value, as Jimmy does, wit, vitality, and, most of
all, love, they can begin to cope just a bit better.[32]

IV

THE ENTERTAINER

The Entertainer presents the despairing personal
and public life of Archie Rice, a third rate master of
ceremonies in the English provincial music halls. Not
only does the play reveal the cumulative attrition of
years of personal and public frustration and disappointment, but it also shows the immediate impact of the
events of one terrible weekend in the 1956 Suez crisis
that accentuates such attrition all the more. Although
for most people, Look Back in Anger may remain
Osborne's best known play, some critics, such as Ronald
Bryden,[33] feel that The Entertainer may turn out to
have the most enduring appeal of all Osborne plays
because it presents such a comprehensive and representative vision of many facets of English life through
the public and private experience of Archie Rice as an
entertainer, a family man, and a person very much aware
of the disturbing and confusing present world in which
he lives, as well as earlier ones particularly that of
the Edwardian age, that he appreciates and yet questions.

Structurally, the play resembles Osborne's two earlier plays and yet moves forward in a new direction. In
both Epitaph for George Dillon and Look Back in Anger
music hall routines or skits are means by which George
and Jimmy, respectively, help dramatize themselves.
The same is true of The Entertainer, particularly since
Archie Rice and his father, Billy, are both music hall
performers. However, more important, the basic action
of the play does have something to do with entertainment for it reveals Archie's efforts to remain loyal to
an art form that is dying out and to pursue a career
which, even at best, is a great disappointment, if not
an outright failure.

But music hall routines, or "turns," to use the English phrase, also represent a separate part of the play.
There are some six or eight of these which alternate
with the basic action of the play that centers on the
personal lives of the Rice family. These "turns"
represent typical performances Archie puts on in his
current role, that of Master of Ceremonies of a burlesque show which he owns that is on tour in the
provinces. In these "turns" Archie comes across as a
sexy, corny comedian who twits, shocks, and patronizes

his audience with a line of pattern consisting of songs, self-ridicule, and sardonic comments on British social and political life.

While at the beginning the "turns" remain separate from the central action, by the end they merge with it as it becomes increasingly apparent that Archie's stage life becomes all he has left, and even that comes to an end. Archie begins as a third-rate entertainer, as he well knows, and ends as one. However, because of the way he responds to this outward failure and the disappointments that dominate his private life and the way he remains sensitive and aware of so many different facets of life around him, he realizes himself to the fullest rather than feel, as he well might, defeated.

At the same time another important consequence of the mingling of "turns" and family drama is that it becomes a means by which Osborne scathingly attacks the English establishment in time of crisis. And that crisis was a significant one in history, the 1956 Suez crisis or debacle. After Col. Nasser announced that he was nationalizing the Suez Canal, the British and French seized control of the canal, only to have to withdraw in the face of American, Russian, and United Nations opposition. For the British, Suez represented one of their last efforts to maintain the empire and the imperialist ethic. Its failure made everybody angry. The imperialists felt that the whole thing had been bungled; the anti-imperialists-- and this could include people from center to far left of center--felt that the whole campaign brought out into the open the chauvinism and narrow self interest underlying British public life. In such a context, Osborne is writing as a member of a young generation painfully aware of how empty and stifling the past was, but how powerful it still remains, particularly when the present is confusing and the future is ambiguous.

Osborne mounts his attack in several ways. In the first place, several of Archie's songs call attention to some of the worst British faults: "Why Should I Care" attacks British chauvinism that the Suez debacle reveals; in "I'm Normal" Archie ostensibly identifies himself with good, proper, true blue Englishmen.

> Now I'm just an ordinary bloke
> The same as you out there.
> Not mad for women, I'm not a soak,
> I never really care.

54

I'm what you call a moderate,
I weigh all the pros and the cons.
I don't push and shove
At the thing they call love.
I never go in for goings on.
Thank God I'm normal, normal, normal.
Thank God I'm normal,
I'm just like the rest of you chaps.

But, since in his introductory routine, Archie has been fighting this audience for being so stuffy and dim witted, he is also ridiculing them for liking such songs.

In the second place, one strand of the plot action involves the fate of Archie's son Mick, a British soldier on duty in Suez, who is captured by the Egyptians in a reprisal raid. In being captured, Mick becomes a British hero, which represents another ironical twist, for the British prepare to ransom him and fly him home for public display. But irony turns to tragedy because Mick is killed before ransoming can take place. In one of the most plaintive moments in the play, Archie's other son, Frank, a conscientious objector, who served a year in prison and now works in a hospital, sings a blues memorial that he directs to Archie as the audience. Although throughout the play Archie has satirized his audience and himself as well for "not caring," his behavior during the song contradicts this impression. On this occasion, Archie can barely retain his composure, an indication that he does care, but that too many elements of his society, especially those who make British foreign policy, don't. They are, to paraphrase Archie's description of himself (which he gives later) "dead behind the eyes."

Nevertheless, the most forceful means by which Osborne attacks a dead British society is in the person of Archie himself as an entertainer. The very fact that Archie should be an entertainer represents a slap in the face at the British establishment, for his father spent a great deal of money educating him at the right public schools to become a gentleman. Most of his school classmates, as Archie points out facetiously, were V.I.P.'s, while he is on the burlesque circuit. As a seedy, vulgar man who carries on an adulterous affair with a barmaid (an affair we only hear about rather than witness), Archie can expose his peers much more than if he had accepted their values. Just as important is the tacit suggestion that Archie's vulgarity is obvious, whereas that of his classmates is masked as imperialism. That Archie's cavorting on the

stage can represent a powerful indictment was evident
to anyone who saw Laurence Olivier play the role in the
original production. Having this middle aged man in a
pin stripe double breasted suit twist his cane seduc-
tively at the women and, with his polished but deliberately coarse voice, lampoon the establishment and
yet proclaim that he himself embodied something
authentically English, constituted a powerful criticism
of English public values.

Nevertheless, the play represents much more than a
satirical indictment of the English establishment--
and something less. I say both because, as revivals
of the play have shown, much of the original satirical
thrust has been blunted.[34] Rightly or wrongly, Suez,
for many present day theatre audiences, seems to be
ancient history. Therefore, the "turns" which brought
down the house when Laurence Olivier did them twenty
five years ago merely seem amusing.

But a more important reason why the Suez crisis
seems less important now involves Archie himself.
Except for his personal grief for Mick's death, Archie
doesn't care a great deal about Suez. While the
reasons for his apathy about politics become more pronounced because of Suez, they also exist in their own
right as part of Archie's life experience. Moreover,
while Mick's death does affect Archie deeply, the
other things that happen and Archie's reactions to them
don't result from the Suez fiasco but from Archie's
personal response to the events and circumstances of
his past and present life. These events and reactions
show Archie's efforts to deal with the considerable
failure that has characterized much of his life.

To begin with, not only has Archie disappointed his
father, who gave him all the advantages of an education, but it appears that he hasn't struggled or seemed
to have set high standards for himself. Nor, except
for a brief time when he taught, has he seemed to have
used his considerable intelligence. More subtly, we
can't even say that Archie deliberately rejected his
father's way of life or that he particularly enjoyed
his third rate music hall career. Besides, over the
years he has been consistently unfaithful to Phoebe and
has built a kind of wall around himself by letting his
"show biz" personality, that of the man who keeps throwing away lines, dominate his personal life. For
example, as one stage direction reveals, Archie feeds
his son Frank lines as a straight man, so that he can
keep him at a distance. Archie also has taken flyers

on business ventures which were bad risks, and he seems
to have been indulged, particularly by his wife,
Phoebe, who has forgiven him his women and his alcohol.

If all these faults or failures were not enough,
Archie has disappointed his daughter, Jean, an intelligent, liberal girl who is developing into a political
activist, despite the fact that Archie and her grandfather, to whom she is genuinely devoted, disapprove.
Ultimately, she comes to feel that her father is just
a vulgar, selfish, and callous person who is out for
"Number One."

On the other hand, Archie does care a great deal
for his family. He admires his father for his real
talent, which he knows far surpasses his own. Archie
shows this admiration by encouraging his father to
reminisce about the past because the latter has simply
resigned himself to living in a present he finds
dreary and vulgar. With Phoebe, Archie has a curious
relationship. Though (as indicated) he has been
unfaithful to her, he has always been candid and tactful. Nor is Phoebe easy to live with. A plain, poor
girl who has worked all her life and never known much
pleasure, she has a profound inferiority complex.
Worse still, she keeps reminding herself and the rest
of the family how miserably she has lived and how
little she values herself. As she continually
asserts, all she can hope for is that Archie will just
endure her and she won't have to be buried as a
pauper:

> I don't want to always have to work. I mean
> you want a bit of life before it's all over.
> It takes all the gilt off if you know you've
> got to go on and on till they carry you out
> in a box. It's all right for him, he's all
> right. He's still got his women. While it
> lasts anyway. But I don't want to end up
> being laid out by some stranger in some
> rotten stinking little street in Gateshead, or
> West Hartlepool or another of those dead or
> alive holes!

Nevertheless, Archie tactfully tries to interest
Phoebe in what goes on, makes a point of being affectionate to her, and tries to orchestrate his responses
to her moods. As for Jean, he admires her because
she is intelligent, independent, and considerate of
Phoebe. He very much wishes that she would trust and
respect him, and, during the weekend in which the most

of the present action of the play takes place, he tries
very hard to earn her respect and trust. In fact,
the central or core action of the play consists of
Archie's efforts to get Jean above everyone else to
understand and accept him, as his first wife never
did, and as no one, except possibly Phoebe to a limited extent, does now. Why Archie feels such a compelling need isn't altogether clear. However, one reason
may be that Archie values her approval because she is
intelligent, a quality, which despite his disclaimers,
he too admires. Another, possibly more important
reason is that Archie feels guilty about the failure
of his first marriage--or rather how much he disappointed his first wife whom he loved dearly--and hopes
to alleviate some of those feelings through Jean's
understanding.

In presenting these different perspectives on
Archie, Osborne is exploring (as he does in Epitaph
for George Dillon) the problem of success-failure.
Here he begins with what seems an obvious failure:
Archie's career and his personal life, which Archie
has known for years have been empty. What Osborne
does is show an interesting paradox. At first glance,
Archie seems to be deliberately reckless and indul-
gent. This reveals itself partly in Archie's relationship (as indicated) with the barmaid in a nearby
tavern. Although we never meet the girl, we know that
Archie has been sleeping with her. Archie's family
are shocked but feel that Archie simply is a spoiled
roué, especially when he reveals to Jean that he plans
to marry the girl.

This tendency seems even more evident in the persona he adopts as an entertainer. Here I am referring
to his constant boasts about his sexuality and his
corny taunting of his audience, as in this typical
byplay:

> What about these girls? (Indicates up stage)
> What about them? Smashin'. I bet you think
> I have a marvelous time up here with all these
> posing girls, don't you? (Pause). You're
> dead right! You wouldn't think I was sexy to
> look at me, would you? No, lady. To look at
> me you wouldn't think I was sexy, would you?
> . . . . (Pause). You ask him! (Points to
> conductor's stand). Ask him! (Staring out at
> audience). You think I'm like that, don't
> you? (Points to conductor's stand again).
> I'd rather have a glass of beer anyday! And

> now I'm going to sing you a little song, a
> little song, a little song written by the
> wife's sister, a little song entitled "The Old
> Church bell won't ring tonight as the Verger's
> dropped a clanger!" Thank you, Charlie.

We might think that such a style would appeal to the
audiences before whom he performs, but Archie doesn't
vary his routines enough. In addition, such routines
seem all the more repetitive as they contrast to
changes within the internal plot action. After Archie's
plans to abandon Phoebe have been frustrated, his
father has died, Mick has been killed, and his daughter
Jean refuses to forgive him, these songs and skits with
their heavy-handed jokes seem pathetic.

But in actuality Archie uses this persona to
express what he most believes in as an ideal, namely
the sexuality and vitality he seems to be celebrating
so coarsely in his routines. In this regard, the
coarseness also represents a defense--partly against
the audience because of its hostility and partly to
conceal from them (and perhaps himself) his doubts of
his own worthiness to embody such an ideal. That
Archie feels so ambivalently reveals itself in particular in two crucial episodes, both of them
involving his daughter Jean whom, as indicated, he
wants above all to understand and respect him. The
first occurs at the end of Act I, when the two of them
are alone, after it is apparent that Archie has concealed from the others (who have gone to bed) the
contents of a telegram he received announcing Mick's
capture. (He did so to spare their feelings.) However, since Jean senses what has happened, Archie
reveals the contents to her. Encouraged by her awareness, he begins to try to communicate to her how
lonely and insecure he feels as a male by telling her
one of his stories about the way women flatter him--or
so he hopes. However, just before he gets to the punch
line, he suddenly breaks down. The stage directions
and his unanswered plea to Jean tell us the bitter
truth which Jean doesn't recognize:

> He trails off looking very tired and old. He
> looks across at Jean and pushes the bottle at
> her.
> ARCHIE: Talk to me.

CURTAIN   END OF ACT ONE

The second occurs in a later scene with Jean when

in a half drunken reminiscence Archie vividly recalls
a black blues singer he heard years ago and admired
for the purity and intensity of the emotions she
expressed in her singing:

> ARCHIE: . . . .
> Did I ever tell you the most moving thing
> that I ever heard? It was when I was in
> Canada--I managed to slip over the border
> sometimes to some people I knew, and one
> night I heard some Negress singing in a
> bar. Now you're going to smile at this,
> you're going to smile your educated Eng-
> lish head off, because I suppose you've
> never sat lonely and half slewed in some
> bar among strangers a thousand miles from
> anything you think you understand. But if
> ever I saw any hope or strength in the
> human race, it was in the face of that old
> fat Negress getting up to sing about Jesus
> or something like that. She was poor and
> lonely and oppressed like nobody you've
> ever known. Or me, for that matter. I
> never even liked that kind of music, but to
> see that old black whore singing her heart
> out to the whole world, you knew somehow
> in your heart that it didn't matter how
> much you kick people, the real people, how
> much you despise them, if they can stand
> up and make a pure natural noise like that,
> there's nothing wrong with them, only with
> everybody else. I've never heard anything
> like that since. I've never heard it
> here . . .

For a number of reasons this is one of the most
important speeches in the play. It does articulate
what Archie values and how he himself would like to
feel as a person who is vital, concerned, and creative, or who has "soul." Yet the speech also suggests
that Archie can't really believe that he can be such a
person for it all seems too late. Nevertheless, the
fact that, finally, after he has told Jean how much he
loved her mother, even though she caught him in bed
with Phoebe and left without waiting for any word of
explanation, he can admit he would like to be as
expressive as the singer shows what he really values
for himself. Just as important, the very way he
describes the singer--his appreciation of her and his
awareness that Jean may not quite believe what he is
telling her or agree with him--indicates how many

traits he shares with the woman whose joy he is recapturing. But, most important, Archie's behavior during much of the play itself (when we look back at it more carefully) shows that, whether he realizes it or not, he does in his own way have soul, namely empathy for many kinds of people and experiences.

Ironically, one way Archie shows his empathy is to remind his family of his "badness," when he doesn't really have to, or to act deliberately vulgar when they might express concern for him. Significantly, for all of Archie's talk about his horrendous escapades, we never see him with another woman so that he doesn't seem to be the monster that he makes himself out to be. While his combination of self-deprecation and vulgar boasting seems corny on the stage, in private life it becomes a subtle, tactful method of holding his family together. For example, he may protect one member of the family when another attacks him or defend some one, especially Phoebe, when she feels embarrassed because of Jean's superior intelligence and education. In particular, Archie knows just the right moment when to provide this encouragement for Phoebe. At one point, when Phoebe is despondent, Archie seems to make things worse by starting to sing a song which even she insists is too vulgar. However, by getting Phoebe to protest, Archie can then urge her to sing. Although Phoebe has a terrible voice and is very self-conscious, she greatly wants attention. Consequently, once Archie gets the others to second his suggestion, she does her turn and feels much better.

I could enumerate many other instances, particularly how Archie teases his father to brag about the past, for then the latter seems more energetic. When we consider that throughout much of the play Billy not only keeps putting Archie down but doesn't realize how much over the years this behavior has undermined Archie's sense of his own worth, we can appreciate all the more Archie's tact and consideration in trying to humor his father who feels lonely and out of touch with the present.

There is also the way Archie will use his own self-indulgence to remind others of the same fault within themselves. When Phoebe begins to reminisce about her painful childhood and almost demands sympathy, Archie withholds it. Instead, he threatens a long tirade beginning with, "If I have to listen to this again . ." While this seems unjust, Archie wants Phoebe to realize that she is letting herself off too easily.

We can still better appreciate Archie's empathy and love when we contrast his behavior towards others to that of Jean and Billy, both of whom outwardly are more successful and upstanding than Archie. Not only was Billy a talented performer, but he experienced real personal happiness. For example, at the beginning of the play he is describing to Jean, while they are both waiting for Archie to come back from his evening performance, how different life was in his time:

> . . . I feel sorry for you people. You don't know what it's really like. You haven't lived, most of you. You've never known what it was like, you're all miserable really. You don't know what life can be like . . .

Even though he is now in retirement, he still prides himself on his appearance and manners. While he keeps to himself much of the time, he still cares for what happens to the others. And, if properly encouraged by Archie, Billy joins in the "turns" or informal skits in which the family participate when the discord becomes too great.

But Billy can be difficult and unpleasant. He can't stand his Polish neighbors, regards blacks as sexual libertines, provokes Phoebe, and drifts off into his own private reminiscences. He acts in these ways because he feels that the present world differs so greatly from the Edwardian world which he enjoyed and loved. This was a world in which, as he tells Archie, everyone knew what were the "rules" or norms. Even if entertainers, such as himself, made fun of these "rules," they, together with their audiences, still believed in them. In fact, because they did it was easier to make jokes since no one felt threatened.

Certainly, we can sympathize a lot with Billy, as many critics do, for they see him embodying a kind of moral integrity that Archie seemingly lacks. Yet what underlies this integrity is a considerable intolerance and insensitivity that takes for granted that these "rules" are absolutes which everyone has to accept. When some one refuses, as Archie has, or even Jean when she participated in protest demonstrations in Trafalgar Square, he is acting not only foolishly but destructively. Billy never realizes that a person could respect his values, as Archie does, and yet feel differently himself. Nor does Billy realize that these rules could frustrate Archie in his own life, or even make it difficult for Billy himself to adjust to change now.

Jean, like Billy, also seems to know where she
stands and acts accordingly. Jean wants to change her
society for the better, she is independent enough to
question her father's and fiance's values, and she
cares for her family, even though her life style
differs noticeably from theirs. In her most moving
speech she tries to make clear to her stuffy, former
fiance, Graham, with whom she has broken her engagement because their values differ so much, how indifferent to suffering the British really are:

> JEAN: Have you ever got on a railway train
> here, got on a train from Birmingham to
> West Hartlepool? Or gone from Manches-
> ter to Warrington or Wides. And you
> get out, you go down the street, and on
> one side maybe is a chemical works, and
> on the other side is the railway goods
> yard. Some kids are playing in the
> street, and you walk up to some woman
> standing on her doorstep. It isn't a
> doorstep really because you can walk
> straight from the street into her
> front room. What can you say to her?
> What real piece of information, what
> message can you give to her? Do you say:
> "Madam, d'you know that Jesus died on
> the Cross for you?"

Since at the same time her father seems more concerned
with trying to keep up his quixotic efforts to refuse
paying his income tax, her social awareness stands out
all the more.

But Jean's personal code, like that of Billy, can
be narrow. Although Archie differs with her, he, at
least, shows some charity. For example, Jean doesn't
realize how loyal Archie has been to Phoebe over the
years, or how much he values her [Jean's] good opinion
of him. Nor does it ever dawn on Jean that Archie may
have some reason for wanting to elope with the barmaid.
Curiously enough, Jean in this regard turns out to be
more puritanical than Phoebe and more intolerant than
Billy. For example, after Mick's funeral, when the
family are gathered together, Jean tries to take out
much of her resentment at what has happened on her
father:

You're like everyone else, but you're worse--
you think you can cover yourself by simply not
bothering. (<u>Newspapers</u>.) You think if you
don't bother you can't be humiliated, so you
just roar your life out in four-letter words
and just hope that somehow the perks will turn
up. . . .

Despite Frank's efforts to get her to stop, Jean continues:

I'd like you to know the truth about your
father-- . . . What do you want, two minutes
silence? Not only is your father generous,
understanding and sympathetic, he doesn't give
a damn about anyone. He's two pennorth of
nothing.

Not only by juxtaposition with Billy and Jean do
Archie's tolerance and compassion, which he fashions
out of his outward failure emerge, but also through his
relationship with Phoebe. To a considerable extent,
I have emphasized this in mentioning how Archie knows
how to respect her needs and yet keeps her from wallowing in pathos. But I would also emphasize that
Phoebe counterpoints what Archie does. Yet, in turn,
this very similarity accentuates significant differences. Phoebe would seem to arouse more sympathy than
Archie since she has had little or no schooling and
had terrible looks from the start. Besides, she
drinks too much, cares little for sex and is so apprehensive about the future that she has to go to the
movies every night as an escape.

On the other hand, Phoebe knows that because she
has endured such humiliating experiences and has
struggled so much, she understands areas of human life
that the more respectable and dignified people will
simply never comprehend. Not the last, she knows
that Archie really cares for his family more than anything else and that he understands far more than his
family credit him with. But, most of all, she understands how lonely he is.

Yet these very things I've emphasized about Phoebe
also reveal that, in contrast to Archie, she never has
had anything she aspired to or hoped for, however
understandably such hopes might have become frustrated.
Having felt as she does makes it easier for her to
understand Archie's disappointments because she hasn't
dared believe in anything except dogged endurance. How-

ever, Archie, at least, has his women, his energy, and his absorbing interest in the people around him (such as the blues singer). Phoebe, on the contrary, has only one dominant concern: how to avoid, as indicated, ending up in a pauper's grave. What Osborne in "They Call It Cricket" said about Archie also applies to Phoebe, if not even more accurately, namely that her life shows the "texture of ordinary despair."[35]

To make even more forceful the contrast with Phoebe in particular, I would point to the very last episode in which Archie makes his final appearance in the Music Hall before apparently being apprehended by the Internal Revenue authorities (for not paying any income tax for years, a personal peccadillo). This episode shows how Archie has come to terms with his life and yet how painful it will continue to be.

The scene begins with the usual routine of self deprecation and corny dirty jokes which the audience (and we ourselves) have heard before. If anything, the routine seems longer, as if Archie may seem to be hiding his feelings of disappointment all the more. But, in reality, as the rest of the scene reveals, he is acknowledging them more. Shoftly after singing one of these corny songs, "Say your jelly roll is fine, but it doesn't compare with mine . . . , " he lets down his guard with this comment. "Life's funny, though, isn't it? It is--life's funny. It's like sucking a sweet with the wrapper on." This is the first time that Archie publicly reveals the disappointment that he has been experiencing for many years. Having admitted it, he seems free to go on, as he does, by telling a longer, even cornier story than usual about a man who comes to heaven and discovers that it ⌐heaven⌐ isn't all that it's cracked up to be. However, the man isn't disappointed so long as he can admit what he really sees. Nor is Saint Peter angry because finally some one does tell things the way they are. While we don't know what word the man uttered in Saint Peter's ear (although it could be shit) this doesn't matter. What is important is that the man (like Archie himself now) is unashamed of how he really feels.

Then, to show even more pointedly how he can accept the limitations of his life and his identity, Archie breaks off singing one of his stand bys, "Why Should I Care," and comes before his audience to thank them for listening. We could regard this action as just another corny routine--which it is in part. Yet in doing it, Archie is showing more openly how much he does care and how unashamed he is to reveal this. Moreover, since this audience, like the others before whom he has been playing for many years, is hostile, the effort isn't easy. Just how difficult the effort must be becomes all the more evident if we go back again to the scene in which Archie described to Jean how much he admired the black blues singer. For immediately after that he tells her how he really feels as a performer:

> . . . You know when you're up there you think you love all those people around you out there, but you don't. You don't love them, you're not going to stand up and make a beautiful fuss. If you learn it properly you'll get yourself a technique. You can smile, darn you, smile, and look the friendliest jolliest thing in the world, but you'll be just as dead and smug and used up, and sitting on your hands just like everybody else. You see this face, you see this face, this face can split open with warmth and humanity. It can sing, and tell the worst, unfunniest stories in the world to a great mob of dead, drab jerks and it doesn't matter, it doesn't matter. It doesn't matter because--look at my eyes. I'm dead behind these eyes. I'm dead, just like the whole inert, shoddy lot out there. It doesn't matter because I don't feel a thing, and neither do they. We're just as dead as each other.

Nevertheless, despite the strong feelings Archie is expressing in this speech, he does manage at the end to become more accepting of them and himself, for after concluding his routine, as I've described it, he tells the audience that he will come looking for them to be their audience, "Let me know where you're working tomorrow night--and I'll come and see YOU." After this, he does manage to leave, as the stage directions poignantly reveal: " . . . suddenly the little world of light snaps out, the stage is bare and dark. Archie Rice has gone. There is only the music."

This is a very sad ending for Archie goes out as a lonely little man, no longer able to appear even before a hostile audience. But he also leaves as a bigger man who shows how much he cares, especially for his family, and who reveals, through his many disappointments, how richly he has lived. Moreover, he will continue to do

66

so, despite all the burdens he still has, not the least
of which is Phoebe who, as the stage directions tell
us, stands in the wings waiting for him.

V

LUTHER

To go from the career of a seedy English vaudeville
performer in provincial English towns to that of a
great historical figure in a magnificent historical
setting of the High Renaissance represents quite a
change. And to go from a play that uses revue skits
as a principle of form to one that uses historical
events as a means of externalizing inward conflict is
also quite a departure. Nevertheless, these two
changes occur in Luther, which concerns itself with
selected historical episodes, public and private, in
the career of the great religious performer. Beginning
with Luther's choice of a monastic life in opposition to his father's wish that he pursue a more
worldly career, the play presents well-known episodes
in the great reformer's career. These include celebration of his first mass, his relationship with one
of the older theologians (Staupitz) who became a
second father figure, his opposition to the Church
establishment, particularly over the issue of indulgences, his role in the Peasants' War and its after-
math, and finally his withdrawal from public life and
marriage to a former nun.

At the same time, though Luther seems to go in a
different direction from The Entertainer, it presents
still another variation on success-failure. Luther
is the story of a man who, to quote his old theology
teacher, Staupitz, practically revolutionized Europe.
Yet it is also the account of a man who begins by
rebelling against his father as the embodiment of
authority and the inculcation of simple family values
and the importance of the flesh and yet in the end
acknowledges that he has much more in common with his
father than he ever dared recognize before. However,
in contrast to the earlier plays, in Luther the
failure is hidden beneath success rather than the converse as in The Entertainer.

Nevertheless, if Luther and his world seem poles
apart from those of Archie Rice and Jimmy Porter, some
of the differences may not be so great after all.

First of all, Luther, like Jimmy, feels driven to
be different. He became a monk because, as suggested
previously, he felt a strong need to oppose his
father's domination. Not only did Luther insist upon

leading his own life, which could legitimately differ from that of his father, but, as Erik Erikson points out in his psychoanalytically oriented biographical study, <u>Young Man Luther</u>, a book which influenced Osborne's play, he had to go to fantastic lengths to express this resistance and justify his own stand.[36] Then, having taken that stand and entered the monastery, Luther is driven to affirm his differentness there. While all the other monks recite their sins, they do so like figures out of Walter Pater's <u>Marius the Epicurean</u>. They are effete, stylized, and dilettantish. But Martin's reactions are coarse and elemental. He suffers from constipation and he suffers noisily. Such suffering, as he comes to realize, expresses much of his resistance to authority. Moreover, when Martin became a monk, he began to see the church in terms similar to those in which Jimmy viewed the world he lives in, namely, as a stodgy establishment he has to attack. Martin finds himself horrified at the system of indulgences, particularly when he hears stories about the way that a monk named Tetzel has been rashly promising that indulgences will guarantee forgiveness of sins, even before they are committed.

From this point on, Martin finds himself strongly opposing the church over a fundamental issue, perhaps the most important of all, the basis on which individuals find salvation. According to Roman Catholic doctrine, persons obtain grace as a result of good works. The greater the number of such works they perform, the more likely their salvation. However, for Luther, good works are secondary, even irrelevant, because only the individual's faith matters. If the individual feels that he cares strongly enough for God and values such a feeling, then this response itself suffices. While the individual may not have to perform good works as a result of this feeling, the chances are that he will.

Secondly, like that of Archie Rice, Luther's drive for self realization has strong sexual overtones. Archie consistently asserts that he is a lecher and is proud of it. Old as Archie is, he boasts that he can have "a go" with a barmaid and not be ashamed of it. Although Luther doesn't act this way at the beginning-- in fact, quite the opposite--by the end of the play he asserts that, while we may talk about the spirit, the body comes first. For man to praise God without accepting his sexual nature--or for man to praise God in order to deny his sexual urges, as Luther himself

was doing when he became a monk, is destructive.
Curiously enough, as suggested, Luther's rebellion at
this stage of his life aligns him with his father,
since the latter didn't believe that being a monk was
manly.

Yet, despite these similarities, Luther really does
differ markedly from the earlier plays in exploring
Luther's efforts to cope with his feelings of helplessness and despair in realizing himself. While George
Dillon, Jimmy Porter, and Archie Rice all know too well
what it means to feel isolated and to have doubts,
none of them dares to cope with them as openly and
forcefully, both privately and publicly, as Luther
does. Whereas Descartes asserted, "I think, therefore
I exist," Luther could say, "I am alone and I doubt,
therefore I exist," however painful such isolation
and doubt may be. In fact, the more painful they are,
the more real his existence.

That Osborne explores isolation and doubt as
dynamic forces in Luther's various identity crises or,
to paraphrase, a recent book title, "Different seasons
of his life,"[37] is evident from even the most cursory
analysis of the play's three acts, as shown particularly in a number of crucial episodes. However,
before looking at these, I want to say something about
the play's overall structure, which is one that com-
bines chronicle history elements together with some
features reminiscent of Brecht's Epic Theatre. (Such
a similarity with Brecht is not surprising inasmuch as
one of the great events of the 1956 London Theatrical
season was the visit of the Berliner Ensemble, a visit
which affected the work of other playwrights, such as
John Arden.)

These Epic Theatre features include 1) a choral
figure called the Knight who makes sardonic comments on
the action to dramatize incongruities and clashes of
views and 2) a technique of scene construction based
on ironical clashes of personalities which emphasizes
dissonance and in which many individual scenes are
self-contained units. Through such dissonant, self-
contained scenes, personal and historical forces assert
themselves. Yet, as Simon Trussler justly observes,
this kind of dissonance does not, as it does in
Brecht, result from a clash of the playwright's perspectives and those of the audience who bring to the
theatre their notions of causation and value which
differ from those of the playwright, a clash which
produces the celebrated alienation effect.[38] Rather,

the dissonance results primarily from clashes of
values between Luther and the different characters,
whether enemy or friend. Although many of these
clashes, especially in Act I between Luther and his
father are open and striking, in much of the rest of
the play they are more subdued and almost seem devoid
of tension. Yet tension does result precisely because
such a slight difference of view or understanding
greatly affects Luther's struggles with himself and
those influencing him. In particular, I would mention scenes with Luther's teacher, Staupitz, a man who
greatly influenced Luther and was one of the few to
understand him. In these scenes (as I want to make
clear in more detail later) just the fact that Staupitz only slightly disagrees with Luther accentuates
some of the forces of doubt that Luther is trying to
cope with internally and externally.

When we turn to look at the play in detail, we
notice that in Act I, which involves Luther's ordination, two sets of contrasts emphasize Luther's isolation and his doubt. The first involves him and the
other monks who are, as indicated, less fastidious
than he. In these scenes Luther torments himself
because he doubts his own worth. He confesses far
more sins than all the others put together. Moreover,
as I've previously suggested, Luther expresses
anxiety symptoms in his constipation. Despite the
efforts of Luther's superior, Brother Weinand, to
assure him that he need not torment himself so much,
Luther persists. He does so because of a second contrast, that between himself and his father.

Right after Luther pledges his vows, his father
(who with a friend has been witnessing them) bluntly
asks: "Why? Why has he become a monk?" From this
question and many others that follow, it is apparent
how strongly Hans Luther disapproves. Hans simply
can't believe what Martin is doing, let alone understand it. To a certain extent Hans' reaction is just,
for the painful way in which Martin punishes himself
in his ordination makes clear that he is fighting part
of his own nature. Moreover, it is that very part
which, as I've indicated, resembles his father--his
sensuous, physical self. Yet what Hans Luther
doesn't understand, but which his comments on the
ordination make clear, is that Martin's decision to
become a monk represents a rebellion against Hans himself. Nor is it just a normal rebellion of a son
against a father that growing up involves. Rather,
Martin (to paraphrase Erikson) has to <u>drive</u> himself to

reject all that his father stands for in order to establish his own identity. Given Hans' domineering personality and his ambitions for his son and Martin's
own sensitivity and intelligence, such a powerful
clash is obvious and dramatic. Moreover, after Martin
almost spoils his first mass by forgetting some of
the details, his father persists in taunting him:

> HANS: Anxious moments! I'll say there were.
>   I thought to myself, "he's going to flunk
>   it, he can't get through it, he's going
>   to flunk it." What was that bit, you
>   know, the worst bit where you stopped and
>   Brother--
> MARTIN: Weinand.
> HANS: Weinand, yes, and he very kindly helped
>   you up. He was actually holding you up
>   at one point, wasn't he?
> MARTIN: Yes.
> BRO. WEINAND: It happens often enough when a
>   young priest celebrates Mass for the
>   first time.
> HANS: Looked as though he didn't know if it
>   was Christmas or Wednesday. We thought
>   the whole thing had come to a standstill
>   for a bit, didn't we? Everyone waiting
>   and nothing happening. What was that
>   bit, Martin, what was it?

Yet at the same time that Martin and his father
clash with each other so much, they also are close to
each other. One reason Hans is so disappointed at the
way Martin celebrated his first Mass is that he cares
a great deal about what Martin does. If Martin must
become a monk, then at least he should excel in the
role. For his part, while Martin does feel that he
has to go to such lengths to oppose his father, he can
admit how much he has needed the latter:

> You disappointed me too, and not just a
> few times, but at some time of every day,
> I ever remember hearing or seeing you,
> but, as you say, maybe that was also no
> different from any other boy. But I
> loved you the best. It was always you,
> I wanted. I wanted your love more than
> any one's, and if any one was to hold me,
> I wanted it to be you. Funnily enough,
> my mother disappointed me the most, and
> I loved her less, much less. . . .

Precisely because Martin can admit openly how he really feels, his need to rebel so profoundly becomes all the greater, inasmuch as such feelings conflict with his deep love for his father and therefore cause him to feel he almost has to reject himself for being so articulate. No wonder that, after his father leaves, Martin should doubt the authenticity of his decision to become a monk. "But what," he asks himself, as the act ends, "if it isn't true?"

Act II and most of Act III (as the stage directions reveal) change the focus completely: from the interior personal life of Martin to his outer, public life. Act II begins with a scene in which Tetzel shamelessly tries to sell indulgences to ignorant common people, and it ends with Luther burning a Papal Bull which excommunicates him. Act III, Scene I, shows Luther at the Diet of Worms refusing to recant and thereby resisting authority to the fullest. But then immediately afterwards comes Act III, Scene II, which I regard as the climax of this part of the play, where Luther, the arch individualist and enemy of the establishment, joins with these very forces to put down the Peasants' revolt. Yet at the same time Luther shows himself undeterred by such opposition and proceeds to marry a former nun, thus opposing authority in another area.

For a number of critics this part of the play (which comprises roughly half) seems unsatisfying. One reason is that Osborne, except in brief episodes, doesn't present Luther's inward reactions but only his public responses. A second reason is that these incidents--which include a long discussion about his own problems and views of religion with his superior, Staupitz, his nailing the celebrated ninety-five theses to a church door in Wittenberg, his being summoned to appear before the Papal legate Cajetan to cease and desist, his preaching a sermon which expresses his rejection of such demands, the impact one of his letters makes on Pope Leo X, and his appearance before Emperor Charles V at the Diet of Worms, not to mention his behavior in the Peasants War--don't seem related to Luther's rebellion against his father. Of the two criticisms, the second seems less likely.

Admittedly, Martin doesn't openly connect his feelings about resisting church authority with those involving his resistance to his father. But does he have to? From the way the church authority figures

74

are portrayed, it is clear that they demand total allegiance and won't tolerate any views that differ from their own position, one that is even more extreme than that of Martin's father.

As for the first criticism, I think we simply have to grant its validity. After Act I, particularly Martin's meeting with his father and Martin's expression of his doubts, "But what if it isn't true?", we could expect Martin to have real conflicts with the Catholic hierarchy and to express them openly. Yet not until the end of Act II when Martin burns the Papal Bull excommunicating him and asks God for help, does he reveal any of the anguish that he expressed so consistently in Act I:

> Oh God! Oh God! Oh, thou my God, My God, help me against the reason and wisdom of the world. You must--there's only you--to do it. . . . Breathe into me, Jesus. I rely on no man, only on you. My God, my God do you hear me. Are you dead? Are you dead? No, you can't die. You can only hide yourself, can't you? Lord, I'm afraid. I am a child. . . .

I think, frankly, we can admit that Martin, as we saw him in Act I, could have expressed such doubts more often in Act II. However, we can also ask ourselves whether Osborne might not be trying to accomplish something else by changing his presentation as he does and not having Martin express such doubts until the end of the Act.

When we look at Acts II and III, particularly four scenes I'd like to discuss in detail, we might see that compelling reasons do exist for what Osborne is doing.

The first scene is Act II, Scene I, in which Luther does not even appear. This whole scene consists of a monologue by Tetzel, the monk most active in Germany in the sale of indulgences. Coming immediately after the last scenes of Act I in which Luther first revealed that he was far more concerned about his own integrity than were his fellow monks, the contrast is powerful. Luther really cares about those he is helping, Tetzel only about how much money he takes in. Moreover, just by listening to Tetzel we realize that Luther, as we have watched him in Act I, will surely have to challenge Tetzel. In addition, if Martin in Act I worried about his role as a minister of God in comparison to

other monks, how will he feel when he learns that someone as brazen and unscrupulous as Tetzel shows himself
to be trying to influence the same audience?

> TETZEL: . . . Look at them, all properly sealed,
> an indulgence in every envelope, and one
> of them can be yours today, now, before
> it's too late! Come on, come up as close
> as you like, you won't squash me so eas-
> ily. Take a good look. There isn't any
> one sin so big that one of these letters
> can't remit it. I challenge anyone here,
> any member of this audience, to present
> me with a sin, anything, any kind of a
> sin, I don't care what it is, that I
> can't settle for him with one of these
> precious little envelopes. Why, if any
> one had ever offered violence to the
> blessed Virgin Mary, Mother of God, if
> he'd only pay up--as long as he paid up
> all he could--he'd find himself forgiven.
> You think I'm exaggerating? You do, do
> you? Well, I'm authorized to go even
> further than that . . .

On the other hand, there are some underlying similarities that accentuate Martin's dilemma all the more.
For one thing, Tetzel displays some of the same earthi-
ness as Martin's father and Martin himself. Consequently, as much as Tetzel differs from Martin, his
behavior reveals facets of Martin's own nature which
the latter still can't accept. Even more to the point,
just as Tetzel can sway people, if not mesmerize them,
so Martin might some day, and with what results? As
the Knight, the choral commentator, who introduces each
scene points out in a later episode (about which I will
comment in more detail) only one person could have
exerted enough influence that he might have led the
peasants in their rebellion against authority and so
perhaps avoided much of the bloodshed of that terrible
war. That person was Luther himself. In short, the
apparently irrelevant scene with Tetzel, which the
play's severest critics acknowledge has considerable
power, also anticipates some of its major themes, particularly Luther's need to question his own inner
feelings because of the different kinds of impact he
makes on others.

A second scene which at first glance seems to be
just an historical tableau presents Pope Leo X's reaction to a letter sent him by Luther to request his aid.

76

As one of Pope Leo's aides reads the letter, Leo, an ambitious, Machiavellian politician responds with growing irritation. While the scene seems to focus on Leo's mounting anger, actually it centers on Luther's inner conflicts which the letter unconsciously reveals. Luther sees himself as a simple, innocent monk overwhelmed by forces beyond his control and his understanding. Yet it is apparent from the text and Leo's contemptuous references to Luther as "a doubledealing German" who won't say what he means, that Luther really wants to regard himself as the final interpreter of God's Word. As Staupitz tried to explain to Luther in Act II, Scene I, the latter actually ridicules authority to set himself up as the only authority capable of determining his relationship to God. By doing so, Luther boldly challenges the most basic tenet of Catholicism, that the church hierarchy, of which the Pope is the infallible head, legislates for all men. Notice, for example, how Luther in his letter (which the Pope is reading) seems to be meek, yet he actually puts himself above the Pope--or at least on the same plane:

> "There have always been, as long as I can
> remember, complaints and grumbling in the
> taverns about the avarice of the priests and
> attacks on the power of the keys. And this
> has been happening throughout Germany. When
> I listened to these things my zeal was
> aroused for the glory of Christ, so I warned
> not one, but several princes of the Church.
> But, either they laughed in my face or
> ignored me. The terror of your name was too
> much for everyone. It was then I published
> my disputation, nailing it on the door of the
> Castle Church here in Wittenberg. And now,
> most holy father, the whole world has gone up
> in flames. Tell me what I should do? I
> cannot retract; but this thing has drawn down
> hatred on me from all sides, and I don't know
> where to turn to but to you. I am far too
> insignificant to appear before the world in a
> matter as great as this."

That the Pope's fears are justified becomes evident in the next scene in which (as indicated) Luther, while admitting his childlike fears, publicly casts the Papal Bull into the flames and denounces the Pope:
" . . . My God, my God, do you hear me? Are you dead? Are you dead? No, you can't die, you can only hide yourself can't you? Lord, I'm afraid. I am a child, the lost body of a child. I am stillborn . . . "

Luther may feel like a child and even sound like one, but by admitting such emotions he finds the strength to act as defiantly as he does. At this point, Luther doesn't see this connection, but Pope Leo did when he read the letter and therefore recognized how dangerous Luther was.

However, the public scene which most forcefully reveals the complexity and danger of Luther's isolation and doubt is Act III, Scene 2, in which Luther (as indicated) is first attacked for his pro-establishment role in the Peasants War and yet flouts clerical authority by marrying. In the first place, the stage directions reveal how well Osborne emphasizes the suffering brought on by the war.

> Wittenberg, 1525. A marching hymn, the sound of cannon and shouts of mutilated men. Smoke, a shattered banner bearing the cross and wooden shoe of the Bundschuh, emblem of the Peasants' Movement. A small chapel altar at one side of the stage opposite the pulpit. Centre is a small handcart, and beside it lies the bloody bulk of a peasant's corpse. Downstage stands the KNIGHT, fatigued, despondent, stained and dirty.

Notice in particular the peasants' banner, and at the very center, the peasant's corpse, the visible result of the turmoil for which (as the scene unfolds) it becomes evident that Luther bears considerable responsibility.

In the second place, the Knight who in previous scenes does nothing more than announce the time and place of an episode assumes much greater importance. Now he serves as a chorus that dramatizes the impact that Luther's refusal to recant (at Worms) had upon the common people. In his immortal words Luther declared: "I cannot and will not recant, since to act against one's own conscience is neither safe nor honest. Here I stand; God help me. I can do no more. Amen." The impact was electric. Not only were the people willing to do whatever Luther commanded, even if it meant violence, but they even preferred taking such action. "Obviously," as the Knight states, "we couldn't have all felt quite the same way, but I wanted to burst my ears with shouting and draw my sword, no not draw it, I wanted to pluck it as if it were a flower in my blood and plunge it into whatever he would have told me to."

But, as the Knight begins to reflect, his tone
changes to one of doubt and bewilderment, for who
would have thought that Luther would end up bringing
violence down upon those whom he inspired? And the
more the Knight reflects, the angrier he becomes, particularly when, as he loads the body on a cart, Luther
himself appears with a book in his hands. The contrast
between Luther who seems to exist in his own world of
contemplation and the bloodshed of the revolt provides
the third reason why the scene is so powerful. Now
the Knight denounces Luther for his part in the
Peasants' War and smears blood from the corpse all
over the latter.

Such denunciation emphasizes Luther's isolation for
now, however much he defends his action, the Knight
attacks him on his own ground. By introducing the
principle of doubt, Luther as the Knight points out,
enabled the ordinary person to evaluate his religious
experience for himself rather than rely on authority.
But now, according to the Knight, Luther himself sup-
ports those very authoritarian forces from which he
freed the common people.

Yet exactly at this point when Luther seems most
open to attack, he reveals that his doubt still exists,
except that now it is positive. "I smell because of my
own argument, I smell because I never stop disputing
with Him, and because I expect Him to keep His Word.
. . . " Because of the force of his doubts and the
fact that God answers them, Luther feels an even
stronger trust or faith in God.

But Luther himself pays a heavy price for his
faith. Having to justify himself so much and be aware
of such profound doubts, he can't understand how others
whom he has influenced can trust their own feelings so
readily and therefore attack authority as wholeheartedly
as the Peasants did. Nor does Luther realize that his
doubts are so great that they impel him to try to
resolve them through some belief in order, which in
this case Luther identifies with the political stability of the German Princes. Luther feels that the
common people are really acting dogmatically since they
are trying to impose their feelings of individual conscience on others. Yet Luther doesn't recognize that
by valuing order so much as he does and identifying it
with the establishment, which all along he has
attacked, he himself is making it difficult for individuals to express those very feelings of conscience
that he has helped them discover in themselves. If

anything, at this point he may be the dogmatist.

Nevertheless, for all of the force and justice of the Knight's accusation, it is difficult not to retain at least equal sympathy for Luther. This is so because, as the rest of the scene makes clear, Luther's faith depends upon powerful inner feelings whose force the Knight simply doesn't comprehend. Luther articulates the dynamics of this faith in ascending the pulpit (after the Knight has gone) and retelling the story of the sacrifice of Isaac.

By retelling the story, Luther is affirming that the most intense experience of the reality of God comes through doubt or test. Because Abraham had enough faith, he subjected himself to a test that seemed inhuman--and was. But the test was only inhuman because God set for Himself standards higher than the human. However, it was precisely such standards that inspired the two believers, Abraham and Luther:

> . . . Never, save in Christ, was there such obedience as in that moment, and, if God had blinked, the boy would have died then, but the Angel intervened, and the boy was released, and Abraham took him up in his arms again. In the teeth of life we seem to die, but God says no--in the teeth of death we live. If He butchers us, He makes us live.

Luther is describing an interplay between God and man which keeps growing in intensity as man's feelings change. But the change is gradual for in the prayer that follows, doubt still remains:

> Heart of my Jesus save me; Heart of my Saviour deliver me; Heart of my Shepherd guard me; Heart of my Master teach me; Heart of my King govern me; Heart of my Friend stay with me.

I have described this scene in such detail because it reveals the depth and complexity of Luther's faith and yet the harm that unwittingly it can help bring on. We could feel that, since he is exposed, the scene diminishes Luther's greatness. Yet we could also feel that it enhances such greatness because Luther openly shows how much anguish he feels.

After this long discussion, it might seem anti-

climactic for the play to continue, but it does and
with reason because we see another ramification of
conflict and doubt in the fourth scene that I want to
discuss, namely the last episode in the play. This
takes place a few years later and occurs in Luther's
house (formerly a monastery) when his old teacher and
father figure, Staupitz, comes to visit Luther, his
wife, and their infant son Hans (appropriately named
after Luther's father). During the scene Staupitz
and Luther look back upon some of the past, particularly Luther's dramatic refusal at Worms to recant.
One thing puzzles Staupitz: why Luther insisted upon
asking for a day's delay in answering the charges.
Was there some mysterious purpose or some certainty
Luther attained by so doing? No, answers Luther, he
was just stalling because he really had doubts all
the time, even when he refused to recant. By focussing on this incident, Osborne seems to portray
Staupitz in his familiar role as a warm admirer but
also a critic of Luther's, who still reminds the
latter that he oversimplifies his understanding of
belief.

    While we might read the exchange this way, we
could also regard it as another indication of Luther's
difficulties. Even now, after all these years,
Staupitz still doesn't understand Luther. But if
Luther still remains isolated and has doubts, such
problems are much less trying than they were before.
Now Luther, upon reflection, can admit that on a
public level he failed in his involvement in the
Peasants' War and on a personal level because he
accepts his father's ideas about marriage and family,
rather than those of celibacy and asceticism, which he
affirmed when he became a monk. On the other hand,
the fact that Luther can radily admit that he does
agree with his father means that Luther no longer has
to rebel against the latter and his own earlier life.
Equally important, as the last part of the scene
reveals in which Luther is trying to get his son to
sleep, he can, unlike his own father, accept his son's
individuality and helplessness. Through doubt, isolation, and suffering, Luther has discovered that he
isn't self-sufficient. Consequently, he won't, as he
tells his son at the end, expect anyone else to bear
such a burden:

            . . . So try not to be afraid. The dark isn't
        quite as thick as all that. You know, my
        father had a son, and he'd to learn a hard
        lesson, which is a human being is a helpless

> little animal, but he's not created by his
> father, but by God. It's hard to accept
> you're anyone's son, and you're not the
> father of yourself. So, don't have dreams so
> soon, my son. They'll be having you soon
> enough.

In this speech and succeeding lines, Luther has
expressed his reverence for life through man's continually changing inner conflicts and the values which
they enable him to affirm. These are values to which
each part of a man's life contributes, and yet, as the
plays reveals, in which each part differs considerably
from any other. At the very end, while Luther differentiates himself from his father, he is also accepting
the latter more and accepting himself as a son who has
chosen now to internalize parts of his earlier experience that he formerly had to oppose. In so doing,
Luther is able to come to terms with what Erikson
calls the last identity crisis, that of integrity, in
which a man consciously accepts his past as part of
his present and future and thereby helps strengthen
his sense of his own self worth and its value.[39] For
Luther, this acceptance has not at all been easy.
Rather, as has been painfully clear, it has come
through suffering and doubt. Yet the strength of
these feelings has enabled Luther to respond to the
change in his circumstances and to the internal
changes which arise out of the dynamics of the feelings
I've been emphasizing.

To return to the beginning of this discussion, I
would say that Luther holding his son seems very far
removed from Archie Rice swaggering into his song as
the lights dim out and reveal his little world. Yet
the endings of both plays pointedly reveal how men
accept their own limitations and those of their circumstances. Admittedly, Luther has the much easier
time perhaps because earlier he could, unlike Archie,
openly confront his helplessness and disappointment.

In its emphasis upon identity crises, rebellion
against authority, and the dynamic, changing relationship between different elements in human nature out of
which come affirmation and trust, Luther owes much to
Erikson's book. Nevertheless, Luther is Osborne's
play. Erikson's Luther is not really a character but
a vehicle for the latter's reformulation of Freud's
beliefs about the nature and shape of human life. How-

ever, Osborne's Luther is a compelling man of many
facets. He can be helpless, tender, aggressive,
earthy, and self-deceived. But whatever he is, he is
large, compassionate, and interesting. Moreover,
whereas in Erikson's book the other characters are mere
ideological spokesmen, in the play these characters,
particularly Luther's father, become individualized.
And, while Erikson's book is moving in its specula-
tions, it is not dramatic. Nor does its prose, except
when it is Luther's own, have the force and point of
Osborne's. While Osborne has freely admitted drawing
upon Luther's own words, still in making them a part
of the vital context of the play, he has made them his
own. Although I have quoted at length from the play,
I would cite this one last example as evidence of the
play's language. When in Act I, all the other monks
confess their own pallid sins, Martin describes how
hard he has to struggle to overcome his fears of
bodily dissolution:

> If my flesh would leak and dissolve, and I
> could live as bone, if I were forged bone,
> plucked bone and brain, warm hair and a long
> bony heart, if I were all bone, I could bran-
> dish myself without terror without any terror
> at all--I could be indestructible . . . My
> bones fail. My bones fail, my bones are shat-
> tered and fall away, my bones fail and all
> that's left of me is a scraped marrow and a
> dying jelly.

Even if many of these words should come from Luther's
prose, although from investigation I really doubt
it,[40] still in choosing them Osborne shows a real
talent for vivid, sensuous imagery. As the Knight
tells Martin when he denounces him, "Martin you're a
poet."

VI

INADMISSIBLE EVIDENCE

The central character of this play, Bill Maitland,
is an astute, articulate, and profoundly unhappy London lawyer who finds himself driven to justify his
personal and business life, not merely to his legal
staff, his family, and mistress, but most of all to
himself. And, to put it mildly, such justification is
far from easy. For reasons not made clear initially
but evident enough as the play develops, people begin
to see what they regard as Bill's destructive qualities more clearly and to desert him. Situations with
his clients (particularly those involving women seek-
ing divorces), which he once handled easily, now dis-
turb and threaten him. As they do, his staff leave him,
his relationships with his mistress, daughter, and
wife become more unbearable, and he faces prosecution
by the Legal Society for unscrupulous tactics. If
ever an Osborne play dealt with failure, that play is
Inadmissible Evidence. But, as Osborne points out
about Tennessee Williams' characters, failure is what
makes people interesting.41 And Bill Maitland certainly is interesting.

The play consists of two parts. First, comes a
prologue in which Bill requests to put himself on
trial before his peers. While outwardly he is confident, it becomes more and more apparent, as he
makes the arrangements, that he is confused and harassed. I would regard this Prologue as Bill's near
conscious awareness of something he has been both
fighting and yet half realizing for years--namely how
unbearable his life has become and how powerless he
seems to be to do anything about it. Second, comes
the play proper which simply shows us two ordinary
days in Bill's life at the office. Yet what happens
in these days (as I've hinted) makes alarmingly clear
why Bill is living in such a recurring nightmare.

Although a London barrister's office seems remote
from the high Renaissance--and it is--and Bill Maitland certainly cares nothing about religious reform,
not to speak of salvation, yet Inadmissible Evidence
has real affinities with Luther. If we think of Martin Luther as one of the supreme examples of a man
who insists upon the individual's right to assert at
all costs the primacy and uniqueness of his own conscience, then Bill Maitland compares favorably to
Martin Luther. Although outward appearances are all

on the side of Luther, the essential inner man may be
just as evident in Bill Maitland. I say this because
the latter answers to his conscience more in ordinary,
everyday involvements and without the presence of
Staupitz to support him and alleviate some of his
guilt.

To speak of the affinities is not to deny the differences; in fact, the latter stand out more because
of the comparison. In Luther we see the individual
conscience evolving at different stages in a career in
which great public success sometimes masks private
failure. In Inadmissible Evidence, this conscience
reveals itself only in a personal crisis of two days'
duration. However, this crisis is so intense that it
accentuates all those forces in Bill's nature that
make his public and private life appear such a failure
and his feelings of self worth so low. Yet at just
such a low point Bill begins to value his conscience.
As Luther remarks, "In the face of death we begin to
live." While Luther's own life certainly bears this
out, yet that of Bill Maitland also bears witness to
this. For precisely at these moments when Bill seems
most bent on destroying himself, he realizes how alive
he is and what he values.

Many critics regard Inadmissible Evidence as
Osborne's most impressive and moving play to date.
While I wouldn't necessarily consider this so, I certainly can understand why the play commands such
praise.

To begin with, the Prologue has a Kafkesque quality
reminiscent of The Trial. By this I mean that there
is a literal reality in which all the details have an
everyday authenticity: the defendant standing before
the judge confusedly asking for a hearing and yet
almost obsessively following all the procedures. At
the same time everything is just a bit distorted, as
the defendant, Bill, begins acting with a deceptive
assurance. However, as he proceeds, it is apparent
how driven he feels and how rigorous a judgement he
makes on himself:

         . . . I never hoped or wished for anything
      more than to have the good fortune of friend-
      ship and the excitement and comfort of love
      and the love of women in particular. I made
      a set at both of them in my own way. With
      the first with friendship, I hardly succeeded
      at all. Not really. No. Not at all. With

> the second, with love, I succeeded, I suc-
> ceeded in inflicting, quite certainly
> inflicting, more pain than pleasure. I am
> not equal to any of it. But I can't escape
> it, I can't forget it. And I can't begin
> again. You see?

A second, and more important, reason for the play's impressiveness is the sheer force of Maitland's presence throughout the play. While in almost every Osborne play the central character dominates, in Inadmissible Evidence this tendency seems even more pronounced since, except for one brief episode, Bill is on stage during the entire play. More than that, his role varies. Sometimes he engages in chit chat with his legal associates, yet with an obvious tension underlying it because much of Bill's behavior under- standably offends his associates. At other times, he feels so immobilized about making any decision that he seems compulsively destroying himself. In these moments, he carries on break length monologues with his wife and mistress, each of whom he feels he needs (without realizing what this is doing to him) and yet each of whom he seems compelled to hurt. Then at still other times, he becomes the cool, efficient counsel who encourages clients to recount their diffi- culties at great length. Such questioning does enable the actor playing Bill to rest. Yet even during these episodes Bill dominates, for the characters' dilemmas clearly resemble his own, and within a few moments both he and the client sense this.

Nevertheless, I don't mean to imply that Bill domi- nates merely because of the theatrical virtuosity which his continuous presence makes possible or even demands. Rather, he does so because he is so alive and aware both of others and his own response.

As evidence for now, I cite two speeches in particu- lar. The first occurs early in the play when Bill is describing to Hudson, his chief clerk, how apprehensive he feels about the coming weekend because this threatens to bring to a head his conflicting feelings for his mistress and his wife:

> I've no idea. I don't know which is worse,
> which prospect frightens me more. I keep
> seeing their faces, Ann's. Liz. And some of
> the others. It's even worse when they ring
> up. Not that Liz rings up very often. She
> has an immaculate idea of a mistress's rights.

I want to feel tender, I want to be comforting
and encouraging and full of fun and future
things like that. But all I feel is as if my
head were bigger and bigger, spiked and fal-
ling off like a mace, it gets in my way, or
keeps getting too close. It's not worth the
candle, is it?

On the one hand, he appreciates his mistress because
she seems so concerned with his comfort. On the other,
he describes in vivid images how, despite all her
efforts, he feels worse and worse. I might also add
that Bill's description of his mistress, although he
seems unaware of it here, may also be damaging his
self worth since it could be making him more dependent
on her than he recognizes and therefore feel guilty.
(But more of these points later.)

The second occurs when he tells Liz how unbearable
an evening he has spent with his wife because her
friends were cutting him and he felt so dependent on
her that he almost couldn't believe he existed in his
own right:

. . . What was what like? Oh, last night...
Well, yes there was an Anna situation...oh,
before we went out and afterwards...Yes, that
was bad enough, but the whole thing was very
strange....It's difficult to explain...No, I
can't quite....I'm sorry. I just don't seem
to retain very much of anything, of anything
that happened....I just felt everyone was
cutting me...cutting me....I know, I should
care! I like them as much as they like me.
...I don't know whether they're more afraid
than I am....I think they really want to be
liked...in that sort of way....I don't
exactly do my best do I. No, well, then....
No, Anna quite enjoyed herself while she was
there....Oh, the usual shower....They all seem
to adore her....I know, but more than ever....
it's only all right when I'm with her....
Yes....But it seemed at my expense this time,
it seemed to be out of me....as if they were
disowning me....it's wonderful to hear your
voice....Well, I don't know yet....sometime
this evening....Look, please don't you press
me...Yes. It'll be all right...

One reason he feels so despairing is that he is
vividly aware of what people are doing to him.

particularly because he senses how they must be feeling, not to mention Liz to whom he is talking. As Hudson, his chief clerk begrudgingly admits, Bill has a talent for taking part in others' lives. For this (as will become evident) he pays a very high price because he picks up others' feelings and turns them against himself. Yet this talent also makes clear why he is so alive and interesting.

From the way I have been describing Bill so far, he would sound like a terrible failure, at least publicly or outwardly. Yet he also represents a considerable success story, which, paradoxically, helps account for his feelings of worthlessness and the compulsive need to hurt himself that I have emphasized. To see Bill as he is in the present action of the play, it is necessary to see him as he has evolved--as much as that is possible since he doesn't talk about his past, except only in the Prologue and at the end in a long tirade directed against his daughter.

So far as we can tell about family background, Bill seems to be lower middle class. I say this because he had to go to work as a law clerk at age fifteen. While he didn't find the work compelling or feel that the law represented a calling for him, he determined to become a lawyer. He did so because he felt he had considerable ability in this field, the law represented a source of power in society, and because Bill believed, or thought he did, in the facile notions of progress and technological expertise that underlie the value system of his society. Significantly, Bill begins his 'trial' with a breakneck, confusing resume of what he professes to believe in:

> CLERK: Do you swear and affirm?
> BILL: I swear and affirm...(Pause. Then a hoarse rattle. Clearing his throat at intervals.) I hereby swear and affirm. Affirm. On my...Honour? By my belief. My belief in....in....the technological revolution, the pressing, growing, pressing, urgent need for more and more scientists, and more scientists, for more and more schools and universities and universities and schools, the theme of change, realistic decisions based on a highly developed and professional study of society by people who really know their subject, the overdue need for us to adapt ourselves to different conditions,

the theme and challenge of such rapid
change, change, rapid change. (Flails.
The Judge looks at him reassuringly and he
picks up again.) In the ninety seven per
cent, ninety seven, of all the scientists
who have ever lived in the history of the
world since the days of Euclid, Pythagoras
and Archimedes. Who, who are alive and at
work today, today, now, at this time, in
the inevitability of automation and the
ever increasing need, need, oh, need....

But, as the rest of the play makes clear, he no longer
believes in these values, if deep down he ever did at
all.

Yet through a combination of astuteness, hard work,
a willingness to cut corners, and sheer gall, Bill (at
the time the play opens) has come a long way. He has a
fairly large practice and a reputation as a tough,
wily lawyer who 'bends' the law when he deems it
advisable or necessary. As for his private life, it is
messy and confusing. To begin with, he has been twice
divorced, although no one mentions this. He has a mistress, whom people do mention because everyone,
including his wife, knows about her. At the same time,
Bill still remains close to his wife. Not only does he
care for her, but he appears with her at all the right
affairs. However, he is accepted at these largely
because of his wife's higher social position and the
sympathy she receives as the wronged woman.

From such a description, Bill would seem to resemble a Humphrey Bogart character--the sensual, opportunistic man of the world who lives more recklessly
and interestingly than do ordinary people. But, with
all due respect to this kind of character, Bill is
more complex and passionate and by the same token more
easily hurt.

As the Prologue suggests, Bill seems to know himself well. He realizes that he isn't a legal genius
and yet appreciates his own virtues, especially his
talent for cross examination and for taking advantage
of loopholes. On the other hand, Bill also deprecates
himself and what he stands for. As he says at one
point in the Prologue, he is "irredeemably mediocre."
He doesn't recognize how quickly he sizes up issues
and how candidly he can deal with clients by encouraging them to be honest with themselves. Most of all,
he doesn't realize until the end of the play, as the

quotations I've cited reveal, how perceptive and aware
he is of his own reactions and those of others and how
wide is his range of interests.

However, Bill's most important self-deprecation
concerns his identification with the law and his own
motives for becoming a lawyer. When he asserts that he
has no sense of a calling and that the law as it
exists in London exploits people, he seems to know
what he's talking about. Consequently, to survive as
a lawyer one may have to exploit the law. Nevertheless, Bill doesn't recognize the price he has paid for
such an identification. One such result is that he
encourages others to accept his own cynical self-
estimate and give themselves grounds, if they so choose,
to turn on him. For example, his secretary, Shirley,
with whom he had had an affair several months ago, now
has suddenly decided that she wants to quit. When previously she insisted that she was quitting, no one
took her seriously--and with good reason since the
threats sounded vague. But now Shirley can't stand
Bill any more, despite the fact that he ended their
affair three months ago. It is true she is engaged
and pregnant, but, as Bill points out, she could easily
stay on for several months. Apparently, Shirley is
quitting because Bill's sensuality disgusts her, as
is evident from the way she taunts him about some of
their typical assignations; "one weekend in Leicester
on client's business. Two weekends in Southend on
client's business. Moss Mansions--remember them? Four
days in Hamburg on client's business. One crummy
client's crummy flat in Chiswick. And three times on
this floor . . . " Nor is Shirley the only one to
desert Bill. Mrs. Garnsey, one of his clients, after
one interview, withdraws her case from him, and Joy,
the receptionist, who previously enjoyed sex with him
because as she admits, she wants it constantly,
threatens to leave. Later still, Winters, the barrister, who for years has pleaded all of Bill's cases in
court,* won't speak to him on the phone, and the Legal
Society begins to investigate him.

Why do all these rejections occur? Is Bill really
so corrupt--or so threatening that people finally have
to turn on him? Certainly much of the "evidence" I've
cited would seem to corroborate this. He taunts and
wheedles his associates, Hudson and Jones, he is not

---
*In England solicitors can only prepare cases;
barristers try them in court.

averse to producing false witnesses to get a client acquitted, at times he lies to his wife and mistress, and he betrays both of them with girls at the office.

But all this "evidence" represents just one side of the coin. To begin with, just before Shirley recounts what seem like such disgusting details of their relationship, Bill presents a different view. In answer to her question as to what he has ever done for her, he has this to say:

> BILL: Nothing, I suppose. But I do know we had some affection for one another, beneath all the arguing and banter and waste of breath. I know I liked you. And when we were in bed together you dropped all your pretences and deceits, after a while anyway. Perhaps I did even. I don't think I let you think it was an enduring love affair--in the sense of well of endless, wheedling obligations and summonses and things. But, if you think back on it, detail by detail, I don't think you can say it was fraudulent. Can you?
> SHIRLEY: No.
> BILL: You can't <u>disown</u> it. If you do that, you are helping, you are conspiring to kill me.

Granted there may be some exaggeration in his last response, he is trying to get her to understand how much he needs some kind of feedback. Although she accepts his description, she persists, as indicated, and then walks out.

In contrast, Bill's mistress, Liz, when she does appear in his office, out of concern for what has been happening to him and to propose that he may wish to be alone, recognizes that much of the time most people, himself included, don't judge him accurately:

> You pretend to be ill and ignorant just so you can escape reproach. You beggar and belittle yourself just to get out of the game.

Because Bill can't stand criticism, Liz feels that he seems compelled to force people to reject him. For this reason, he is, to quote her again, "a dishonest little creep," who has been deceiving everyone for years.

Certainly Bill's relationship with his wife Anna seems to bear out what Liz says. Not only does he talk indiscreetly about Liz to his wife, but insults the latter's friends at their dinner parties. Worst of all, as I've indicated, Bill insists on telling Anna over the phone how much he depends on her for his existence. In doing so, he would seem to be embarrassing his wife and adding to her guilt.

However, is Liz as insightful as she believes herself to be? True enough, Bill sets higher ethical standards than he lets on to others. But is it because he is afraid of harsh judgments or that he realizes that none of his judges, even Liz, understands his motives and actions?

Clearly his wife doesn't for she assumes that the reason Bill insists upon wanting to spend a weekend with Liz rather than with his daughter Jane (when she celebrates her seventeenth birthday) is just to indulge his own pleasure. In reality, he makes this decision because it would bring everything out into the open—particularly his own ambivalence towards his daughter and the way his wife is using the party to play upon Bill's guilt feelings. By forcing the issue at this time, Bill is making it easier for his wife to break with him, if she wishes, since now she has more reason to do so. Only Liz, in offering to release Bill from spending the weekend with her, realizes some of the conflicts involved in his decision. Yet even she assumes that he prefers to be alone to avoid further reproach for his actions. But, in reality, Bill accepts her suggestion because he realizes that all along she never wanted to go. She doesn't want to go, not because she doesn't care for him but that in going she would be committing herself more to their relationship than she is prepared to do. Or, to use her term, she would be vulnerable to reproach. As she admits, unlike Bill, she considers herself free of guilt: "I've always managed to avoid guilt. It's a real peasant's pleasure, you know. For people without a sliver of self knowledge or courage." For these reasons, she acknowledges she may be paying a heavy price for her pleasure. Considering what Liz has said and done, we might expect Bill to turn on her. But instead he affirms his love for her: "And I shall never forget your face or anything about you. It won't be possible. I think, I'm quite certain, not that it matters, I loved you more than anyone." When Liz in reply asks, "More than Jane?" Bill answers "yes."

Admittedly, Bill derives a lot of pleasure from what

Liz calls his "impeccable assessments," and this one is his pride and joy, especially since it may be his last for some time. But he is also helping her to maintain her ideal self image and to relieve herself of responsibility for her decision. Then immediately afterwards he calls his wife and gets her to agree that it is pointless for him to come home. In this way he makes it appear that they have both made the decision. However, Bill alone has decided in order to make it easier for the other person. (More of this later.)

In short, Bill acts far more responsibly and compassionately than others, including Liz, recognize. However, the only way he can do so is to withdraw from all the people with whom he is involved and endure even greater loneliness and frustration than he has known in his life.

To mention loneliness and frustration is to bring us back to what is really the climax of the play, an incident that occurs before the encounter with Liz, and one that seems to contradict all that I've just been asserting about Bill's principled behavior. I refer to his painful and apparently cruel rejection of his daughter Jane, whom he has called to his office to inform her why, instead of coming to her seventeenth birthday party that her mother, as mentioned, is arranging for her, he is going to spend the weekend with Liz. In itself, just to tell Jane that seems cruel. Yet, in what is the longest speech of this and all Osborne's plays to date, he denounces her for her coldness and indifference and drives her away from him. (For now I quote only the end):

> You know what God is supposed to have said, well in Sunday School, anyway? God said, He said: Be fruitful and multiply and replenish the earth. And subdue it. It seems to me Jane, little Jane, you don't look little any longer, you are on your way at last, all, to doing all four of them. For the first time. Go on now.

Why, we ask, could he do something like this to his own daughter, whom he loves and who is standing there mute and helpless?

However, when we look back at what has been happening to Bill, particularly as he has been dealing with the clients who have been appearing before him, it is apparent that these interviews have been crystallizing

in him deep and conflicting feelings which others
never really perceived and that he himself only begins
to realize.

The first of these, Mrs. Garnsey, describes how
unbearable her life has become because she senses that
her husband is failing and she can't help him:

> MRS. G.: But what, what kills me is that he is
> being hurt so much.
> BILL: How do you mean?
> MRS. G.: By everyone. He comes home to me,
> and I know that nothing really works for
> him. Not at the office, not his friends,
> not even his girls. I wish they would.
> God knows, he tries hard enough. I wish
> I could help him. But I can't, and
> everyone, everyone, wherever, we go
> together, whether it's a night out, or an
> evening at our club, or an outing with
> the children, everyone's, I know, every-
> one's drawing away from him. And the
> more people have been good and kind and
> thoughtful to me, the worse it's been
> for him. I know. And now. Now: I'm
> doing the same thing. The children
> hardly notice him. And now it's me. I
> can't bear to see him rejected and laughed
> at and scorned behind his back and
> ignored--(All this last is scarcely audi-
> ble.) I've got to leave him. (Nothing
> more meaningful comes from her. BILL
> gets up to comfort her but is paralysed.)

From the stage directions, as well as the fact
that Mrs. Garnsey can't (as indicated) bear to come
back to the office again, it is clear that what she
says also applies to Bill, namely how ignored and
worthless he feels. This is evident by the fact that
immediately afterwards Bill begs his receptionist, Joy,
to stay on afterwards and have sex with him because,
although he can't admit it, he feels Mrs. Garnsey's
guilt and her husband's failure.

Why does Bill feel as he does? The subsequent
meetings with the other clients and the first part of
his speech to Jane, before he sends her away, show why.
As the clients come before him, they describe how,
despite their own and their partner's effort, the real
attachment they felt for each other and their mutual
consideration, they can't go on as they are. We have

no reason to doubt what these people say for they seem
open, and they are in such great pain that at times
their accounts cause Bill to drift off into private
fantasies. Simon Trussler regards these reactions as
evidence of Bill's solipsism to people, as a result of
which Liz leaves him and he can't face going home to
his wife.[42] But is this so?

Undeniably, Bill is withdrawing and for a time
denying these women support. Yet I think he is doing
so because their accounts reveal, by comparison, how
much emptier his life is than he ever dared realize.
He isn't loved as are the husbands of these women, and
he isn't being loving, at least towards his wife. Yet
for these reasons, as this exchange with a later
client reveals, he is beginning to understand that he
wants something different out of life and how valuable and yet difficult love must be if it is to work:

>MRS. A: I have never been with anyone apart
>from my husband.
>BILL: That's what's wrong with all of you, you
>dim deluded little loving things. You
>listen to promiscuous lady journalists and
>bishops and your mother. And hang on to
>it.
>MRS. A: But he's always saying these things.
>BILL: He listens.
>MRS. A: It's as if he can't help it. When he
>wanted to, he would have intercourse two
>or three times a day. He would, he would
>go as far as he could but that was all.
>But it's not only that, it's not even that.
>If it were only that, I could put up with
>all kinds of things. Because I know he is
>a good man, really, and a kind man. He
>can be, and he has been kind to me.
>BILL: I love you. He never said, he hardly
>ever said, he stopped saying, he found it
>difficult to say I love you. It has to be
>heaved and dropped into the pool after you,
>a great rock of I love you, and then you
>have to duck down below the surface and
>bring it up, like some gasping, grateful,
>stupid dog.
>MRS. A: He loves the children, and is always
>making a fuss of them, and giving them
>things. My sister used to come in to watch
>T.V., but I hardly ever went out while she
>was there. We went to the doctor and he
>made me go to Weymouth for two weeks for a

complete rest.

However, Bill doesn't have anyone who feels about
him, as Mrs. A. does about her husband, even though,
as his comment about love reveals, he seems capable
of more empathy than does the latter's husband.
Instead, because of the cold, indifferent, exploitive
atmosphere in which he grew up and worked and in his
own acceptance of such values, he has come to depre-
cate himself so profoundly that, as he told his wife,
he can't feel he exists without her being there. It
is no wonder that his marriage seems to have reached
the point where his wife, knowingly or unknowingly,
holds him to her through guilt, and he holds on to her
to punish himself. At the same time he compounds such
feelings by his relationship with his mistress whom he
has to call for feedback. While he does receive
some, the reaction that Liz expresses, as shown by
her comment that she prides herself on not feeling
guilt, actually could make Bill feel even guiltier
than he has before he called her.

By the time that Jane arrives, Bill's awareness of
the value of love, particularly when people admit how
they really feel becomes stronger. Significantly, just
before the scene with Jane, Bill spends a lot of time
with Maples, a young married man charged with homosexual behavior. (This was before the days of the
Wolfenden report which forbade such discrimination.)
While Bill proposes ways of getting Maples off, particularly since the latter really was framed by the
police, Maples refuses. He does so because, although
he is being punished unfairly, at least in acknowledging what occurred, he is accepting his identity as a
homosexual who can feel genuine love, however painful
are the consequences, rather than go on, as he has
been doing, simulating such feelings to his wife to
satisfy his mother in particular that he is "normal."
Moreover, since Maples' wife knows of his homosexuality and still accepts him, he really won't be hurting
her any more than he has already. At the same time he
is treating himself more kindly, since he has _less_ to
feel guilty about.

It is against this background that we need to
look in more detail at the rejection of Jane, for
through it Bill is trying to acknowledge openly the
conflicts that have been wracking him and by so doing
affirming a greater sense of his own worth and to pay
whatever price he has to sustain that awareness. He
pours out these feelings to Jane both as the person

for whom he has cared the most (at least until his
relationship with Liz) and yet the one who has disappointed him the most. Nevertheless, that very disappointment helps him appreciate more of the qualities
which he deprecated in himself and which for those
reasons are taking such a toll on him:

> BILL: They're all pretending to ignore me. No
> they're not pretending. And that'll be the
> going of you except that it's happened
> already. Of course, it has, ages ago.
> Look at me. Why you can't have looked at
> me and seen anything, what, not for years,
> not since you were a little tiny girl and
> I used to take you out and hold your hand
> in the street. I always used to think
> then when you're the age you are now, I'd
> take you out to restaurants for dinner,
> big restaurants like I used to think posh
> restaurants were like, with marble columns
> and glass and orchestras. Like Lyons used
> to be before you knew it. And I thought
> we'd behave like a rather grand married
> couple, a bit casual but with lots and
> lots of signals for one another. And
> waves of waiters would pass in front of us
> and admire us and envy us and we'd dance
> together. (holds her to him.) Very slow-
> ly. (pause.) And when we got back to our
> table, and when it was all over, we'd lean
> forward and look at each other with such,
> such oh, pleasure--we'd hardly be able to
> eat our dinner. (releases her.) So that
> when we got up, after a bit too much
> champagne, we'd have to hang on to each
> other very tightly indeed. And then: go
> home...I always wish I'd been brought up in
> the country you know. Won't be possible
> much longer. There isn't any place for
> me, not like you. In the law, in the
> country, or, indeed, in any place in this
> city. My old father lives in the country,
> as you know, but he doesn't want to see me
> these days. Can't say I blame him. When
> I went to see him the other day--whenever
> it was, do you know, I tried to remind him
> of all sorts of things we'd done together,
> but he simply wouldn't, he wouldn't remem-
> ber. And then the old devil got mad and
> told me I was imagining it. I had to go
> in the end. He was tired and he wanted me

to go. When I bent down and kissed him, he
didn't look up...Your other grandparents
can hardly bring themselves to acknowledge
me. The old woman crossed to the other
side of the street once when I was pushing
you in the pram so as to avoid speaking to
me. Which surprised me. With you, I mean.
They have you over there and your mother
goes, I know, and they still give you
generous presents Christmas and birthday,
but to you know when they write to your
mother, they never even mention me by
name, love to Bill, how's Bill, nothing,
not for ten years, and they only did it in
the early years after you were born because
they thought they had to if they were going
to be able to see you! And then they discovered that they didn't even have to mime
that genteel little courtesy. How much do
you think your safety depends on the good-
will of others? Well? Tell me. Or your
safety? How safe do you think you are?
Safe? (She turns away increasingly frightened.)   Do you want to get rid of me? Do
you? Um? Because I want to get rid of
you. (She moves to the door.) (toweringly
cool for a while.) Just a moment, Jane.
You can't go yet. Till I tell you. About
this famous weekend. (She shrugs impatient-
ly.) Oh, I know it's none of your fault.
But you should know I shan't be with you,
or, at least, your mother then, just
because I shall be with Liz--a subject that
bores you, I know, as much as it's beginning to her, if you see--I'll be with her
for three whole days or something, if she'll
have me, I don't know that she will, but
I'll be with her instead of you on your
seventeenth--is it seventeen?--anyway,
birthday and the reason for that is because
I know: that when I see you, I cause you
little else but distaste or distress, or,
at the least, your own vintage, swinging
indifference. But nothing, certainly not
your swinging distaste can match what I
feel for you. (Small pause as he changes
tack.) Or any of those who are more and
more like you. Oh, I read about you, I see
you in the streets. I hear what you say,
the sounds you make, the few jokes you make,
the wounds you inflict without even longing

to hurt, there is no lather or fear in you,
all cool, dreamy, young, cool and not a
proper blemish, forthright, unimpressed,
contemptuous of ambition but good and
pushy all the same. You've no shame of
what you are, and, very little, well, not
much doubt as to what you'll become. And
quite right, at least so I used to think.
They're young, I said, and for the first
time they're being allowed to roll about
in it and have clothes and money and music
and sex, and you can take or leave any of
it. No one before has been able to do
such things with such charm, such ease,
such frozen innocence as all of you seem to
have, to me. Only you, and girls like you,
naturally, could get on that poor old
erotic carthouse, the well known plastic
mac and manage to make it look pretty.
Pretty, mark you! Chic. Lively. You've
stopped its lumbering, indecent, slobber-
ing ancient longing and banged it into the
middle of the Daily Express--where they're
only allowed to say the word 'rape' if a
black African's involved. Or perhaps a
nun. You don't even, not moved, to wear
make-up any longer. Your hair looks like
a Yorkshire terrier's come in from out of
the monsoon. And, yet, somehow, perverse-
ly, you are more beautiful and certainly
more dashing than any of the girls I used
to know and lust after from morning to
night, with their sweety, tacky lipsticks
and silk stockings on coupons and permanent waves and thick hipped heavy skirts.
I don't know what you have to do with me
at all, and soon you won't, you'll go out
of that door and I'll not see you again.
I am quite sure of that by this time if
nothing else. You hardly drink except for
some wine and pintfuls of murky coffee.
You'll go anywhere and more or less seem to
do anything, you've already permanent sun-
less, bleached stains beneath your breasts
and two, likewise, crescents, on your
buttocks. You'll read any menu without
bothering, order what you want, and, what's
more, get it. Then maybe leave it.
You'll hitch hike and make your young
noises from one end of Europe to the other
without a thought of having the correct

100

currency or the necessary language. And
you're right. And you dance with each
other, in such a way I, would never have
been able to master. (He gazes longingly
across.) But, and this is the but, I still
don't think what you're doing will ever,
even, even, even approach the fibbing, mum-
ping, pinched little worm of energy eating
away in this me, of mine, I mean. That is:
which is that of being slowly munched and
then diminished altogether. That worm,
thank heaven, is not in your little cherry
rose. You are unselfconscious, which I am
not. You are without guilt, which I am
not. Quite rightly. Of course, you are
stuffed full of paltry relief for emer-
gent countries, and marches and boycotts
and rallies, you, you kink your innocent
way along tirelessly to all that poetry and
endless jazz and folk worship, and looking
gay and touching and stylish all at the
same time. But there isn't much loving in
any of your kindnesses, Jane, not much
kindness, not even cruelty, really, in any
of you, not much craving for the harm of
others, perhaps just a very easy, controlled
sharp, I mean 'sharp' pleasure in discom-
fiture. You're flip and offhand and if
you are the unfeeling things you appear to
be, no one can really accuse you of being
cruel in the proper sense. If you should
ever, and I hope you shan't, my dear, I
truly do for I've leapt at the very idea
of you, before you were ever born, let
alone the sight and smell of you; if you
should one day start to shrink slowly into
an unremarkable, gummy little hole into a
world outside the care or consciousness of
anyone, you'll have no rattlings of shame
or death, there'll be no little sweating,
eruptions of blood, no fevers or clots or
flesh splitting anywhere or hemorrhage.
You'll have done everything well and sen-
sibly and stylishly. You'll know it
wasn't worth any candle that ever burned.
You will have to be blown out, snuffed,
decently, and not be watched spluttering
and spilling and hardening. . . .

I quote this very long speech because it crystal-
lizes what has been happening to Bill and shows how

101

acutely he feels it, as his descriptions of his yearning for Jane, his rejection by his father, his consciousness of the life style of Jane and her generation, his awareness of the energies he feels throbbing in him, and his description at the end of what it is like to be dying emotionally (" . . . if you should one day start to shrink slowly into an unremarkable, gummy little hole into a world outside the care or consciousness of anyone . . . ") all reveal so articulately.

Admittedly, some--or even most--of the hostility he feels towards Jane and her generation seems overdone. That it does may suggest that Bill's remarkable talent for absorbing himself in others' lives (as mentioned earlier) may be causing him to distort what he perceives. Or he may, without realizing it, be punishing himself by driving away some one for whom he cares so much. Yet the fact that Bill does shows he could go on hurting Jane and others even more were he to remain in their lives.

On the other hand, Bill is showing how much energy he does possess, particularly by the range of his observations; how much he cares for what is happening in his society; and how much he needs others to stimulate him, give him affection and understanding, and enable him to express his concern for them. Yet by the same token the failure of these people causes him to be destroying himself inwardly (" . . . that of being slowly munched and then diminished altogether. .)" not to mention others in the play who are less aware than he of what is happening to themselves as their relationships aren't working out. At least, by withdrawing from Jane, Liz, and Anna, his wife, and letting the Legal Society prosecute him, even if such action may to a certain extent be unfair, because, as his clerk Hudson acknowledges, prestigious firms are corrupt in more discrete ways, Bill, like Maples, is affirming openly who he is and what he values and acting accordingly. To that extent, he is trying to take over control of his life in contrast to the anxiety he expresses in his trial. "But I can't escape it, I can't forget it: and I can't begin again . . . "). At least he is trying to be equal to it, and, even if he can't begin again, he is trying to arrest what has been happening. In particular, he is doing these things by breaking with his wife in the manner in which he does. Not only is he making it easier for her by saying, "I, I think it must be better if you don't see me, don't see me . . . yes . . .

don't . . . ") but also for himself since he will be making himself less vulnerable to Anna's judgments and therefore feel less guilt. As a result, he is taking an important first step towards developing a healthy conscience and a more just sense of his own worth.

VII

A PATRIOT FOR ME

Like <u>Luther</u>, <u>A Patriot for Me</u> concerns the career
of an actual historical figure who in his day rose
from obscurity to great prominence. However, in place
of a great religious reformer, Osborne presents an
Austrian Intelligence Officer, Col. Alfred Redl (1863-
1903) who was involved in a case as celebrated as that
of the Dreyfus Affair--although admittedly Redl had no
Zola to defend him.[43] The son of a poor railway clerk,
Redl showed such ability, determination, and finesse,
that, despite his lower class, and, as we discover at
the end, possible Jewish background, he became the
most celebrated and talented Counter-Intelligence
Officer in the pre-World War I Austro-Hungarian
General Staff Corps. Not only did he make Austrian
Intelligence highly respected, but he also succeeded
in rounding up a record number of Russian spies.
Though he lived on a grand scale, no one questioned
this because officers naturally were considered gentle-
men whose private lives (so long as they remained
hidden from public view) were beyond scrutiny and
above reproach as members of an elite. Yet, in
reality, Redl was a notorious homosexual and counterspy for the Russians, to whom, as the price of blackmail for not revealing his homosexuality, he betrayed
many important secrets. When the Austrians finally
did discover his treachery, they concealed it as much
as possible by permitting Redl as an officer and gentleman to take the "honorable way" out, namely to
commit suicide. But, despite all their caution, the
details became known and sent shock waves throughout
Central Europe. For if at the very center of the
Empire such treachery could occur, then who could
really feel safe?

From my account so far, one important thrust of
the play is the crucial importance of role playing both
for the individual and for the society in which he is
operating or fulfilling himself. A significant reason
Redl succeeded was that he was able to reflect back to
his superiors just what they wanted to hear about the
officer elite that could enable them to feel proud of
what the corps stood for and therefore reassured about
their own worth and that of their society itself. Such
reassurance was crucial inasmuch as the Empire had
really done very little since 1517 when at the Battle
of Lepanto the Austrians saved Europe from conquest by
the Saracens. From that time on, the Empire just

managed to hold itself together through the force of appearances. This involved pointing to the Officer Corps as proof that at least one group was performing a valuable function by providing role models as a source of inspiration for society. It is not surprising, then, that Redl's treachery provoked uneasiness.

Yet, while the play does emphasize society's dependence upon the elite, primarily it shows us what membership can do to someone who, while a super-star in the organization, is vulnerable because of his background and his sensitive, proud, and strong-willed personality.

To begin with, membership in the elite seems to give Redl a golden opportunity to realize himself through satisfying the expectations of his superiors and meeting the challenges involved. A very good example of the potentialities of feedback of this sort occurs in a scene in Act I when Redl appears at the annual ball given by the Emperor in honor of the Officer Corps. Since at this point Redl has already demonstrated considerable achievement (he had graduated from the prestigious Intelligence school to which only a few were sent, and he had just returned from a tour of duty in St. Petersburg where he had learned Russian), the ball presents him with a great opportunity to further his career and to display his talent for impressing his superiors. So far as the former is concerned, the high point of the scene would be the announcement that the Archbuke Franz Ferdinand, heir to the throne, wishes to meet Redl. Yet just as important (and certainly more interesting for what it reveals of Redl's talents) is an episode in which Redl along with the Countess Sophia Delyanoff, a beautiful woman attracted to him (but, unknown to anyone at the ball, actually a Russian agent sent to lure Redl into marriage so that she might set him up in some way) chats with Colonel Von Mohl, Redl's former commanding officer who hasn't seen the latter since he selected him as one of three candidates for Command Staff Training. Since Von Mohl is having a good time and is proud of Redl, the latter can talk more openly than he usually does. As for Sophia, she wants to flatter Von Mohl and charm Redl into becoming interested in her. I quote a passage that begins after one officer, Kunz, has so sharply criticized the Army that General Von Hotzendorff, Von Mohl's superior, has politely excused himself and left. While Kunz insists that he was only joking and everyone should have known this, he does apologize and apparently departs. At this point Sophia moves in and turns her charm on both Redl and Von Mohl, although in different ways:

> COUNTESS: Well. What tempers you men do have! What about you, Captain, we've not heard much out of you yet? I've a feeling you're full of shocking things.
> REDL: What about?
> COUNTESS: Why, what we've been talking about.
> REDL: Like the army, you mean? I'm afraid I don't agree with the Major.
> COUNTESS: No?
> REDL: No. I mean, for myself, I didn't want to be, or mean to be: rigid or fixed.
> COUNTESS: But you're not.
> REDL: No. At the same time, there must be bonds, some bonds that have more meaning than the others.
> COUNTESS: I don't follow.
> MOHL: Now you're baiting, Countess. Of course he's right. No officer should be allowed to speak in the way of Major Kunz.
> COUNTESS: He offends against blood. He--
> MOHL: Against himself; it's like being a Pole or a Slovak or a Jew, I suppose. All these things have more meaning than being, say, a civil servant, or a watchmaker. And all these things are brought together in the army like nowhere else. It's the same experience as friendship or loving a woman, speaking the same tongue, that is a proper bond, it's human, you can see it and experience it, more than 'all men are brothers' or some such nonsense.
> COUNTESS: And do you agree with that, Captain Redl?
> REDL: I don't agree that all men are brothers, like Colonel Mohl. We are clearly not. Nor should be, or ever want to be.
> COUNTESS: Spoken like a true aristocrat.
> REDL: Which, as you must know, I am not--
> COUNTESS: Oh, but I believe you are. Don't you, Colonel?
> REDL: We're meant to clash. And often and violently. I am proud to be despised by some men, no perhaps most men. Others are to be tolerated or ignored. And if they do the same for me, I am gratified, or, at least, relieved.

Sophia cleverly plays Redl off against Von Mohl in

order to give the latter a chance to reaffirm his
admiration for Redl and the former to earn it. Yet
she also challenges Redl to talk more interestingly and
openly than he customarily does because she senses that
he would also appreciate more stimulation than Von Mohl
affords. Redl, in turn, can accept her challenge
because he knows that he can differ with Von Mohl here
since this will enable the latter to praise Redl for
style--the supreme achievement of an officer. Yet in
differing in the way that he does, Redl chooses to take
a considerable risk since he offers an explanation for
his views that may be too penetrating for Von Mohl to
understand. However, he does so because he senses
that Sophia is demanding proof that he can show real
independence. In insisting that he is a snob, he
satisfies that demand and yet because of loyalty to
Von Mohl takes the risk of offending her as well.
Clearly his performance, and to a lesser extent hers,
show how much energy, wit, tact, and candor a person
can express through enacting a role with style.

Nevertheless, such appearances are deceptive.
Sophia, as indicated, has to work for the Russians so
that she has no real choices she can make. As for
Redl, when we follow the curve of his career, as
Osborne presents it through a formal structure very
much like that of Luther, of contrasting, self contained scenes of varying length which show the pressures operating on him at each stage of his career,
we see how oppressive and degrading such role playing
can be. Yet, we also see how strong Redl has to
become to survive under such conditions, as he fights
back and also acknowledges feelings within himself
that he scarcely knew he possessed. In particular, I
want to focus on five episodes: the opening scene, a
large extravagant annual masked ball (which takes up
most of Act II) only given for homosexuals, Redl's
encounters with the Chief of Russian intelligence, his
passionate denunciation of one of his lovers, and
Redl's final meeting with his superiors.

Act I, Scene I, which takes place in a gymnasium
early in the morning where a duel is to occur, is both
delicate and violent as it foreshadows many of the conflicts to come. At considerable personal risk, since
duels are outlawed, Redl has agreed to serve as second
for a comrade, Lt. Syzinski because he has been insul-
ted by another officer, Von Kupfer, who taunted him
about his Jewishness and his homosexuality ("Fraulein
Rothschild" as he called him). Redl has done so partly
because he likes Syzinski and feels sorry for him

since he has no other friends. Yet Redl has also
done so, as the scene reveals, because he identifies
to a considerable extent with Syzinski and senses that
the latter really understands him. Both come from a
lower class background (about which, however, Redl is
more secretive) and both are warm and sensitive
(although again Redl conceals these qualities from
most people). As they wait for Von Kupfer, an aristocrat, to arrive, Syzinski encourages Redl to persist
in his career and not act destructively and recklessly
as he himself is doing in challenging a master swords-
man against whom he has no real chance of success.
Encouraged by Syzinski's empathy (and wishing to dis-
tract him), Redl reveals to the latter a recurring
dream he has, which he professes to dismiss but which
clearly troubles him:

> REDL: It's too dull. So is this too. Anyway:
> I was attending a court martial. Not mine.
> Someone else's. I don't quite know
> whose. But a friend of some sort, some-
> one I liked. Someone upright, frank,
> respected, but upright. It was quite
> clear from the start what the outcome
> would be, and I was immediately worrying
> about having to go and visit him in gaol.
> And it wasn't just because I knew I would
> be arrested myself as soon as I got in
> there. It wasn't for that. Anyhow,
> there I was, and I went and started to
> talk to him. He didn't say anything.
> There was just the wire netting between
> us...and then of course, they arrested me.
> I couldn't tell whether he was pleased or
> not. Pleased that I'd come to see him or
> that they'd got me too. They touched me
> on the shoulder and told me to stand up,
> which I did. And by that time he'd gone.
> Somehow.

The dream expresses Redl's hopes that he might be a
good person--frank and upright like the friends with
whom he is imprisoned. Yet the very situation of
imprisonment expresses Redl's fears of being trapped
and failing. Then, before either he or Syzinski can
elaborate on the dream, Von Kupfer brusquely enters.
Without deigning to recognize Syzinski's existence, he
draws his sword and, despite Redl's efforts to inter-
vene, quickly cuts Syzinski up and without a word
leaves. The scene ends with Redl holding (or cradling,
as the stage directions tell us) Syzinski in his arms.

This scene in miniature presents much of the basic thrust of the entire play. For it shows the involvement of a sensitive, compassionate person in a system in which he thrives but in which he can be highly vulnerable. The system rewards talent and provides opportunities inasmuch as both Syzinski and Redl are part of the elite. Yet it also rests on open inequality and contempt as shown by Von Kupfer's behavior, and it profoundly distrusts warmth, compassion, and hope. Because Syzinski is partly Jewish, he remains defensive about his background since otherwise he would be completely excluded. Nevertheless, he is only half tolerated--which, though he doesn't recognize it, is perhaps the worst of all because he has internalized much of the contempt felt for him. This is shown by his acknowledgement of Kupfer's insult and insistence upon a duel, a basic part of the very code by which Kupfer and other aristocrats operate. While Redl seems more confident and self-possessed than Syzinski, he is also more ambitious. And, as the end of the scene shows, he is openly affectionate so that he may possibly experience stronger loyalty conflicts than his dead comrade.

Following this episode, come in quick succession scenes which reveal how Redl, unlike Syzinski, does flourish in the system, as the scene at the annual Hofbrau ball brilliantly reveals. Yet each step of the way the demands placed on Redl become greater. As Col. Von Mohl (in I,II) congratulates him for being selected as one of three candidates for Intelligence School, he also reminds him that he (Redl) differs from the others because of his lower birth and therefore will always have to work harder. At the same time, Von Mohl admits more openly how unfair the system really is because one of the three chosen is Von Kupfer primarily because of his aristocratic birth. Nevertheless, most disquieting of all is Von Mohl's description of what constitutes worth in an officer:

> MOHL: Some men have a style of living like bad
> skins. Coarse grained, erupting, spotty.
> Let me put it this way: I don't have to
> tell you that, even in this modern age of
> what they call democracy, the army is still
> a place of privilege. Redl is the rare
> type that redeems that privilege. And why?
> Because he overpowers it, overpowers it by
> force, not mob trained force, but natural,
> disciplined character, ability and honour.
> And that's all I've got to say on the

subject.

Not only does Von Mohl have a naive notion about judging worth, but he rules out many of the qualities that Redl, as we have seen in the last episode, obviously possesses.

Yet Redl's difficulties don't end here. We see how painful it is for him to act like the other officers in celebrating good fortune by getting drunk and sleeping with a whore, how hard he drives himself to improve various skills and yet how little satisfaction he derives, and how lonely he is, even though he is a very popular officer. Worse yet, the Russians as indicated, decide to single him out for surveillance because they sense that, as a poor boy, he will be at a social disadvantage in the elite, especially since he affects a very expensive life style which he clearly can't afford. As part of their plan, the Russians arrange to have the Countess Delyanoff (as suggested) get Redl to become interested in her. Although she is beautiful, sophisticated, and clever, personifying these attributes that would make her a desirable wife in the eyes of Redl's superiors, unlike Syzinski, she has no empathy for Redl's sensitivity. In what is a very painful scene (and one which has recurred), Redl wakes up, after they have made love, because he finds himself crying and is so embarrassed that he feels he must dress and leave. Granted that Sophia could feel hurt, she makes no effort to understand him or, at least, try to control some of her irritation. Instead, she tries to make him feel guilty by acting as the injured party who will be embarrassed if people know he is leaving before dawn. Finally, in a burst of anger, he does leave. To make matters worse, it is possible that, while he really cares for Sophia, Redl was also trying to act a part since she obviously was a very desirable woman for him to be seen with, as well as to consider marrying. Then in the next scene a young man in a cafe makes insinuating remarks to him, "I know what you want," that make Redl become so angry that he hits him. The point of the scene, which certainly is one sided and even crude, is that Redl doesn't realize that he has homosexual desires. Immediately after this comes an even more abbreviated and overdone scene in which Redl wakes up in bed (after having had an assignation with a young soldier) to find himself being beaten and robbed.

Undeniably, these last two scenes with which the act ends are the least satisfying in the play because they

are so short and simplistic. Yet what they are emphasizing is not that Redl has suddenly found that he is
a homosexual or has resisted such a discovery for a
long time, but that the pressures building up in him
because of his role playing in the elite have become
so unbearable that something had to give. That the
outlet was homosexuality is perhaps less important than
the urgency of the need that has been driving Redl.
However, what is also important is how contradictory
the experience of being a homosexual is from the
beginning. Redl clearly enjoys himself; yet he is
victimized just as he is in the Army, although in a
different way.

Where Act I ends with a short, violent scene, Act II
begins with a long, exuberant one. Instead of a sordid
hotel room, the setting is a lavish palace, and instead
of a beating and robbery, there are dancing and elaborate entertainment. Nevertheless, both scenes center on
homosexuality. The lavish entertainment of Act II is
part of a grand masked ball that is given each year by
Baron Von Epp, a celebrated and yet, because of his
position, accepted Viennese homosexual. The ball
represents one of the great social events of the year;
all invitations are carefully controlled; all guests
come in drag (or some other appropriate costume); and
a special feature of the evening is an all male performance of an opera (generally by Mozart). Yet what
dominates the ball is not so much the entertainment as
the opportunity the occasion affords for people to
release their inhibitions and be their natural selves,
whatever these may be, a need that obviously is great
because of the rigidity and pressures of the role playing that dominates the life of the elite. As Baron Von
Epp makes clear, he sees his life for what it is,
whereas Von Mohl and the generals do not so far as
theirs is concerned:

> BARON: I understand the inner secrets of my
> nature perfectly well. I don't admire them,
> but I do know them, anyway better than this
> Dr. Schoepfer. [A charlatan who gives lec-
> tures on homosexuality.]
> FERDY: Silly mare!
> BARON: And I'm quite happy as I am, I'm no
> criminal, thank you, and I don't corrupt
> anything that isn't already quite clearly
> corrupt, like this ghastly city. On the
> contrary, I bring style, wit, pleasure,
> energy, and good humour to it that it
> wouldn't otherwise have.

Although one important purpose of the ball is to
contrast it to that at the Hofbrau, the main one is to
show how much Redl has changed by becoming a homosexual. Where all the others choose elaborate cos-
tumes that conceal their identities, Redl appears in
his military uniform. Yet, more than that, he comes in
his dress uniform, which is to say as plainly as possible that he is not merely an officer but a very
distinguished one, high in Military Intelligence, who
is not ashamed to let people know his identity. As
further evidence of his boldness and courage, Redl
brings with him (also in his uniform) his latest loved
one, Lt. Stefan Kovacs. Not only does Redl let everyone know that he openly lives as a homosexual, but he
is willing to run the risk of losing Stefan, since the
latter is handsome and others immediately begin to
flirt with him.

It is true at the Hofbrau Redl, as indicated, enjoyed
himself. However, on this occasion he goes much further. He tells jokes, flirts, and drinks a lot--
although still maintaining self control. Clearly Redl
shows that he can let himself go and still exhibit his
"style" which makes him stand out on any occasion.
Here he does so by being spontaneous; at the Hofbrau
and possibly much of the time with Sophia he may have
been acting out another of his roles.

Nevertheless, although so much has changed, a great
deal hasn't. As the scene goes on, it becomes
apparent that, while the conversation is livelier than
at the Hofbrau, it is also predictable in its own way,
as many of the young men (or bum boys as they are
called) prattle on with stock jokes about homosexuals
and the establishment. If the bum boys are more open
than the Army elite, in their own way they act offen-
sively as they jest insultingly and flirt indiscrimi-
nately. Nor can Redl forget the past since he meets
Von Kupfer and other officers connected with the
Syzinski duel. Most disturbing of all, Redl realizes
that he is not as free from guilt or shame as he
imagined. As a proud member of the elite, he is disgusted at what is going on, although most of all with
himself for participating. This explains why, when a
bum boy makes a slightly offensive remark, Redl
unexpectedly strikes him and knocks him down. It is
true that he immediately apologizes and leaves so that
he really hasn't interrupted festivities. Still, it is
apparent that Redl is not as liberated as he would like
to be--an impression that is painfully reinforced by
the next crucial scene, that in which at the end of

Act II the head of Russian Intelligence, Col. Oblonsky,
meets Redl and (as indicated) threatens to expose him
for his homosexuality if he doesn't become a counterspy.

At first glance, this scene, which is much shorter
than that of the Drag Ball, is incredibly crude on both
sides. Oblonsky is a cynical, aggressive man who
enjoys exposing people, especially those who in some
way dare to be different as Redl is by being a homosexual. Moreover, since Redl is his counterpart in
Intelligence and a very resourceful enemy at that,
Oblonsky has gone to great lengths to embarrass Redl
by presenting him with massive evidence of his homosexuality. His crowning example turns out to be an
Eton boater (or straw hat) belonging to a young English
aristocrat with whom Redl had an affair and which the
latter kept over his bed. Actually, Oblonsky need not
have presented· this since Redl had already acknowledged
that he was caught and was accepting Oblonsky's terms.
However, the latter, as he admits, just couldn't
resist. Nor can he resist denouncing Redl in the most
vitriolic and condescending manner for acting so
stupidly and letting himself be trapped:

> OBLONSKY: What can you do? Change your way of
> life? It's getting desperate already,
> isn't it? You don't know which way to
> turn, you're up to your eyeballs in debts.
> What could you do? Get thrown out, exposed
> for everything you are, or what the world
> would say you are. Would you, do you
> think, could you change your way of life,
> what else do you want after all these
> years, what would you do at your age, go
> back to base and become a waiter or a
> washer up, sit all alone in cafes again
> constantly watching? What are you fit
> for? . . .

For his part, Redl at first tries the most obvious ploys,
such as that the love letters Oblonsky reads don't have
the names of the loved one written on them but only on
the envelope and therefore are not fool proof evidence
or that in a show down there would only be the word of
his accusers against his own name and rank as a privi-
leged member of the elite. His embarrassment becomes
all the greater since he seems to be responding to Oblonsky on the latter's level.

However, when it becomes apparent that these tactics
don't work because Oblonsky is so cynical and well

prepared, Redl insists on taking over the investigation himself and incriminating himself. Then, when Oblon- sky hands him an envelope containing a bribe (the first of many he is to receive) Redl accepts it without a word. That he agrees so quickly and undramatically (as compared to the real life Redl who in a similar situa- tion stalled and threatened)44 may seem odd, not to mention the fact that he showed no remorse or even thought of resigning from the service and living unobtrusively in exile. After all, the elite have recognized his merit and he does have high standards on which he prides himself. As he told Sophia at the Hofbrau, he is a snob who thinks that some men are better than others.

Yet actually to answer one question helps answer the other. That Redl acts as he does results, first of all, from the fact that, as has been shown, he tailors his response to those he is dealing with. After Oblonsky's naive and one sided denunciation of him, Redl would find it pointless, at least now, to explain to him all the forces that caused him to become a homosexual, let alone that homosexuality is not at all what Oblonsky insists that it is. In the second place, Redl, as he feared in his dream, is trapped and through no fault of his own. By that I mean that he hasn't really committed any crimes. If anything, granting that some of his actions as Oblonsky detailed them, seem excessive and flamboyant, they result from the fact that whatever he does, he does wholeheartedly. Therefore, if he chooses to be a homosexual, he will do so without reservation. In the third place, he is honest. After investigating the evidence that Oblonsky has presented, he has to agree that it proves him to be a homosexual. Conse- quently, by not saying anything and accepting the money, he is acknowledging the truth of the allegations. Yet being honest also means admitting one's own desires and weighing them against the priorities and values of his society and acting accordingly. Clearly Redl, as we have seen him develop, enjoys power, responsibility, recognition, and material comfort of his society, especially since the latter help him to compensate for some of the feelings of inferiority that he has experi- enced as a person who has made it into the elite the "hard way" but has never been fully accepted as an equal. For him to resign and live in gentile poverty would make him reject what he has striven for and cause him to reexperience the humiliation that he felt about his early life. On the other hand, acting in such self interest, however honestly he acknowledges such feel- ings, would seem to conflict with other feelings, principally that of responsibility to the elite whose interests he is defending as a soldier. Therefore, to accept the money and to do so without deliberation would seem to suggest that Redl is just as corrupt, if not more so, than the generals who, while they rationalize inequality as a basis for membership in the elite, at least believe in the latter as some ideal of human worth and community.

But, if we look more closely, we might see that the very fact that the generals rationalize inequality as they do is itself very destructive. Not only does it justify the maintenance of privilege, as shown in the special consideration that Von Kupfer received in being chosen to go to the Command school, even though he killed Syzinski, but it creates among those others in the elite, such as Redl, not to mention those outside it, feelings of inferiority. What is more, the very fact that the system accepts some poor boys of unusual merit, like Redl and even those who are partly Jewish as Syzinski is, really accentuates the cruelty. The reason is that such exceptions feel even more acutely the limitations of their position, for they must always remain subordinate to those of higher birth. For example, while Syzinski could be an officer, he could not rise very high in the ranks. Consequently, he was in a double bind. He couldn't resist not opting for the system since few other possibilities for self realization existed elsewhere. Yet once within it (as indicated), he internalized the system's values and turned them against himself. Similarly, this is what was happening to Redl, except that he fought it much harder than did Syzinski. And one way he did so was to become a homosexual, for at least in this life style some of the time he was able to feel freer. Yet as the end of the ball scene and the encounter with Oblonsky and, as we shall see, many of the events of Act III show, this choice has destructive consequences. Not only does it threaten the elite since many of the values of the elite surface in this alternative life style, but it also makes Redl, who is one of the elite, ashamed of some of his behavior as a homosexual.

However, there is another aspect to consider. That is, that the inequality on which the elite rests with its reliance upon role playing and adherence to forms as manifestations of that equality, may itself represent an effort to cope with, or even conceal, some basic failure and fear in society. I refer in particular to an illuminating and despairing comment that Von Mohl makes to Sophia about marriage while dancing with her

116

at the Hofbrau. Ostensibly, he is all for it because
it is proper and respects the forms, but in reality he
is acknowledging that it is all his society, for want
of something better, has to cling to:

> It really is the most lamentable thing for
> most of us, isn't it? I mean, as you say,
> it doesn't work really. Only the appear-
> ances function. Eh? Everyone knows the
> feelings, but what's the answer, what's the
> answer do you think?

His defense of marriage represents a pathetic confession
of failure, namely that people can't love or trust one
another. Instead, they act cynically: as Oblonsky does
when he berates Redl for his homosexuality, or as
Sophia does in her reply when she tells Von Mohl that
marriage doesn't really serve any purpose (although
interestingly later in the play she does marry, and,
ironically enough, one of Redl's former loved ones).
Or they act despairingly: as does the prostitute with
whom Redl spends the night when she confesses that she
would like to marry and have children but yet doesn't
expect that this will happen.

    And why is society in such shape? Granted the ques-
tion is not easy to answer, for up to a point I agree
with Irving Wardle in his review in The Times, London,
that Osborne doesn't bring into a single consistent
focus his views about the individual and society.[45]
However, one very clear suggestion, as Redl's own contrasting behavior in I and in his reply to Hilde's comment about wanting marriage and children reveals, is
fear or embarrassment in being sensitive and caring.
In I, Redl describes in his dream how he wants to be
frank and upright, and he treats Syzinski compassionately as he cradles him in his arms after the duel.
Yet, in response to Hilde, Redl puts down love, marriage, and children as disgusting or pointless. The
reason he does, I think, is that he has become part of
the system and, without realizing it, has internalized
some of the insensitivity and rigid self control which
Von Mohl admires and which have enabled Redl to advance
his career. Nor is the fear just that of tenderness
but also of vitality and sexuality. The officers have
sex mainly to convince themselves they are not strange,
different, or homosexual. And when Von Mohl laments
the state of marriage, he also wishes that he could
let himself go more as he is just in dancing with
Sophia.

Considering then the full context of choices and values in which Redl has been trying to realize himself at this point in the play, we could feel that it would be difficult for him to have deep loyalties to a regime that has treated him as it has and is as repressive and despairing in its outlook. Yet at the same time, since he has internalized many of these reactions, it is difficult for him at this stage to reject his society, especially when even homosexuality, which does violate the forms and the established role playing, still maintains its existence within this same society. Moreover, whatever else we can say about Redl, although outwardly he does conform, yet inwardly and privately, he tries to find his own way of coping with these pressures. As a very proud man who tries to meet each challenge in its own terms, he would feel at least at this point in his career that he would have to explore all the options: continuing his career and yet trying to deal with Oblonsky, and trying to live his personal life to the hilt.

Act III shows, first of all, some of the destructive consequences of Redl's efforts to maintain his career, his personal life, and his involvement with Oblonsky. Career-wise, he distinguishes himself even more as he obtains a citation and commendation from his superiors and becomes the Head of the Prague Bureau, the number two position in the entire hierarchy. When we consider Redl's humble beginnings, we can certainly feel that he has come very far and can feel proud of himself, as his superiors obviously do. Yet at the very moment Gen. Von Hotzendorff and Col. Mohl tell Redl the good news about his promotion, they also tell him that some one else will have the number one position in Vienna, and that someone else, not surprisingly, is an aristocrat who in all probability is less qualified for the position than Redl. For someone as proud as Redl, this is, as he makes clear by his bitter private comments afterwards, an insult.

As for Redl's life as a counter spy, it becomes more precarious and degrading. To protect himself from exposure, he had to trump up charges against the Russians and seize several of their best agents. In turn, he has to agree to give the Russians one of his own top men. His choice for this is Von Kupfer who, for reasons never made quite clear, has been living with Redl apparently as some kind of aide or confidant. But most degrading of all, he has to listen to Oblonsky ridicule him even more grossly than he did when the latter threatened exposure. Since at this

118

point Redl has been in Oblonsky's employ for a long
time, he can't just walk away or even not bother to
reply.

So far as Redl's private life is concerned, much of
it is painful and humiliating. His loved ones shamelessly exploit him as they accept lavish gifts from
him, such as the Daimler which he really purchased for
Viktor, his newest beloved. With anger and disgust,
Redl denounces Viktor for his selfishness and ingrati-
tude. Before this, he has also had to endure (as
indicated) the humiliation of losing another loved one,
Lt. Kovacs (whom he brought to the Drag Ball) to Sophia
in marriage. If those don't hurt enough, he has to
listen to Sophia, like Oblonsky, ridicule him viciously
and foolishly. In fact, her attack sounds much like
his--and possibly with reason since at one time she
served in his employ. Yet still another humiliation
occurs when Redl visits the hospital bed of Mischa
(another former loved one) who is lying in a crazy
stupor, while his girl friend is keeping a vigil.
Although the circumstances are not made clear, Redl
obviously is deeply embarrassed, both for what has
happened to Mischa (whether or not he is in any way
responsible) and because he cares for him, even though
the girl friend is present.

Yet the most terrible humiliation derives from the
circumstances of his exposure. I refer first of all to
the fact that the Officers, when they learn about it,
express no concern for Redl but simply determine that
he must save them from embarrassment. Consequently,
they arrange as quickly and coldly as possible to have
him take his own life. Not once, while they work out
the details with him, do they show any interest in why
he acted as he did. Conversely, Redl for his part seems
fastidiously concerned with appearances. At no time
does he seem to assume responsibility for what he has
done. Instead, he offers them champagne and lectures
them about the reasons for the decadence of the Austro-
Hungarian Empire!

Yet these moments in which he seems most corrupt and
is most humiliated are also those in which he shows how
open he can finally be and how even in his very corruption, if it is that, he has transcended the cynicism
and despair of his society.

Since Sophia has hurt Redl a great deal, and clearly
has no idea what his life is like, we might expect him
simply to ignore her denunciation. Instead, he lets

her know that he is unashamed of what he is and how
sexually intimate he has been with Stefan:

> REDL: . . . I tell you this: you'll never know
> that body like I know it. The lines
> beneath his eyes. Do you know how many
> there are, do you know one has less than
> the other? And the scar behind his ear,
> and the hairs in his nostrils, which has
> the most, what colour they are in what
> light? The mole on where? Where, Sophia?
> I know the place here, between the eyes,
> the dark patches like slate--like blue
> when he's tired, really tired, the place
> for a blow or a kiss or a bullet. You'll
> never know like I know, you can't. The
> backs of his knees, the pattern on the
> soles of his feet. Which trouble him, and
> so I used to wash them and bathe them for
> hours. His thick waist, and how long are
> his thighs, compared to his calves, you've
> not looked at him, you never will.

Comparably, just as Redl could have politely disagreed
with Oblonsky or ridiculed him for his narrow, stupid
prejudice, here he admits how painful his life really
is and yet again how unashamed of it he is.

   Whereas in the confrontation with Sophia and Oblonsky, Redl at least can defend his homosexuality, with
Viktor he finds himself doing almost the opposite. It
is bad enough that the latter, as indicated, should be
so selfish, but, worse yet, he isn't even beautiful
any more and, like Redl himself, can only look forward
to a lonely and sordid life in years to come:

> REDL: . . . You are thick, thick, a sponge,
> soaking up. No recall, no fear. You're a
> few blots...All you are is young. There's
> no soft fat up here in the shoulder and
> belly and buttocks yet. But it will.
> Nobody loves an old, squeezed, wrinkled
> pip of a boy who was gay once. Least of
> all people like me or yourself. You'll
> be a vulgar fake, someone even toothless
> housewives in the market place can bait.
> (Grabs his hair and drags him.)
> You little painted toy, you puppet, you
> poor duffer, you'll be, with your disease
> and paunch and silliness and curlers and
> dyed wispy hair and long legs and varicose

veins like bunches of grapes and prostate and thick waist and rolling thighs and big bottom that's where we all go. (Slaps his own.) In the bottom, that's where we all go and you can't mistake it. Everyone'll see it! (He pauses, exhausted. His dressing gown has flown open. VIKTOR is sobbing very softly and genuinely. REDL stands breathless, then takes the boy's head in his arms. He rocks him. And whispers): It's not true. Not true. You are beautiful...You always will be...There, baby, there...Baby,...It won't last...All over, baby...

After all that Redl has done to maintain his life as a homosexual, to seem to have to reject it--and with such disgust--seems the cruelest irony of all--or the clearest indication of how corrupt Redl has become. Yet the very intensity of his disgust shows how deeply hurt he is and, ultimately, as the last lines reveal, how much he cares. More than that, as with Syzinski, Redl again embraces him, and perhaps most important, Viktor shows that he also cares. This may be why the following scenes in which Redl is discovered are so short and generally undramatic because, now that Redl has finally admitted to himself and some one else how deeply he can feel, his life is not that important.

Still, his very last speech to the generals also represents in its own way, although this may not seem so at first glance, an affirmation. After passing out champagne, Redl seems almost facetious and irresponsible as he tells his fellow officers that the Spanish Bourbons, from whom the Habsburgs have descended, ruined the Empire:

REDL: . . . But I think I hate the Spaniards most of all. Perhaps that's the flaw...of my character...they are Catholics. Those damned Spaniards were the worst marriage bargain the Habsburgs ever made. Inventing bridal lace to line coffins with. They really are the worst. They stink of death, I mean. It's in their clothes and their armpits, quite stained with it, and the worst is they're so proud of it, insufferably. Like people with stinking breath always puff and blow and bellow an inch away from your face. No, the Spaniards are, you must admit, a musty lot, the

121

entire nation from top to bottom smells of
old clothes in the bottom of trunks . . .

In talking like this, he almost seems to be parodying
his fellow officers for insisting on the uniqueness of
the Empire. But what he is really doing is trying to
explain to them, tactfully by placing the blame on the
Bourbons rather than they themselves, their Emperor, or
their society, how corrupt their life really is. Because they are afraid of vital energies, such as love,
sexuality, and empathy, they try to stifle them through
forms and role playing. At the same time, since this
isn't enough, they displace the guilt which they feel
onto those whom they brand as inferior and/or different,
namely people from the lower classes, homosexuals, and
Jews. As the son of a railway porter, a homosexual,
and presumably a Jew, Redl understands just how insidi-
ous and destructive such fear can be, as his own public
and private life shows. But he also demonstrated that
in being so deeply affected by the repression and fear
in his society he was able finally because of his own
kind of honesty and determination to transcend these
and know what it is like to live rather than concentrate his energies on 'lining coffins with bridal
lace.' Equally important, I should add, he is unashamed
of whatever he does, whether it is sipping champagne
before taking his life, or even sacrificing Von Kupfer
to the Russians. After all, in Redl's corrupt society,
how terrible is it, if one must sacrifice some one,
to choose Von Kupfer who epitomizes the worst that
society embodies?

    By the time the play ends, it is very clear how much
the society Osborne presents, particularly the elitist
officer corps, can jeopardize, if not fatally corrupt,
human worth, and how difficult it is to resist the
temptation. Yet in his own way Redl does manage to a
considerable extent, mainly by his insistence upon
exploring every choice to the fullest and at the same
time trying to be true to his particular standard of
integrity, which is part of that society and yet
strongly opposed to it. His effort is formidable under
any circumstances, but all the more so, since Redl, in
many ways, despite all of his public involvement and
yet because of it, is very lonely. The results of his
efforts aren't wholly admirable. But Redl himself
would be the first to admit this...

    Although the play takes place far away from the Bri-
tish Isles, its relevance to a highly structured class
system such as that of England, is all too obvious.

VIII

A BOND HONOURED

A Bond Honoured is an adaptation of Lope de Vega's
La Fianza Satisfecha (A Credit Acknowledged). As
Osborne explains in a brief introductory note, he under-
took the project because Kenneth Tynan (who was then
Artistic Manager of the National Theatre) was looking
for interesting dramatic experiments and because some
of the play's issues appealed to him personally:
"What did interest me was the Christian framework of
the play and the potentially fascinating dialectic
with the principal character."[46] Tynan may have been
drawn to the play because it appeared in translation
by Willis Barnstone in The Tulane Drama Review (September 1962) along with a brief note by Barnstone
which emphasized the play's contemporary relevance.[47]
Its hero, Leonido, is a Sicilian nobleman who violates all the mores of his society--raping his sister
and his mother, blinding his father, renouncing his
religion for Mohammedanism--but then finally acknowledges his guilt and repents before Christ. From my
account, Leonido may sound like another Raskolnikov
who can acknowledge his meekness of spirit only after
he has committed violence. If anything, Leonido goes
even further because he himself becomes a Christ-like
figure who is humbled by the burden of the suffering
he chooses to assume. Yet Barnstone feels that
Leonido is an Existentialist hero because he violates
all the laws of his society in order to discover
where his own morality begins.[48] Actually I can't see
how Barnstone's analysis fits Lope's play at all,
because the Christian feeling underlying the play dominates Leonido's actions, even before he repents.

If doubts may exist about what Tynan and Osborne
may have been attempting in doing such a play, critics
who reviewed it seemed to have few of their own.
Either they blasted it or they ignored it and concentrated their attention on the other play which appeared
on the same bill, Peter Shaffer's Black Comedy.[49]
Simon Trussler in a more detailed analysis in his book
concludes that two reasons exist for the failure of
A Bond Honoured. In the first place, Osborne lost the
consistency of viewpoint of the original, which for
Trussler represents a Christian dramatization of sin
and repentance. In the second place, Osborne didn't
know how to use for his own purposes the play's
Renaissance dramatic conventions, such as disguise

plots, allegory, and stock characters like Tizon,
the faithful but truculent servant, similar to Sancho
Panza.[50] On the other hand, Alan Carter and Martin
Banham in their books don't know what to make of the
play. Carter feels that the play vaguely refers to
contemporary England because at one point Leonido
remarks, "Me, I had an overstrong instinct, you
understand and this is an island of overprotected
people. The range of possibilities in living here
shrinks with every year."[51] Banham suggests that, like
the play Luther, A Bond Honoured concerns itself with a
need for faith so overwhelming that the individual
involved demands the strongest possible proof, namely
direct confrontation with Christ.[52] However, neither
Carter nor Banham explore the play to any extent so
that their discussions remain fragmentary.

I have to admit that my own initial response to the
play was negative since I felt that Osborne used
Leonido's tirades mainly as a vehicle to attack as many
taboo subjects as possible. Compared to Leonido's fulminations against parents, religion, and sex, those of
Jimmy Porter or Bill Maitland seemed mild. Tizon's
final comment to the Moorish King after Leonido's body
has been carted off (a comment which is not in the
original) summed up for me what the play was all
about--or rather all that it was about. "Well, King,
he played a good tune on vituperation."

However, after carefully comparing Barnstone's
translation with Osborne's play and reading a two part
review by Mervyn Jones in Tribune[53] and a long article
by Daniel Rogers in The Durham Review,[54] I came to see
the play much differently. To begin with, Rogers
points out that Osborne did not use Barnstone's translation but worked closely from a more accurate and
literal one supplied by the National Theatre.[55] Yet
at the same time much of Osborne's wording of passages
which he retained represents, as Jones also feels,[56]
a poetic rendering of the original. But, even more
important, he points out that Osborne has deliberately
changed the play, adding some six scenes at the beginning, as well as modifying others. Even if Osborne's
play may be too compressed, especially in the climactic encounter between Leonido and Christ, it is far
better than I previously recognized. While Barnstone's comments about Lope's hero are highly questionable, they do tell us something important about
Osborne's, for his Leonido, as I hope to make clear,
does find the private and public morality of his
society unacceptable. As a result, he feels a ter-

rible need to fashion a morality of his own--a task
which he finds extraordinarily difficult because he
discovers that he is far more deeply affected by the
morality of his society than he ever realized. The
more Leonido rebels outwardly the more he discovers
inwardly how dependent he is. Yet for that very
reason he realizes how much further he has to go
should he wish to do more than just sing a song of
vituperation.

   If Tizon's comment about vituperation doesn't
take us far enough into the play, I would suggest
another opener, Leonido's criticism of his family and
their society as overprotected. Like Antonioni in
some of his early movies, Osborne is portraying a
decadent aristocratic society in which people care
only about self interest. However, they don't
acknowledge such feelings directly but mask them
through their religion and social morality. They
either accept what happens with Christian resignation
or regard it as the result of divine retribution.
Either way, they hold some one else responsible for
their decisions and actions. Given such behavior by
those in authority, it isn't any wonder that a sensitive, passionate, and intelligent person like
Leonido should feel so strong a need to attack these
standards that he would try to invert them.

   Yet at the same time he is doing so he may be discovering that he hasn't had any supportive role models
he can respect who can help him understand the reality
of his own feelings or have given him any real love to
provide some basic sense of self worth.

   The most dramatic evidence as to how much Osborne
has changed the original reveals itself in the treatment of Leonido's relationship with his sister,
Marcela. In Lope's version when Leonido tells his
father he tried to rape his sister, he says that he
did it to defile his blood--that is to punish and
degrade himself even more. While Leonido's assertion
sounds emphatic, it remains just an assertion, and
therefore not important in the dynamics of the play.

   However, in Osborne's version the relationship
with Marcela becomes the most important one in the
play and incest an actuality. From consistent innuendo
and repartee with Tizon, it is clear almost from the
beginning that Leonido has been sleeping with Marcela.
Nor is it just a sexual relationship for, when in Act
I, Scene II, he visits her in her bedroom, he tells

her how much she means to him:

> I can't see your face . . . What defect is
> there in me? I find beauty and comfort . . .
> and sustenance . . . only . . . in you.
> There's no light from the sea tonight. I
> can't see your face. I don't care what
> people may speculate. I do <u>not</u> want them
> to know. Not words or movements or moments.
> Those are for our pleasure, only. Marcela?
> Secrecy <u>is</u> the nerve of love. Can you see me?
> Marcela? Are you asleep? . . .

Not only does this scene reveal the force of their
sexual attraction, but it also shows Leonido's great
dependence on his sister, for like George Dillon when
he is playing up to Ruth, Leonido can't even be sure
he exists at all away from Marcela's presence. Nor
does he realize that, while he seems to be very independent in rejecting his father's morality, he is only
defining himself negatively in opposition to the latter.
In reality, Leonido would rather have a loving and supportive father whom he can admire and who can understand him.

After Leonido has committed himself so openly, he
hopes that at least his father, when he learned of his
relationship with Marcela, would feel outraged and
concerned for her sake. By such responses, Leonido
would feel that his father cared for him and could help
him. But no such thing happens. Gerardo piously proclaims his own virtues and absolves himself from
responsibility by warning Leonido that God will punish
him. Not surprisingly, Leonido becomes all the more
outraged because his father not only has turned his
back on his children but doesn't even know it.

If Leonido's father's reactions, as I've described
them, aren't disheartening enough, Marcela herself
makes things even worse by agreeing to marry someone
like Dionisio. Not only will this be just a marriage
of economic and social convenience or, as Leonido
describes it so well, "all dowries and benefits," but
it will be boring. As Marcela herself half jokingly
admits, Dionisio is cowardly and dim witted. Then, to
make matters worse, when Dionisio does appear, he
threatens to revenge himself on Leonido for trying to
dishonor Marcela. However, when Leonido challenges
him to a duel, Dionisio never shows up. Yet Dionisio
doesn't stop being difficult here. After Leonido is

forced to flee his father's house because he attacked
Marcela on her wedding night (an incident I want to comment on shortly), Dionisio now has the gall to proclaim
himself as Gerardo's true son:

> "Be calm, father. You have a new son here.
> In me. Take a little pleasure in your son
> and daughter and what's to come from both of
> them. Let me lift you. There. On my
> shoulder. There."

And Gerardo with just as much self-pity accepts his
offer.

Yet worst of all, from Leonido's point of view,
are Marcela's changed feelings toward him after her
marriage. Leonido doesn't demand that she not marry
Dionisio, for he realizes that, once the match is
made, familial and social pressures are too strong for
her to resist. But when Marcela matter of factly tells
him that all is over with them, Leonido feels shattered. For in telling him this, she is denying him the
only part of his existence that he has felt has been
real to him. Unfortunately, Leonido can't separate
his sense of self and the precarious reality of his
existence from Marcela's feelings toward him. In this
respect she is his bond--what literally holds him
together. This helps explain why he reacts as violently as he does in assaulting her and then rushing
out and hoping to find some way to assert himself. At
first he hopes to do so through accepting the challenge
to a duel from Dionisio. However, since the latter (as
indicated) is too cowardly to appear and Leonido is
worn out by frustration, all that happens is that he
falls asleep in sheer exhaustion. But, when he
awakens, his whole life seems to change dramatically,
for he finds himself involved with a raiding party of
Moors who are out looking for Christians.

The entire sequence of events which then begins here
contains many of the stock ingredients of Roman comedy,
such as shipwrecks, love at first sight, and discovery
of long lost brothers and sisters (Lidora, the Moorish
princess at whose request the Moorish King Berlebeyo,
is hunting Christians turns out at the end to be
Gerardo's daughter and therefore a Christian whom the
King's father implores him not to marry). When I
first read the play, I felt that Osborne had to use
this material for the sake of the plot. But, in actuality, I think he uses this material cleverly to show

other aspects of Leonido's dilemma in trying to establish an accurate sense of his identity and self worth.

In both Lope's and Osborne's plays, Leonido overpowers King Berlebeyo, agrees to become a Moslem, appears before Lidora, and rejects her protestations of love. Lope uses all of these incidents, and others such as that in which Marcela appears before Lidora as a captive and the latter welcomes her as a sister, to show that even the Moors have chivalric ideals worthy of Christians. Appropriately, by the time Lidora discovers her true birth, she has already been receiving instructions from Tizon about Christianity.

However, Osborne uses these same details amusingly to portray the Moors as hypocrites, who, like Leonido's family, mask their self interest. But they do so more ingeniously than the Christians. When Leonido overcomes Berlebeyo with a tree he has uprooted, the latter immediately offers him his entire kingdom as proof of his loyalty. However, Berlebeyo really expects that Leonido in return will swear his loyalty to the King and massacre Christians if so ordered. As for Lidora, when she meets Leonido, she throws herself at his feet and proclaims that she will be his slave. But, in turn, she would like him to be her master and therefore to care for her as he would a child or a dependent. With a mixture of frankness and barbed insult, Leonido vainly tries to show Lidora what are her real motives.

Even more amusingly, when Lidora discovers that she is Gerardo's daughter, she seems happy because she has found a father. However, she seems unaware of what kind of father she has found, one who welcomes her because she encourages him to pity himself. Nor does she see that in preferring Gerardo to Berlebeyo (whom she willingly gives up as her fiance), she may be doing so because, by becoming a Christian, she can dissociate herself even more from any responsibility for what she does. Such behavior on her part may explain why Berlebayo gladly permits Lidora and the other Christians to take Leonido's dead body back to Sicily. "Take it [the body]. Go. Bloody Christians all of you. Go. Back to Alicarte and your blood and Sicily. Help them take him." Now he sees how hypocritical Christians are, perhaps more so than Moslems.

Since Leonido, before meeting the Moslems, has been rejected by Marcela, his one source of positive feedback and approval, we might expect that the welcome he received from Berlebeyo and Lidora would do wonders for his ego. However, Leonido recognizes that the Moslems want far more than they are giving by trying to impose on him a self or persona that suits their purposes not his. Therefore, although Leonido could feel that he has received considerable recognition from these people, he isn't free to react as he wishes. Just as important, in imposing such a role (or self) on him, the Moslems are ignoring his basic need to be accepted as some one who is groping to find an accurate sense of self and an honest relationship in which he can admit his true needs.

For these reasons the encounter with the Moslems accentuates Leonido's difficulties rather than alleviates them. Consequently, when he suddenly meets Marcela and his father his resentment, confusion, and need for some honest relationship become all the greater. Admittedly, the opposite might seem true initially, for Leonido now has Marcela in his power.

However, by refusing to ask Leonido for mercy but instead saying, "Do you not know me?" Marcela really compounds Leonido's identity crisis. Since at their last meeting, she was refusing to know him as her lover, now she is going further and acting as though even that never occurred. By doing so, she is trying to absolve herself from responsibility again by playing upon Leonido's guilt. For this reason he feels compelled to do something drastic to force Marcela to acknowledge the reality of their previous relationship, namely that she will submit to him sexually or he will order Gerardo killed. By making such a demand (cruel as it is), Leonido is desperately trying to get Marcela to admit how she has felt about him before. Instead, she refuses either option. By doing so, we might feel that Marcela is really helping Leonido since, by forcing him to decide, she is helping him define himself through making choices. In theory, this may seem plausible for Leonido certainly can't have much of a sense of self so long as he needs others to authenticate his feelings of his own worth. Yet before Leonido can rely more on himself, he has to admit unashamedly how much he needs others, particularly his sister. As Martin Luther observed (as quoted in Erikson's Young Man Luther), it is difficult for a person to master one area of his experience until he can admit how much it dominates him.[57]

However, Marcela, by refusing both options, is also refusing to take seriously Leonido's feelings of

profound insecurity. Not surprisingly, as the next
scene begins which involves Leonido's meeting with a
shepherd (the counterpart to the meeting with Christ in
Lope's play), Marcela dominates Leonido's consciousness. Leonido keeps hearing voices which may be his
own thoughts or the hidden presence of Christ:

> LEONIDO: Marcela. I feel the bond tighten-
> ing. Yes. it's tightening.
> VOICE: Calm.
> LEONIDO: Beyond logic so beyond doubt.
> Marcela, miserable, deluded and deluding
> family. Where are you? Where's your
> timorous Dionisio? Where is your memory
> of me? It shall soon fail. My imprint
> will have died out of all hearts inside
> a month. Discard. A discard. I have
> been mostly, a fair mixture of intelli-
> gence, mostly, self-criticism and, yes,
> gullibility. Yes, that's a hesitating
> assessment.

Now Leonido feels that he has to give up on his sister
and consequently on any separate, enduring identity for
himself. "My imprint," he laments, "will have died
out of all hearts inside a month. . . . "

Yet something else is happening. Actually by
making such a hesitating self-assessment, Leonido is
beginning to accept some kind of self, even if it is,
as he says, "a discard." Or, to paraphrase Erikson,
by admitting how much his fears dominate him, he is
beginning to try to overcome them. Then in subsequent
speeches (in which the voices seem to pose questions
to him as in a catechism) he begins to show a clearer
awareness of what that self is--one in which, as he
says, desire and will, reason and instinct, good and
evil, are at war. Nevertheless, at this stage all
that Leonido can do is intellectualize his dilemma.
Although this is a necessary first step, he can't feel
such conflicts deeply enough to try to resolve them or
live openly with them. Instead he needs some one to
help him to begin to feel these conflicts openly and
unashamedly. Just at this moment some one does appear
who might conceivably help him, namely Christ as the
shepherd.

But, before going on, it is necessary to point out
in more detail how much Osborne has changed the original. In Lope's play, Leonido has no such problems
concerning himself. At first he is just a proud

revenger who, when Christ appears as a loving figure, dismisses him. However, when Christ suddenly becomes powerful and angry, Leonido becomes frightened and falls at Christ's feet. Then, after a long pause, he rises (to quote Barnstone's stage directions), "no longer fearful, he appears relieved, as one who has found his identity, and speaks in a clear, soft voice."58 His identity, as is soon made clear, is that of a repentant Christian who wants only to emulate Christ by assuming a burden of suffering, expressing his love for his father, and dying in a state of grace.

However, none of these events occur in Osborne's play. Christ as the shepherd mainly seems anxious to get Leonido to acknowledge the real source of his difficulties, his guilt feelings about his father and Marcela, and because of these to realize that he has to pay the consequences of what he has done by repenting and doing good. To a certain extent this insistence seems just, for Christ is trying to get Leonido to accept responsibility for what he has done. However, what Christ doesn't understand, but what Leonido (and Martin Luther) do is that repentance doesn't come from good works alone, if it comes from them at all. Rather, it comes from a desire to want to do such works. To paraphrase Luther, "If the faith is right, the works will be right." At this stage Leonido doesn't feel his own worth strongly enough to have faith that he can be saved. For him, repayment, as Christ conceives of it, means denying the reality of his conflicts and therefore accentuating his feelings of self worthlessness. Consequently, Christ's insistence on repayment constitutes (as we shall see) another rejection or failure for Leonido.

With painful insight, Leonido points out to Christ that he is willing to pay the debt. However, he is bankrupt emotionally and ethically, so that, unless some provision is made for that, the payment will not save him but only kill him:

> I am overspent. It's not in your interest to believe me. But it is the case. I always knew it would be so. You will get, if you are so fortunate, a bankrupt's farewell, which is somewhat less than a penny in the pound. So be it then. You will have had access to my books, so there is nothing for me to do but acknowledge each item, which might give satisfaction to you as a kind of

131

divine lawyer's fee, but as wearisome to me
as the hell I go to and the hell I came from.
You shall have my life, which is what you came
for. It's no more than fluff at the bottom of
the pocket.

Unfortunately, Christ doesn't understand for He
insists upon embracing Leonido, which really means forgiving him and therefore denying the reality of the
feelings which Leonido is trying to accept in himself.
In so doing, whether Christ realizes it or not, He,
like the others, is absolving Himself from responsibility and instead placing more guilt upon Leonido.

At this point, we could expect Leonido to give up
for what little sense of self worth he has begun to
feel is being eroded by Christ. But Leonido is not an
Osborne hero for nothing. Consequently he tries to
establish some honest basis for his relationships (or
bonds) with those around him. Since by now the Moors
have made it clear that they intend to kill Leonido,
he begins with them. First, he insists upon fighting
the Moors bravely--but only for a while because, as he
makes clear, to escape would be to give himself false
hopes (as he has said, he is spent). Then Leonido
tries to reach his father by throwing himself at the
latter's feet. Through such a gesture, I take him to
be saying in effect, 'Look--here is what being debased
really means, not what you think it is. The truth is
that I need you to love me as a son, and I to respect
and love you as a father.' Then, just as in Lope, at
this point Gerardo's sight miraculously returns. However, the difference is that in Osborne's play the
results are ironical. Although Gerardo asks that he
might approach Leonido, nobody seems willing enough to
help him. Apparently, they don't care enough for
Leonido, or even for Gerardo; yet they won't admit it
openly. This is evident by the fact that, when Leonido
urges Tizon to help his father, "Give him his sight,
Tizon?" the latter doesn't respond.

However, in another respect Leonido does make head-
way. Throughout the play, Leonido has taunted his
servant for his cowardice but without getting any
response. "You would like to kill me," he says, "but
you wouldn't dare." But this time Leonido succeeds.
Instead of helping Gerardo, Tizon acts as he really
feels and stabs Leonido. In what I take to be grati-
tude for this authentic reaction by Tizon, Leonido
before dying remarks, "Ah, if there is remembrance, I

132

shall remember you." It is true that, before dying, Leonido doesn't succeed in redefining his relationship with Marcela, but that would be to ask of him more than he can accomplish.

At the end Leonido has become neither the Existentialist hero I referred to at the beginning of this discussion nor Lope's Christ-like figure, nor even a Bill Maitland able to try existing on his own for the first time. Yet, considering the kind of society in which Leonido lived, even to do what he manages represents an achievement. Just to accept the fact that one feels little sense of personal worth but would like to do so represents at least an honest expression of feeling and to that extent, especially in contrast to the others who could never acknowledge such needs in themselves, represents an affirmation.

To take so long to discuss such a short play may seem unnecessary. Yet I don't think so. The reason is that, while Osborne foreshortens much of Lope's dialogue and action, he changes the dialectic but then compresses it as well. As a result, the play is more complex and ironic than it may appear to be but yet not fully realized. For these reasons, <u>A Bond Honoured</u> is an uneven and difficult play.

However, it deserves better notices than it has received. In the first place, it has racy, energetic, and witty dialogue often laced with hyperbole, as shown particularly in many of Leonido's attacks on Tizon:

> One day, one day of your lifetime I shall kill you with this sword. Now? No. Tonight or tomorrow or in a year. Whenever, you affront me most or I'm most impatient. Don't misjudge the time by my mood. It may be when I'm gasping for want of enemies or running idly up to a joke.

In the second place, it has a considerable range of characterization: Gerardo resembles a "heavy" in an Italian opera; Tizon is a sluggish, artful, and yet latently savage, peasant; and Marcela, at least in the two bedroom scenes, alternates between being open and sensitive and indifferent and proper. And in the third place, <u>A Bond Honoured</u> is an interesting presentation of how pervasive, complex, and little understood rejection can be. On the face of it, Leonido seems to be going to great lengths to reject his family (except Marcela) and his society. Yet he is doing so because that society and his family (as only he realizes) have gone to even greater lengths to reject those who, like himself, want to be honest and open and admit some of the most child-like needs that they as adults still feel.

IX

TIME PRESENT

To turn from Inadmissible Evidence, A Patriot For Me, and A Bond Honoured, to Osborne's next two plays, Time Present and The Hotel in Amsterdam, may seem like too great a change of pace. True, these two plays, like the other three, concern themselves with frustrated, unhappy, main characters who need feedback, loving relations with others, and adequate feelings of self worth. Yet these two plays are also slighter in action and less despairing in outcome. Neither main character endures the daily hell of Bill Maitland and neither finds himself so cornered that he has to take his own life. Rather the main characters of these plays, for all of their unhappiness, still retain personal lives of some stability and pursue ongoing careers. On the other hand, the fact that Osborne writes about such characters shows the range of his awareness of how many lives can be troubled.

To an even greater extent than possibly any two other Osborne plays, Time Present and The Hotel in Amsterdam have a great deal in common. Just to begin with, they appear in the same printed volume and ran concurrently for several months in London. Besides, both are short (almost one long act) and have an early middle aged character who is creative and in some ways quite successful (in the former play, Pamela, an actress, and in the other, Laurie a film writer) and both have a significant background figure who never appears but whose death affects the action. Yet what links the plays together even more is that they both concern themselves with how much (to paraphrase a line from The Hotel in Amsterdam) 'people need people' and yet how difficult and painful trying to satisfy such needs can become, particularly when the people involved live in a materialist, success-oriented society that both blunts and yet accentuates such needs. As Ronald Bryden pointed out in his review of these plays in The Observer, the subtitle Osborne gives to these works, Plays for the Meantime, applies in more ways than one. Both concern themselves with people living in a precarious, indeterminate present in which little can be resolved and in which people are corrupt or spoiled by affluence and, to use a word that recurs in both, "bitchiness" or mean-ness.[59]

Nevertheless, the plays do differ considerably, especially since Time Present is more ambiguous in its

implications and more difficult to assess in impact.
For these reasons, despite all the similarities, it is
better to consider them separately.

Whatever may be unclear about **Time Present**, certain
things <u>are</u> evident. To begin with, unlike any other
Osborne play to date, its main character is a woman.
Pamela, the heroine, is an actress of considerable
talent, if we can judge by the favorable comments of
those around her and her own way "of coming on strong."
She knows just what she wants to do in a role and why
and how close she comes to her objective. But, most
important, she prides herself on emulating her father,
a famous actor, who consistently emphasized the need
for pure, authentic feeling appropriate to the role, a
mode of acting that, as we discover later in the play,
now seems out of vogue. Not that he always achieved
this goal, but at least he knew when he did. Despite
Pamela's talent, or rather because it is so cerebral
and she herself seems such a distinct personality, she
has had a very limited success. Nor, apparently, are
her prospects likely to improve since what she can do
best simply isn't appreciated.

If she is distinctive because she is Osborne's
first female central character, she does resemble the
Osborne heroes. She is articulate, histrionic,
intensely self-aware, alone, and inclined to hide or
perhaps not even always know her deepest feelings.

As for the basic action of the play, it occurs in
an apartment which Pamela shares with a Labour M.P.
and it centers primarily on the relationship of
Pamela with those around her from whom she needs feedback and yet the toll this exacts from her. While
those around her include a number of people, such as
her mother, half sister, and some assorted young men,
the two most important figures are her father and Constance, her apartment mate. That Pamela should be
living with Constance has resulted partly from mutual
need and partly from affection and respect. Since
Pamela had just broken with a man who had been living
with her at her house for some time, she wanted to
make the break as dramatic as possible. For this
reason she was looking for a new place to live. Inasmuch as Constance had just recently divorced (or been
divorced from) her husband, she also had to find a new
place to live. Apparently she asked Pamela to join her
because she liked and admired her; Pamela accepted
because she had comparable feelings about Constance.

What is also clear is that the play, like those of Chekhov, is deceptively shapeless. In The Cherry Orchard, nothing seems to be happening except that people are arriving and departing. In the background, however, is the threat of the sale of the cherry orchard and then the reaction to that sale. Even further in the background, but present in the characters' consciousness, as Margaret Marshall commented in reviewing a 1944 production of the play, is a basic change in society. "Nothing happens," she remarks, "except that a world comes to an end."[60] In Act I of Time Present the foreground action consists of arrivals and departures; the background action involves the impending death of Pamela's father and the growing intimacy of Pamela and Constance and the hopes this arouses in each as well as the dangers. In Act II at least one aspect of the background action is the death itself. Pamela's mother, who divorced her father many years ago and subsequently remarried a now-prominent M.P., feels, and, with some justification, that the illness and death represented an unfair intrusion into her life. Therefore, she wants to resume her normal existence. To make this easier, she has organized a memorial service (another outer action we only hear about), to which everyone except Pamela has come. In this way she hopes that everyone involved can feel some release from grief more quickly. However, for Pamela the death created such an emotional trauma that she spends most of Act II almost immobilized. At the same time other things have happened in the background that add to her pain. From hints Pamela drops about the availability of abortion services, it seems, for reasons not made explicit but which do become clear, that after the death she had an affair with Constance's lover, Murray, and has become pregnant. And from the way Constance seems to notice Pamela's physical presence, it is also possible that Constance may have some latent Lesbian feelings for Pamela. However, rather than confront these additional crises directly (the affair and the increasingly complex relationship with Constance), Pamela chooses to withdraw by arranging to stay temporarily with her agent, presumably until she can have the abortion and then live by herself again.

In Chekhov's plays, the miniutiae of everyday life and the social involvements of the aristocrats provide the catalysts which enable the characters both to express some of their deeper feelings and concerns about their lives as well as to conceal some of them, both from others and possibly themselves. In Time Present the characters' reactions to Pamela's father's

impending death and ruminations about his career and
Pamela's own achieve a similar purpose. In these
circumstances, Pamela seizes the opportunity to
express her opinions and attack those of others. She
taunts her mother and her half-sister for their bad
taste and has a field day exposing to Constance the
naïvete of her actress rival, Abigail, who is now the
critics' darling:

> . . . She [Abigail] moons about on street cor-
> ners in a French movie, looks listless and
> beautiful in her own big, beady way while you
> hear a Mozart Requiem in the background. She
> plays with herself, gets the giggles while
> she's doing it and they say she's a cross
> between Garbo and Buster Keaton. Abigail--
> who's never seen a joke in her life when it
> was chalked on a blackboard for her, who was
> the only person in the entire world who didn't
> know the truth about her Daddy until she found
> him tucked up with a Greek cabin steward and
> the family's pet bulldog! And that was before
> she got engaged to the biggest poove in the
> business. . . .

Nor does Pamela restrict herself to character assassi-
nation, for which she has undeniable talents. She
also denounces student radicals, newspaper drama
critics, tricks of the trade in acting and play-
writing, and assorted sexual habits of her contemporaries.

Considering Pamela's venom and gusto, we can understand why some critics interpreted the play mainly as
a personal vehicle for Osborne's own criticisms of his
times and/or a defense of himself. Pamela's fulminations against student radicals do parallel Osborne's
own remarks to Kenneth Tynan in The Observer interviews
I have mentioned in the Introduction. As for Pamela's
attacks on actresses and critics, these may seem like
veiled references to Osborne's contemporaries. Wide-
eyed Abigail trudging around made up like Fidel Castro
suspiciously resembles Vanessa Redgrave doing left-wing
politicking (although in the Tynan interviews Osborne
denied this).

Yet to regard the play merely as such a vehicle, or
even as that, is to ignore the real personal dilemma
that Pamela faces in her relationship with all those
around her, and to fail to realize that Pamela's put
downs, like Jimmy Porter's harangues, are means of

138

expressing her own sensibility and yet protecting it. Just as Jimmy Porter's long harangues embody his desire for love and yet his terrible insecurity, so do Pamela's fulminations express her yearning for love and self fulfillment and yet real doubts and fears. Even the attack on Abigail, when we place it in its dramatic context, derives much of its force and energy from Pamela's desire to please Constance who has asked for her impression of her rival. At this point in the play Pamela mistakenly believes that Constance can appreciate her wit and also realize that she is, as she believes her voice tone makes clear, exaggerating.

Like Jimmy, Pamela derives many of her basic values and much of her sense of identity from close personal relationships. In Jimmy's case (as indicated) his father and the mother of his friend Hugh (who helped start him out in his sweet shop) were his chief sources of inspiration; with Pamela, of course, it is her father, both as she remembers him from the past and as she experiences the ordeal of his dying. From her love for her father, she derives her feeling that she is a special person with a distinct aesthetic and ethical sensibility. Where she differs from Jimmy is that she sees herself more objectively in her inter-play with others, as well as the fact that she has achieved some success in her career. If she is not, like Abigail, the newest rage, she is not, like Jimmy, 'so full of fire and so frail.' On the other hand, Jimmy, for all of his frailty, as well as because of it, knows his basic emotions and expresses them passionately. However, Pamela for reasons not altogether clear, but which seem to involve her father and her particular kind of need for feedback, can't really do this. Two very short speeches in the play reveal Pamela's difficulty. The first occurs in Act I when Pamela is describing some of the problems that will confront her after her father's death. Constance, wanting to help her, asks Pamela if she believes in friendship (presumably to show her own capacity for providing it). To this Pamela ultimately answers:

> Oh of course. Yes, I believe in friendship, I believe in friendship. I believe in love. Just because I don't know how to doesn't mean I don't. I don't or can't . . .

The second is an entreaty Constance makes in Act II to try to dissuade Pamela from leaving: "Darling, please stay. You need love more than anyone I've ever known. And looking after. We'll both Murray and I do it."

Granted that Constance may have an ulterior motive or not even, as I think more likely, realize she does, she still hits home. Although Pamela's grand manner, her fulminations against critics and mediocre performers may suggest great assurance and love of self, the opposite may be nearer the truth. No matter how hard Pamela tries, no matter how engaging and concerned she may be, she just can't wholly believe that she can love and be loved.

While the play never openly dramatizes why Pamela feels as she does, I think it largely involves her relationship with her father. In revering him, she seems to be internalizing his values and establishing an identity for herself. However, this identity may be one that she doesn't feel she can wholly claim as her own. The reason is that so much of her sense of herself depends upon her attachment to her father. From Pamela's descriptions of her father, particularly her very detailed and exhilarating account to Constance of just how he acquired his stage name, it is clear that he was an open, honest, charismatic, and perceptive man with a clear sense of himself, and yet modest and remarkably free of jealousy. At the same time, he also had a strong empathy that enabled him both to project himself into greatly varied roles and to stimulate others to express themselves freely and interestingly in his presence. Since Pamela herself is a sensitive and discerning person, we can understand why she should admire him so much. Besides, he needed feedback himself. One reason he needed it is that her mother (who as indicated has been divorced from him for over twenty years) never seemed to appreciate him, perhaps because as a bluestocking she looked down on him. Being so close to her father and also having, as suggested, a temperament much like his (although more analytical and intellectual) Pamela felt inspired to emulate him by internalizing his values. Moreover, her particular gift, as well as her greatest need, is to feel so stimulated by others' concerns and responses that in their presence she expresses herself freely and passionately. The stronger the concern of these others, the stronger is her response. In having such sport with Abigail, Pamela really is (as indicated) performing for Constance. But of all the people who can stimulate her to be most alive and interesting, the most important is her father. In his presence, as is clear from the excitement she projects to her mother and Constance when she returns from visiting him in the hospital, she has felt so transported that she will have to take time to wind down as she does from a performance.

From what I've said so far, it is evident how much Pamela has gained from her father, but yet how vulnerable she also is. Patterning herself on her father stimulates her to demand a lot from herself in her career and personal life. Yet such patterning can cause her to put herself too much in her father's shadow or make her question her self worth, particularly when others around her don't properly appreciate her. While she feels most alive in his presence, this could also make her feel that her own identity may not exist wholly apart from him. All this is not to consider what can happen to her when she has to bear his loss and feel the need to give of herself, but to have to turn to those who give of themselves much less than her father and herself do and yet want much more in return. Moreover, these other people are not only shallow and play roles but keep changing them without realizing they are doing so.

One such example is Pamela's half sister, Pauline, who keeps trying out a variety of life styles one after another in an effort to keep up with current trends. She tries drugs, sloppy clothes and sloppier boyfriends, and a variety of dead end jobs. Murray, Constance's lover, is a playwright with a talent for rendering the surface of social behavior amusingly. However, he doesn't explore or question; he just soaks up what seems fashionable. Nevertheless, he takes himself very seriously and considers himself irresistible to women. Therefore he is willing to let them indulge him as a special person in their lives. He simply can't comprehend that Pamela should find him uninteresting. As for Abigail, she seems spontaneous and unaffected because she acts without inhibition. Yet one reason she can do so is that, without knowing it, she apes fashions from leftist counter culture (as in her Castro-like garb). As for the critics, they mistake her naïvete for naturalness. Yet, as Pamela makes clear in another speech to Constance, Abigail's lack of self awareness does enable her to let herself go as Pamela herself, who is more exacting, can't.

But of all the other characters, Constance is the one who stands out most in contrast to Pamela. While she doesn't indulge herself or let others do so for her, as Murray does, Constance has no doubts about the value of whatever she undertakes. In her mind, she is both a dedicated and able M.P. and yet a woman who is very attractive to men, and with reason because she is

beautiful, poised, and ingratiating. While she may
sound egotistical, she really isn't; she is earnest
and takes herself much too seriously and uncritically.
As Pamela points out to her, much to her surprise, Constance has little idea about what really motivates
her or how she actually feels about others, especially
Pamela herself:

> PAMELA: I think you should pay more attention
> to tones of voice. They are very concrete.
> You have plenty of them.
> CONSTANCE: You mean I dissemble?
> PAMELA: I mean you are many things to different
> people.
> CONSTANCE: A trimmer?
> PAMELA: In the House, to your constituency, in
> the papers, on the telephone, in bed; I
> don't know about that but you're deter-
> mined not to be caught out. You've read
> the books the others have, the reports,
> the things in the air at the moment, the
> present codes and ciphers. It all has to
> be broken down. The information has to be
> kept flowing. Or you'll feel cut off,
> left behind. You keep trying.
> CONSTANCE: What should I do then?
> PAMELA: What your fears and desires tell you
> together, I imagine . . .

What Pamela means, as the even more critical comments she makes about Constance to Murray later in the
play make clear (when she is trying to make him see
that Constance can take advantage of him), is that Constance lets other people's aspirations, particularly
those who are successful, determine her own goals. As
Pamela explains to her, Constance is a "trimmer" and
one who "doesn't want to be found out." Pamela doesn't
mean that Constance fears exposure but simply that she
lacks any real convictions of her own, except one, and
that is a belief that she has a right to be herself in
any number of ways. She does so not because she wants
to have lived a full, rich life, but rather that she
believes she is entitled to have her share of anything
that is available in her society so far as career,
income, and personal life are concerned. Being persistent, hard working, adaptable, and (as indicated)
earnest, Constance impresses people as some one of
good will who is eager to learn and try new experiences.
But she is also, as Pamela comes to realize, unself
critical and manipulative so that she ends up using
people without knowing it. As Pamela remarks to

142

Murray, right now Constance has staked out politics for her domain; next year she will probably write a novel based on her relationship with Pamela; and after that, without even realizing what drives her, she will probably go on the stage.

Just how shallow, exploitive, and unself aware Constance can be, is evident from her very last speech which comes after Pamela has left to stay temporarily with her agent and after Constance has implored her to stay on so that, as indicated, she and Murray can give Pamela the love she needs:

> CONSTANCE: (on phone): Darling? You're there...No, I'm o.k... I arranged a dinner for Pamela and she's gone...Yes, left... I don't know...How do I know...I don't know what she's bent on or anything...come on over...yes, now, please...I love you... I ache for you...Do you? Thank heaven for that...Darling...oh, my darling...Pamela's going to give me a lesson...yes, right... Don't be long...

At this point Constance's main interest in Pamela seems to be to get her, as the latter did promise just before leaving, to come back and give her a lesson in how to cry without running her mascara! In expressing this wish, Constance is not really being greedy so much as being petty or insensitive. While at the same time she seems to be giving herself wholly to Murray, it is also clear that she is making very sure that she has a firm hold on him.

Considering the way in which Constance has just revealed herself, we could feel that Pamela is fortunate in getting away as quickly and unobtrusively as she has. She doesn't have to remain, as she might have been, a sexual object for both Murray and Constance since the latter (as indicated) has expressed interest in Pamela's body, although again without realizing what she may have intimated. Besides, Pamela can be more open with her agent, Bernard, who freely acknowledges that he is a homosexual and genuinely admires her for her particular kind of talent. Also she does have her career of sorts. Yet her possibilities in this regard have become more limited as an incident just before the end reveals. While Pamela is waiting for Bernard, suddenly she gets a visit from Abigail, who, disguised as a man, has been up all night celebrating the great reviews she received in the opening of her

143

new play the night before. Inasmuch as the two women's
acting styles differ so noticeably, Abigail's resounding
success indicates how much more difficult it will be
for Pamela to achieve recognition that is due her.

However, what is far more painful is the toll that
the relationship with Constance took on Pamela. I
don't mean simply that Pamela feels disappointed that
she misjudged Constance's nature so that a friendship
didn't develop. Rather it is that Pamela found herself
caring a great deal for Constance and in doing so
stimulated to want to please her, as even the put down
of Abigail revealed. Yet, as has become evident in
Act II, the only way Pamela could do so was on Constance's terms, which meant compromising many of her
own values and internalizing those of Constance and
Murray, as Pamela's abortive affair with the latter
made clear. What is more, such changes were occurring
so quickly that Pamela couldn't resist them. Then,
having discovered what had happened, Pamela found herself, while ostensibly closer to these people, really
more alone and isolated than before since she couldn't
communicate to either of them how she really felt.
Being so isolated, she missed her father all the more
as some one to whom she could really feel close. Moreover, because she found herself violating so much of
what she valued in herself that she derived from her
father, Pamela felt compelled all the more to identify
her sense of herself with her loyalty to her father
and what he stood for. This explains why, as this
example reveals, just before leaving with Bernard,
Pamela looks through some of her father's clippings
and reminisces about his performances even in mediocre
plays:

> PAMELA: Don't know yet. I expect I'll do a
> telly. Here we are: "The Real Thing."
> "Think Ella, there is no inheritance,
> nothing, only my debts and no career. Just
> the poor son of a parson, an ex-capitan.
> Now that Jock Crawley has deprived me of my
> one chance, my one hope of happiness, and
> redeeming myself, there is nothing left for
> me to do. Only go out of your life. No,
> I want you. I want you to be my wife.
> That is not possible, I want your life.
> Ella, oh Ella, you are a magnificent
> woman. A gem." She had mystery behind the
> eyes even then. "And so are you David.
> All that a woman could ever want. A real
> gem. Not paste. But the real thing,

Davie, the real thing."

Yet when we notice how she reminisces, we see that, while she may be emphasizing her father's achievements at the expense of her own, she is remembering him happily and therefore easing her pain. At the same time by doing this, while waiting for Bernard to come, she is making things easier for Constance who doesn't have to say much.

While almost every Osborne play depends heavily upon the performance of the main character, Time Present does so to an unusual degree. In the first place, the other characters, except possibly for Constance, are obvious caricatures. They do serve as targets for Pamela's wit, but, since they don't effectively counter her remarks or provide any effective, ironical contrast through their actions, they aren't particularly interesting to listen to or watch. In the second place, the contrast between Pamela's surface self-assurance and her underlying self doubts depends largely upon voice tone. As Pamela remarks to Constance, it is the tone of voice not the words that counts; or rather it is the tone that tells us how to interpret the words. Some of Pamela's conversations with her mother and sister are deliberate verbal pyrotechnics in which she is playing the role they expect her to play in order to remind herself that it is pointless to communicate any other way. With Constance, it would be necessary to suggest that sometimes Pamela, as in Act I, attempts some real communication involving trust and understanding, but that at other times, particularly in Act II, she knows it is too late for such communication. On these latter occasions Pamela is trying to be gracious but guarded. Through such nuances in voice tone, Pamela can project her awareness of the complexities of her dilemma in which she is trying to keep from hurting Constance and yet avoid turning against herself the hostility and aggression that Constance's exploitiveness and shallowness arouse in her.

X

THE HOTEL IN AMSTERDAM

A good way to describe The Hotel in Amsterdam is to
call it a holiday away from Hell or being in Limbo.
The play concerns itself with three affluent, middle-
aged couples on weekend holiday in Amsterdam to escape,
so they hope, from the domineering presence of their
employer, K.L., a well known movie producer for whom
two of the husbands and one of the wives work.
Although the couples like the high salaries, they feel
trapped because the producer considers their private
lives simply to be extensions of their jobs. Therefore, they regard it as a great coup just to have
gotten away without his knowledge of their whereabouts.
Most of the play's conversation seems even more casual
than that of Time Present, for it consists of chitchat
about the best restaurants, mutual admiration for
their great escape, and backbiting at the producer
because of their dependence upon him. However, as it
turns out, the casualness is cruelly deceptive.

While there is considerable interplay of the
characters, the most important and interesting one
clearly is Laurie, who does the scenarios for the producer. Originally from a working class background, he
now does so well financially that he has a large house
and a retinue of servants. Though he complains about
all the dunning letters he receives from relatives, he
would never dream of returning to his working class
origins. He feels that he works hard for his money
and so is entitled to enjoy it, particularly since so
many ordinary things cause him pain. He can't tip
waiters, he is nervous about flying, and he hates
being alone even for short periods of time. At the
same time Laurie does pride himself on his film writing
because it involves literary artistry. That artistry,
as he describes it, is a heightened sensitivity to the
life around him. "What I do, I get out of the air,"
he explains. "Even if it's not so hot always, I put
my little hand out there in that void, that empty air.
Look at it. It's like being a bleeding conjuror, with
no white tie and tails..."

Yet Laurie also feels very defensive about what he
does. He keeps reminding himself that critics assert
that he has never fulfilled his early promise as a
novelist. Moreover, he also admits how much he needs
society's approval. Every year he just has to see if

<u>The Times</u>, London, lists his birthday. When on one
occasion it did not, he wasn't sure he really existed.

But even more directly than generalized approval,
Laurie needs to have people close to him. Although
the others also wanted to get away, they have come
mainly for his benefit. They listen to his parodies
(spontaneous and rehearsed), confessions, and his
character assassinations. Like Jimmy Porter, Laurie
is fascinating and even compelling, but he also
<u>demands</u> approval and understanding. At first glance,
it would seem that Laurie, like Pamela, has far less
need than Jimmy for such demands since he does have a
reputation, a considerable income, and a family. Yet
gradually Laurie becomes aware how profoundly unhappy
he is, and how even more dependent he is than he ever
realized.

Consequently, as the play progresses, it becomes
clear that Laurie, in particular, really isn't on
holiday at all. Three events in particular bring home
to him this bitter truth. The first is the appearance
of Laurie's sister-in-law, Gillian. Out of concern
for the latter, who goes from one exaggerated personal
crisis to another, Laurie's wife, Margaret, has left
her their Amsterdam address and telephone number.
While the others don't welcome Gillian's appearance,
they quietly accept it. However, Laurie stoutly
refuses. Not only does he expose Gillian's white
lies (which everyone knows anyway) but also reduces
her to tears. Certainly one reason he does so is that
her appearance reminds him of his own dependency needs.
But, as I want to point out later, there just might be
other reasons.

The second is a cryptic phone call from K. L.'s
butler announcing that the latter has committed suicide. As Margaret reveals, K. L. cleverly had
persuaded Gillian to disclose to him where the three
couples had gone. However, instead of harassing them,
as Laurie would have had us believe, K. L. was so shattered by being abandoned that he killed himself.
K. L.'s death may, as some critics assert, be a contrivance to bring the play to an end.[61] However, it
certainly shows how ironical have been the characters'
efforts to escape from their dependency on the latter.
While they are free from his physical presence, they
will no longer have the income with which he provided
them nor the sense of common purpose derived from
uniting against him. All this is not to mention that
now they have to rely more on each other.

The third episode which reveals Laurie's dependence is his declaration of love to Annie, the wife
of one of his collaborators, Gus, and a man Laurie
greatly admires. Throughout the play it is obvious
how, though Laurie is talking to all the others, he is
talking most of all to Annie. For example, early in
the play she facetiously remarks, "You know what: I
think people who need people are the ghastliest people
in the world." With his histrionic instinct, Laurie
uses this epigram to begin an exchange which is also
a skit:

> LAURIE: Absolutely. We all just happened to
> find one another. At the right time.
> ANNIE: It sounds a bit Jewish show biz.
> LAURIE: I thought it was a rather tense Anglo-
> Saxon sentiment myself. I mean you
> couldn't sing it.
> ANNIE: Well, you could. It would be rather
> mediocre.
> LAURIE: I mean you couldn't belt out a rather
> halting little comment like that. It's
> not poetic. It's just a smallish state-
> ment. About six unusually pleasing
> people. Well five. God, I'm getting fat.

Yet more than "show biz" is involved here for Annie
has announced a major theme of the play, which Laurie
then picks up and expands. By stating this theme and
then mocking it as they do, they are trying to deny a
painful contradiction. On the one hand, they are
saying how could anyone dare believe that we six desperately need each other. On the other hand, they are
saying, even if we do, don't we carry it off in style?
To have things both ways, or play them both ways,
seems to be what Laurie tries to do all along, but the
going becomes increasingly difficult.

The fact that he surfaces more of his deeper
feeling largely results because Annie understands him
much more than do the others. That Laurie should also
reveal his love to Annie is appropriate, since she has
given him the courage to admit his deepest anxieties.
She, in turn, admits that she feels the same about him.
In admitting their love for each other, Laurie and
Annie seem to resemble Masha and Vershinin in Chekhov's
Three Sisters, who, while still preserving the facades
of their marriages, dare to take their happiness when
they can find it. On the other hand, where Vershinin
and Masha at least enjoy their love, however briefly,
Laurie and Annie decide to keep theirs to themselves.

Moreover, as Annie points out, now that she knows how Laurie feels, she isn't sure she can endure the ordeal of being near him on the journey back to London. Even more important, Laurie and Annie wouldn't dare reveal their love to others because they need them too much. Ironically, Annie herself seems to be proving the truth of her earlier statement, "People who need people are the ghastliest of people..." At the end, she and Laurie haven't escaped from London at all; they have to return to a London which, with K. L. gone, could be more of a hell than ever.

The play, as I've been describing it so far, seems primarily to represent just an ironical reversal. At the beginning the characters have made a get away; at the end they somberly prepare to return. Yet much more comes out because of Osborne's understanding portrayal of the many facets of Laurie's dependency, that make him such an appealing character. While many such facets exist, I would emphasize three.

In the first place, Laurie's particular gifts as a writer heighten his dependency. Despite his earlier disclaimer, as indicated, he does more than just reach out and sniff the air. What he really does, as his vivid, sensory account of why he hates holidays reveals, is articulate the underlying feelings of despair of all the people present at K. L.'s pool when everyone was supposedly enjoying himself:

> LAURIE: . . . Finish your drink first. I am glad it's snowing. How I hate holidays. Those endless, clouded days by the pool even when it's blazing sun. Do you remember doing it? All together--at K. L.'s villa? We drank everything you could think of from breakfast onwards after that vile French coffee. The deadly chink of ice in steaming glasses all day. Luxury, spoiled people. Lounging together, basting themselves with comfort, staring into pools. A swimming pool is a terrible thing to look into on a holiday. It's no past and no future. You can stare into a stream or a river or a ditch. Who wouldn't rather die in a ditch than in a pool? I'm too fat for pools and the pretty girls with their straps down and their long legs just make me long for something quite different. I always want someone to write me long, exhilarating

149

> love-letters when I lie there with the
> others...A handwritten envelope by your
> towel, curling up.

Through images of taste, smell, and sight, Laurie brings
a whole scene to life. Yet, in doing so, he feels all
the more unhappy. From this example, it is fair to
conclude that, when Laurie writes a scenario, he takes
a considerable toll on himself and one which K. L. in
all probability doesn't appreciate.

In the second place, Laurie is, for an Osborne hero,
almost embarrassingly modest and gentle, and this
doesn't make things easy for him. It is true that at
first glance he hardly seems this way as his strong
attacks on people such as his mother ("I mean," he
says early in the play, "just to think of swimming
about inside that repulsive thing for nine months") or
K. L. ("Where would K. L. be without me--where will he
be without me to write his loving pictures. Pretty all
right, I guess. And without Gus to edit them into
making sense and cover up his howlers") suggest. But,
significantly, nobody really objects to either description. All Margaret says after another of Laurie's
more vehement attacks on his mother ("Mine's got a
very mean, little face. Celebrates every effect,
plays up all the time to the gallery, do anything for
anything. Self involved, bullying..") is reply, "I
don't know why nice men don't like their mothers."
More to the point, when in Act II Laurie describes his
other relatives as grubby hypocrites who like to make
him feel guilty, no one objects. The reason could
simply be that Laurie is accurate, and, as I want to
show later, this has much to do with Laurie's sources
of unhappiness.

As for Laurie's attacks on K. L., notice that his
most bitter and sustained condemnation, the longest
speech of the entire play, comes only at the end of
Act I, after Laurie has had to spend most of the act
building up to it:

> LAURIE: He takes nothing out of the air round
>   his head. Only us. Insinuates his grit
>   into all the available oysters. And if
>   ever any tiny pearls should appear from
>   these tight, invaded creatures, he whips
>   off with them, appropriates them and
>   strings them together for his own neck-
>   lace. And the pearls have to be switched
>   or changed about. Otherwise the trick,

the oyster rustling would be transparent
and the last thing he wants made known is
his own function or how he goes about it.
Where does he get the damned energy and
duplicity? Where? He's tried to split us
up but here we are in Amsterdam. He has
made himself the endless object of specu-
lation. Useful to him but humiliating
for us. Well, no more, my friend. We
will no longer be useful to you and be
put up and put down. We deserve a little
better, not much but better. We have been
your friends. Your stock in trade is
marked down and your blackmailing sneering,
your callousness, your malingering, your
emotional gun-slinging, your shooting in
the dark places of affection. You trade
on the forbearance, kindliness and talent
of your friends. Go on, go on playing
the big market of all those meretricious
ambition hankers, plodding hirelings,
grafters and intriguers. I simply hope
tonight that you are alone--I know you
won't be. But I hope, at least, you will
feel alone, alone as I feel it, as we all
in our time feel it, without burdening our
friends. I hope the G.P.O. telephone system is collapsed, that your chauffeur is
dead and the housekeeper drunk and that
there isn't one con-man, camp follower,
pimp, mercenary, or procurer of all things
possible or one globe trotting bum boy at
your side to pour you a drink on this dark
January evening . . .

Notice also that when Laurie finishes, what does he
say? Something to top it? Not at all. He merely
says, and obviously with relief, "I think I'm the only
one who believed all that. Good, all the better. We
can get snowed up." Laurie's last comment indicates
that these feelings of frustration had been building up
for months, and that it took a great effort of the
will finally to express them. Again, I should add, no
one contradicts him. In fact, earlier one of the
others made it clear that Laurie had cause for feeling
badly treated by K. L.

In the third place, even for an Osborne hero,
Laurie feels isolated and self-punitive. One such
revealing episode occurs when he asks Annie if she
wishes she could live alone. After she says <u>no</u>, he

goes on to describe why this has been so painful for him. "I have lived alone sometimes. It can be all right for weeks on end even. But then, you have to crawl out of the well. Just a circle of light and your own voice and your own effort. People under-estimate Gus, I think . . . " Later, he reveals why he admires Gus so much: "Gus has created himself. Think he's nobody, thinks he behaves like it. Result himself." And still later he adds, "I love Gus very much. I think he really believes most people are better than him. I only suspect it."

That Laurie immediately associates his feelings about not wanting to live alone with his admiration for Gus because the latter seems so at ease with him-self, even at the expense of greatly underrating him-self, suggests that Laurie, in contrast, is very hard on himself. When he doesn't have people around him, towards whom he can feel affection and can be suppor-tive, he punishes himself, as his description of a typical working day reveals:

> LAURIE: I'm afraid I usually need a drink. It's the only thing that burns it out. Need to weld my guts with a torch. Then about nine, it eases off. I read the post. Try to put off work. Have a so-called business lunch. That's a good waste of time. Then I know I'll have to sleep in the afternoon.

Worse still, he expects such punishment to become more severe. Later in Act I, he asks Gus and Dan (a painter and husband of Amy, who is K. L.'s secretary) an apparently trivial question; whether or not they keep an annual appointment book as a daily reminder. After Gus merely says <u>yes</u>, and Dan <u>no</u>, (which indi-cates that neither attaches any great importance to the question) Laurie indicates why for him getting such a diary is a necessary but painful affair:

> LAURIE: Well then, Gus. I wonder if this happens to you. You know how just after Christmas and you've got nothing to do except feel ill and miserable and dread those last days of December? If you haven't got to hell out of it. Well, I always start my new diary off before the New Year. Put my licence number in it because I can't remember it. Why <u>should</u> I

remember it? Then you put in your telephone numbers--I even put in my own in.
Otherwise I might ring one I had years
ago...Well, and then there are the names of
all those people, not all those people but
some people because I don't keep many in
there and then you know--every year I sit
down and there's not just one I don't put
in again, there's four, five, six. I think
there are only about eleven in this year--
and that includes people like you and Dan
and K. L. He'll be out next year. And my
agent. And that's about it. Oh, and my
mother...Hey, what are you all doing in
there?

He seems to be saying that he expects to lose contact
even with those he cares most about and that the process
seems irreversible. Next year, K. L. will be out;
maybe the following year, although Laurie doesn't say
so, Dan and Gus will be out.

Why does Laurie feel that he is becoming more isolated and has to punish himself more? Although he
never directly answers these questions, he does provide
us with enough clues, several of which I've already
mentioned. For one thing, the very way he talks about
his mother and the rest of his family indicates how
much he has wanted to break away from them and assert
himself because otherwise he feared he would end up
like them. In such put downs, he might also be expressing feelings of shame about his family, comparable to
those that Redl expressed when Hilde, the prostitute,
asked him about his background.

Besides, what he has done has not been easy, for
one of the most terrible things about his family, as
he reveals in one of his longest, funniest, and yet
bitterest speeches, is that they have a great talent
for making him (and perhaps others) feel guilty long
after he has gone away from them:

LAURIE: Retired rotten, grafting publicans,
shop assistants, ex-waitresses. They live
on and on. Having hernias and arthritic
hips and strokes. But they go on: writing
poisonous letters to one another. Complaining and wheedling and paying off the
same old scores with the same illiterate
signs. "Dear Laurie, thank you very
kindly for the cheque. It was most wel-

153

come and I was able to get us one or two
things we'd had to go without for quite
some time and the doctor sends me to the
hospital twice a week. They tell me it's
improving but I can't say I feel much
improvement. How are you, old son? Old
son? We saw your name in the paper about
something you were doing the other day and
the people next door said they thought you
were on the telly one night but we didn't
see it, and Rose won't buy the television
papers so we always switch on to the same
programme. Rose doesn't get any better,
I'm afraid. I brought her a quarter
bottle the other day with your kind remit-
tance which served to buck her up a bit.
Your Auntie Grace wrote and said she'd
heard Margaret was having another baby.
That must be very nice for you both. We
send our best wishes to you both and the
other little ones. Hope you're all well.
Must close now as I have to take down the
front room curtains and wash them as Rose
can't do it any longer, but you know what
she is. Bung ho and all the very best.
Excuse writing but my hand is still bad.
Ever. Your Uncle Ted. P.S. Rose says
Auntie Grace said something about a letter
from your mother which she sent on but
I'm afraid she sent it back unopened. She
just refuses to pass any comment. She
told me not to say anything about it to
you but I thought I'd just--PASS IT ON TO
YOU! (He gestures towards them.) Pass
that on!

I don't think it an accident that just before this
speech Laurie was complaining that he can't enjoy having servants because they make him feel guilty. As he
remarks, "The mistake is to feel guilty. That's always
been my mistake. He's driving you about because
you're cleverer than he is and though I say it, he
can't even drive as well as I can . . . "

That Laurie should speak so knowledgeably about
guilt might indicate how well he has been coping with
it. But since this speech comes just before Gillian's
appearance late in Act II, it more accurately reveals
how much he has been trying to understand such feelings,
let alone deal with them effectively. That Laurie in
fact is far from confident about dealing with guilt

becomes clearer after he has, as indicated, criticized his family so harshly. When Margaret, in reply, insists that all one needs to say about them is that they are boring, Laurie objects strongly, "They're not that even. They're not even boring. Now I am boring. I am quite certainly the most boring person you have ever met in your lives . . . " Despite the fact that Gus insists that he is infinitely more boring, Laurie goes on to run himself down even more: "There you are. I am just as boring drunk as I am sober. There is no appreciable difference. If I could tell you, if I could, how much I bore myself. I am really fed up with the whole subject . . . I am a meager, pilfering bore."

In escaping from his family, Laurie has gained considerable freedom. Yet he feels guilty about what he has done and possibly ashamed. At the same time, he feels just as strongly that he hasn't done enough-- that, as his critics attest, not lived up to his promise. Throughout much of Act I, he vacillates between insisting how hard he works and how little people understand what he does and trying to convince himself that he really is doing something worthwhile to justify his high salary:

> LAURIE: But what goods? I ask myself: can any- thing manufactured out of this chaos and rapacious timidity and scolding carry on really be the goods. Should it not be, I ask myself. What do I ask myself, perhaps I shouldn't be rhetorical and clutter con- versations with what-do-I-ask-myselfs? Won't they be shown up by the way of the manner of their manufacture? How can they become aloof, materials shaped with precision, design, logical detail, cunning, formality. And so on and so on.

The very awkward, self conscious tone clearly indicates how bothered Laurie really is by his particular suc- cess. Fortunately, Annie, as she does so regularly, rescues him by asking supportively, 'if the cloth isn't really very good?' While Laurie agrees, he still feels guilty and ashamed. In fact, such feelings may also help explain the ferocity of his long tirade (already quoted) directed against K. L. For one of the things Laurie feels most ashamed of is that he has found himself, because of his own feelings of low self worth, having to feel so dependent on K. L. and there- fore hate the latter, and even more himself, for doing so.

From what I've been pointing out, it is clear that the play does far more than just show that the characters, particularly Laurie, can't get away at all. If anything, the three incidents at the end, coming after all I've described, would seem to make Laurie's dilemma even more despairing than originally indicated. Yet, if we look again at these incidents, especially after we have noticed how throughout the play Laurie has admitted how unhappy he is and how harshly he treats himself, we can see something else that occurs: an effort to be honest at an even deeper level and to cope with some of his feelings of guilt and shame.

For example, when Gillian appears because she clearly has been unhappy in London, we might expect Laurie as a fellow sufferer to show some compassion for her. But instead, in striking contrast to the others, he, as indicated, taunts her. Yet he does so because he recognizes that, while she does need help, she is also making them feel guilty unfairly by her behavior. Therefore, by attacking Gillian, Laurie is beginning to protect himself from having to be made to feel guilty. Equally important, he makes it possible for Gillian herself to admit how she really feels. By brusquely insisting, "For Christ sake, Gillian burst into tears," he enables her to do so and permits Margaret to take her into her bedroom and find out what really bothers her. Comparably, Laurie's apparently even more irresponsible reaction to the news of K. L.'s suicide:

> LAURIE: Come in. Have a drink. You too, Gillian. Dan...Sleeping pills, aspirin, bottle of whisky, half a loaf of bread to keep it all down...give the housekeeper the weekend off, turn the extension off in your study and lock the front door... Well, cheers...(Silence.)

provides a far more important release of guilt. By mocking the details of the suicide, Laurie is helping the others to diminish their understandable feelings of guilt in having left him alone for the weekend (feelings that would be accentuated by the fact that he left their address by his bedside before taking his own life). Moreover, through his mockery, Laurie is enabling the others to feel grateful that they are alive because at least they admitted how intolerable their life had become and had done something about it. True, they had to spend most of Act I in alleviating their guilt feelings for having dared to do so. Never-

156

theless, they did take a step that helped them ease
some of their frustrations.

However, the incident that most clearly shows the
extent to which Laurie begins doing something to change
his life, although it may not at first seem that way,
is the one in which, as indicated, he reveals his love
for Annie. While his declaration comes out spontaneously and haltingly, it isn't something that appears out
of the blue. For one thing, as I've emphasized earlier,
Annie has consistently been supportive to Laurie, both
through witty repartee and open, but tactful concern.
Moreover, at the end of Act I, Laurie does kiss her,
though as the stage directions tell us, "lightly."
But what I really mean is that in the scene itself
both Laurie and Annie build up very carefully to this
declaration, although this may not be evident at
first, particularly since the scene begins with what
appears to be bitchy cocktail party talk, not unlike
that of London. Laurie starts things off by asking
Annie if she has ever been married before. After she
has answered no, and he has acknowledged that he has,
the replies on both sides become caustic:

> ANNIE: It's quite a well known fact.
> LAURIE: Yes. It's like having had a previous
>   conviction...
> ANNIE: Of course, I lived with people before
>   Gus.
> LAURIE: Many?
> ANNIE: I don't think so; some would. But I
>   don't think it was inordinate--no. I
>   lived with each one an inordinate time.

Yet, by commenting as she does about his first marriage
and admitting what she has done, Annie helps Laurie
relieve himself of more of his guilt, as his comment
about having a previous marriage reveals. In turn,
this enables him to admit something far more painful
about his first marriage that apparently has been
bothering him, how much he dreads meeting his ex-wife
unexpectedly:

> ANNIE: Why do you dread it?
> LAURIE: I don't think she likes me.
> ANNIE: Why not?
> LAURIE: I imagine I wasn't very kind to her.
> ANNIE: Weren't you?
> LAURIE: I don't know. I wish I could really
>   remember. I try to. I hope not. But I'm
>   sure I was.

```
ANNIE:   It doesn't mean that you're unkind.
LAURIE:  Doesn't it?
ANNIE:   Oh, come.  Just capable of it.  Like
         everyone.
LAURIE:  Amy is never unkind.
ANNIE:   You don't want to be like Amy.
```

In confessing that he fears his ex-wife might not like
him because he imagines he wasn't very kind to her,
Laurie is not merely admitting how much her rejection
bothers him but how much he blames himself for what
took place during the marriage. For someone who can
criticize others as harshly as Laurie has done, we
might expect him to say something hostile about his
ex-wife as he did about K. L. That he doesn't may
indicate that he can be more forgiving about his ex-
wife, or that he feels so much guilt that he can't
recognize any other emotion. Significantly, Annie
seems to understand both his kindness and yet the
strength of his guilt by her replies. "It doesn't
mean that you're unkind" and "Oh, come. Just capable
of it. Like everyone." On the one hand, she recognizes that Laurie needs to accept the reality of his
guilt feelings and, on the other, to accept himself as
a good person since he has only felt a certain way
towards his ex-wife rather than acted in this manner.
Moreover, in assuring him that he doesn't want to be
like Amy, whom he has been looking up to all the way
through the play as the perfect secretary, friend,
wife, and sexually healthy woman, Annie is telling him
that he is undervaluing and punishing himself by
making such a comparison. Through such understanding,
Annie helps Laurie feel free or freer about his first
marriage, as well as to begin to admit how difficult a
bind he felt himself in when he married his present
wife, particularly because he felt such a strong need
of others' approval:

```
LAURIE:  You live with someone for five, six
         years.  And you begin to feel you don't
         know them.  Perhaps you didn't make the
         right kind of effort.  You have to make
         choices, adjustments, you have requirements
         to answer.  Then you see someone you love
         through other eyes.  First, one pair of
         eyes.  Then another and more.  I was afraid
         to marry but afraid not to.  You see, I'm
         not really promiscuous.  I'm a moulting old
         bourgeois.  I'm not very good at legerde-
         main affairs...Do you like Margaret?
```

How quickly Annie understands his unhappiness becomes evident by her reply, "Have you been unfaithful to her?" That she also asks him how often and if he enjoyed it, and when was the last time, may seem like prying, but such questions permit him to become more open and forgiving for what he has done. Moreover, as his answer to the question about the last time, namely, "When she was in the nursing home" and Annie's complete unawareness that this occurred reveals, he may have had reason because Margaret had a nervous breakdown. In any event, living with her has not been easy, particularly since, as Laurie revealed to Annie earlier in the play, he and Margaret have gone on having children mainly because each felt that this was what the other wanted.

Since Laurie's disclosure about Margaret's stay in the nursing home was such a closely guarded secret, Annie at this point might understandably have pressed him for more details. But doing so would have pained him. That, instead, she immediately asks, "Why did you tell me this?" shows him not only how she wants to spare him any such embarrassment but how much she cares that he has told her. This encourages him to take his deepest plunge and express, as his combination of yearning and doubt reveals, his deep love for her and yet hope that she will respond in kind:

> Why? Because...to me...you have always been the most dashing...romantic...friendly...playful... loving...impetuous...larky...fearful...detached ...constant...woman I have ever met...and I love you...I don't know how else one says it... one shouldn't...and I've always thought you felt...perhaps...the same about me.

While this speech in its piling up of adjectives may seem high flown, yet it does suggest how much Laurie has held back, how much he now dares to admit, and yet at the end how modest and undemanding he actually is. In addition, the striking contrasts also accentuate his vulnerability, for, if she doesn't give him some hope, he would feel not only greatly embarrassed but guilty and depressed. However, Annie quickly, but also gently reassures him with, "I do, I do" and later goes on to reveal that for a long time she has wanted to tell him she has loved him. Still, immediately after this climax, each makes it clear that they will keep their love secret because neither wants to hurt the others involved. As Annie points out, since Gus is so trusting and innocent, he would never guess that

159

this could be. Laurie, in turn, reveals how bound he is in obligation to Margaret and how much he cares for her. Besides, as he has admitted earlier, he loves Gus.

That Laurie and Annie choose to do nothing may raise the question as to why Laurie should ever have bothered to tell Annie since now they could feel more trapped than ever. Yet, just by admitting his love, Laurie is showing that he dares hope for something more out of his life. At the same time in taking so long to express it, he acknowledges how much others' reactions can affect him, but that at least he has begun to cope more effectively with such feelings. Finally, if in not doing anything to change his present situation Laurie may be acknowledging how much he needs Gus and Margaret, as well as Dan and Amy, he is also showing how much he cares for them and how responsible he feels for Margaret. Since at the beginning of the play, Laurie seemed to feel that he deserved some special consideration and the others responded in kind, his behavior at the end represents a noticeable change.

XI

WEST OF SUEZ

i

West of Suez centers on the Christmas-time reunion
of a prominent English upper middle class family, consisting of a widower and his four daughters, at a West
Indian island villa belonging to the oldest daughter.
The island, a former British Crown Colony, is now a
combination tax shelter for wealthy English refugees
and a haven for British colonials who want to preserve
as much as they can of the good old days of imperialism. The father, Wyatt Gillman, is a writer with a
considerable reputation, based as much, if not more,
on his being a celebrity rather than on his writing,
most of which he has done years ago and about which
people talk only in general terms. Now in his seventies, Wyatt enjoys playing to the hilt his current
role as a star on a television talk show. As he is
the first to admit, Wyatt adopts poses or attitudes in
order, as he says, to make life easier. By that, he
means that he can cover up his self doubts and nurse
his talent, even at the expense of family responsibilities.

Robin, the oldest, is married for the second time
to a retired Army Brigadier who spends his time cook-
ing, puttering in the garden, and socializing at the
club. Largely occupied with indulging her husband's
whims, Robin feels that she never did have much of a
grasp on her own life, although she doesn't seem to
know why. In any event, she now believes that it is
too late to change things. Mary, the youngest and the
only one to have children, is married to Robert, a
Scottish school teacher. That she has children
strengthens a dominant impression she creates, that of
being the "normal" and "happy" member, the one with
few self doubts and the one who probably believes in
the "right causes" (though without defining what they
are). Evangie, the second youngest and the only one
not married, is a prolific writer, particularly on
occasional or topical subjects. While she may have
other reasons for being a writer, most of them have to
do with her father. Ostensibly she writes because her
father has encouraged her by calling her "the bright
one." However, because she senses that he doesn't
really mean what he says, she writes to try to convince
him (as well as herself) that she does have talent.

161

Yet all the while she senses that she is pushing herself but can't do anything else.

Finally, there is Frederica who is married to Edward, a successful, intelligent, and witty London pathologist. Although he comes from a good family, he really has made it on his own and believes that this is what life is all about. As for Frederica herself, she is (as I indicated in the Introduction) a beautiful, intelligent, and outspoken woman who feels strongly that the private and public behavior of people close to her and that of the society in which she lives smacks too much of role playing and snobbish condescension. In addition, she feels greatly frustrated because, unlike Pamela whom she resembles in many respects, she has no career or outlet for her talents, largely because of having been brought up in the kind of society she seeks to expose. As a result, she feels herself in pain much of the time. However, unlike other Osborne main characters who are also in pain and are outspoken, she conceals much of her anguish partly out of pride and partly because she is herself a victim of what she is attacking. Instead, she spends most of her time trying to satisfy her restless curiosity and (as again indicated) to get people around her to be more honest, open, and loving as she herself wants to be. Like Pamela, she cares a great deal for her father, except that her feelings for Wyatt are more ambivalent than those of Pamela for her father. In particular, Frederica is very critical of her father's dishonest and patronizing treatment of others, not only for what it has done to them but, as she realizes during the play, to herself and even to her father as well.

While the play centers on the family's interaction with one another (as Robert says at one point there is something fascinating about a father's relationship with so many daughters because it is like a closed circle), it is both wider and narrower in focus than my description so far might suggest. The focus is wider because it includes the family's interaction with several representative English and American people living on the island who also are bored, restless, and in pain. These include Alastair, a middle aged hairdresser and homosexual who feels particularly insecure in such a role but tries to cover this up by making a show of it; Harry, a sickly, hulking businessman who, though American, seems a permanent part of the scene; and Lamb, a writer of almost the same age and reputation as Wyatt. Like Wyatt, Lamb also protects himself behind poses, though he is more cautious and honest in

the way he employs them. Like Alastair, Lamb also is
a homosexual but more discreet and yet more secure, as
he is the first to admit, because of his upper class
birth. Finally, there are two other non-English people
who stand out in striking contrast to the English on
whom they openly look down. The first is Mrs. James,
an intelligent, courteous but also outspoken black
journalist who appears in just one scene to interview
Wyatt for a local radio station. The other is Jed, a
vociferously rude and dissident young American hippie
who, for reasons never made clear, happens to be on
the island. During most of the play he scarcely seems
visible, but at the end he bursts in and denounces the
English in a vicious tirade which is the longest and
most dramatic speech in the play.

Yet the play is even narrower in focus because it
centers on the impact of two characters, Frederica and
her father, both on each other as well as the rest I've
mentioned. From Frederica's point of view, she is
trying, as indicated, to get her husband and to a
greater extent her father, as well as others around,
to be more open and caring. From Wyatt's point of view,
he is trying to continue acting as he has all these
years. However, he is having increasing difficulty,
mainly because of Frederica but also because of the
impact of Mrs. James, Jed, the natives on the island,
and long submerged self doubts.

That Osborne should have an English family travel
so far and to such a small place to explore and yet
conceal even more, if possible, the dynamics of its
private and public attitudes and relationships may
seem round about. But actually it isn't. For one
thing, the family as well as all of the English on
the island, are colonials (although from east rather
than west of Suez). Therefore, in visiting this former crown colony, they are coming closer to their
roots, such as they are. For another, colonial life
accentuates some important aspects of English personal
and public life. In leaving England, colonials seem
to be denying some of their strongest feelings of
community and family. Yet living so far away also
makes them acutely aware of these, as the many
references to England as home in the play suggest.
Equally important, they have left England because,
paradoxically, they believe strongly in many features
of English life which they have transplanted to the
colonies as part of imperialism. These include privilege and its accompanying exploitation of natives and
elaborate attention to forms or rituals as a basic

part of private and public behavior. In this sense the
colonials are, if possible, more quintessentially English than those who stayed behind. Therefore, just as
in The Hotel in Amsterdam, the characters turn out not
to be on holiday at all but very much a part of what is
all too enduring in English life.

The fact that the play focuses both on the family
as well as a larger group of characters around them as
they sip their drinks and idly but facetiously converse
helps account for a considerable looseness, even apparent shapelessness, because much of the play seems just
like talk. Nor is the talk just restricted to the
large circle of English people but is interrupted by
outsiders who themselves have a great deal to say.
Then, if these interruptions aren't disconcerting enough,
at the end comes an even more intrusive one, that of a
group of armed natives who suddenly appear uninvited
and bring the play to a quick, shattering end in which
conversation seems anti-climactic.

Yet this kind of play is not so strange after all
for it significantly resembles Shavian discussion plays,
especially Heartbreak House. In both plays, characters representing many viewpoints (but all part of a
bored ruling class) sit around and talk leisurely
about their own private lives and their secrets to
help relieve their frustration. The conversation
flows freely enough to permit characters to convey many
of their feelings and yet to conceal them through
repartee, digression, and displacement. Because the
talk both explores the attitudes and feelings and yet
tries to contain them, it creates, though not obvious
immediately, escalating tensions which finally express
themselves in violence that may seem to strain credibility. Nevertheless, the violence in both plays does
bring into sharper focus what has been happening, as
well as convey a clear warning as to what could happen
if something isn't done and done quickly.

Although comparisons with Heartbreak House are
illuminating, especially formally, they can be overdone because they can make us overlook significant
differences between the visions of both plays. Granted
that both plays have a central father figure, interesting daughters, considerable repartee and, most important, present a highly critical view of a society that
is stultifying, they do differ in many ways. Shaw's
play presents more fantastic elements and different
tonal contrasts, family configuration, historical
periods, and issues. Since the plays do differ so

much, it is unnecessary to ask which is better or, more to the point, to attack Osborne, as some critics have done, because he hasn't written Shaw's play.[62]

In the same vein it is also unfair to attack Osborne because he hasn't written his version of another play which West of Suez resembles, though to a lesser degree, and that is Chekhov's The Cherry Orchard.[63] Admittedly, Osborne has stated in the Tynan Observer interviews how much he wishes he could have written The Cherry Orchard.[64] More to the point, both plays do portray pained aristocrats who react confusedly to change. But again the family configuration and social backgrounds differ even more than they do in comparison to Heartbreak House. Besides, West of Suez is not, like The Cherry Orchard, a play of indirect action. Most important, in The Cherry Orchard characters are reacting confusedly because they have already experienced so much of the pain brought about by change that they are trying to accommodate themselves to it. However, in West of Suez the pain results to a considerable extent because not enough change has occurred, the time is growing shorter, and the resistance still remains pretty strong.

Therefore, it is enough to say that West of Suez represents Osborne's version of a discussion play that strikingly juxtaposes extensive, free flowing conversation and sudden, concentrated action. Yet in such plays, whether by Shaw or Osborne, the conversation, though varied, extensive, and discursive is also structured. In West of Suez, while Osborne uses a number of means to structure his talk, at least three stand out.

The first is simply that of repetition, whether of topics or image. For example, recurrent references to the sounds or birds or to seasonal changes emphasize the characters' yearning for home. At the same time repeated strange noises emphasize, in contrast, an ominous, disquieting atmosphere underneath the surface calm of social conversation. A more subtle and interesting type of repetition is that of leitmotif, or thematic recurrences. At the beginning of the play, for example, Frederica talks about the natives as an interesting mixture of lethargy and hysteria, and brutality and sentimentality. Much later in the play when Mrs. James asks Wyatt what he thinks about the islanders, he speaks of the people as a "very unappealing mixture of hysteria and lethargy, brutality and sentimentality." This repetition shows that even two people who differ widely still share common attitudes which contribute to the violence that erupts at the end.

The second, and more obvious and important, means is that of centering each episode around a clash of characters or of one character versus just about all the others. While Edward and Frederica begin the play (as I want to show in greater detail later) with glib repartee about island life that sounds like a revue skit, shortly afterwards the tone shifts to that of acerbic confrontation. Elsewhere in the play there is Mrs. James' interview with Wyatt which develops into a confrontation of another kind and Jed's frenetic outburst at the end in which he denounces all of the English. Furthermore, even two long episodes that seem the most discursive and low keyed, Wyatt's appearance in the second half of Act I and the extended after dinner conversation before Mrs. James arrives, depend upon a dramatic clash, which, though less apparent initially than the foregoing, is nonetheless real. In coming on the scene and taking over as he does, Wyatt (as I want to show later) is really trying to forestall any opposition to his performing to the hilt and so keeping things the way they've always been with his family. In the first part of Act II Frederica both organizes the conversation so that it will flow freely to enable people to surface feelings mainly about the past and yet disrupts it to prod her father and, to a lesser extent, the others to level with themselves. Her father, in turn, resists with all of his skill.

The third, and most important, has to do with the relation of these episodes to each other. While Act I plays as a continuous unit, it really consists of the two long episodes I've mentioned, each of which stands out in sharp contrast to the other, and each of which seems like a fresh start or even a separate one act in itself. Although Act II, i, also plays as a continuous unit, it contains two isolated but very different parts, Frederica's control of the conversation and Mrs. James's interview with Wyatt and his resistance to her questions. It is true that II, ii, which contains Jed's appearance also has a short, preliminary encounter between Frederica and Christopher (Wyatt's secretary). However, the encounter moves so fast that the whole scene appears as a unit. By this technique of scenic juxtaposition, Osborne creates five distinct episodes which build upon each other and which show in successive stages and in varied detail just how difficult it is to get people to be open, honest, and caring, and how equally difficult it is

166

to contain those forces both within characters and
within their society that have been submerged for so
long. The play keeps starting, stopping, expanding
and yet contracting its energies. As a result, as I
want to show by looking at each of these five distinct
episodes in some detail, while the end is sudden and
violent, it is not accidental or meretricious. Moreover, although Frederica and Wyatt do not appear
together in every scene, the play really centers on
both of them for, even while Frederica is struggling
with her husband, she is trying to clarify her feelings
about her father. Granted also that Frederica isn't
present while Wyatt is playing to his family in the
latter half of Act I, it is apparent that one reason
he can do so is that Frederica isn't there to challenge him.

ii

The first phase begins with lively, witty, far
ranging repartee, which seems almost like a playlet in
itself. The repartee includes epigrams about the
weather, the natives (as indicated), impressions of
Frederica's family, male ane female role relationships,
and the influence of the past, especially when one is
a colonial. Such a list might suggest that the dialogue merely provides an opportunity for two articulate
people to display their wit and to keep themselves
from being bored. But the repartee also shows that
both Frederica and Edward, while interested in fighting
boredom, are really acutely aware of each others' frustrations and their own defenses against these feelings.
At first, Frederica just seems to be looking for ways
to hurt Edward as she taunts him with comments such as,
"I think doctors are an oddly narrow lot, on the whole,"
or later with "Doctors are to be used." Coming out of
the blue, these comments just seem to express unfounded
malice, particularly since Edward in reply seems to be
restrained and tactful with such replies as "We try not
to give rise to incident." However, as the conversation goes on, Edward begins to get his own back with,
"Sometimes your tongue does trip over a palpable
truth." While Frederica seems more blunt, her attack
is less personal. Consequently, she does give Edward
a chance to dissociate himself from what she is saying;
he, for his part, gives her no such option.

As the repartee goes on, it becomes increasingly
apparent that Frederica is difficult to live with. She
asks a lot from people, pours out her frustrations
about not having a career, and has a talent for finding

167

red herrings in debate and for sustained verbal aggression:

> FREDERICA: I thought you said you liked him?
>   [The Brigadier]
> EDWARD: I do. I certainly don't hold him in
>   the contempt you do.
> FREDERICA: He's too old and doddery by half.
> EDWARD: He'll outlast her.
> FREDERICA: While the money holds out.
> EDWARD: But then contempt comes easily to you.
> FREDERICA: I keep most of it for myself.
> EDWARD: Then try spreading the load or turning
>   down the pressure or something.
> FREDERICA: I happen to like high standards,
>   starting with number one.
> EDWARD: Perhaps you should have a go at obser-
>   ving them, whatever they are. Like try
>   charity for a bit. Give that a whirl.
> FREDERICA: Don't start giving me St. Paul.
>   That's the prig's first.
> EDWARD: You think you don't sound priggish?
> FREDERICA: The woman was made for the man, not
>   the man for the woman or whatever it is.

Yet it also becomes apparent that Edward is just as
difficult, if not more so. He is so bland and agree-
able because he can limit himself exclusively to his
work and can't understand why Frederica feels so dissatisfied. After all, he can cope with his life, even
if he has to admit that most of the time he is
unhappy. On the other hand, for all of Frederica's
apparent intolerance of Edward, she does understand why
he can be as smug as he is. On the one hand, it is
because he prides himself on being very narrow in his
work; as he willingly admits, he is literally "just a
blood and shit man." As such, he doesn't feel that
he has to make exalted claims for what he does. On the
other hand, while he acknowledges that Frederica clearly has different values from his and has a right to
believe in them, he feels that this gives him the
right to look down on her for having them. This
explains why she asks him what could otherwise seem
like the cruelest and most unfair question of all,
"Why do you hate me?" Significantly, he doesn't deny
it but rather suggests that it is a form of bad manners
to ask such questions. At the heart of Frederica's
attacks is her strong feeling, which Edward's reactions
confirm, that she has married a cold, career oriented
man who really can't empathize with some one because
he is so much engrossed in his own work and really

can't love because he doesn't have much faith or hope.

While Frederica could become indignant at this
point because Edward clearly isn't satisfying what
she needs most of all, yet she values the fact that
they both depend on each other and admits it. Accordingly, she reaches out her hand and asks, "Friends?"
To this he replies, "Married friends." Although again
he is not giving her the love she wants, he is being
honest, and he cares as much as some one with his particular combination of ambition and basic skepticism
can.

This scene first of all shows how hard it is for
Frederica to pierce through the veneer of attitudes
and defenses that Edward possesses (and that she herself also can employ), how much in particular she
wants to be loved but can't openly dare admit, and yet
how hard she tries to find, as she does at last, some
rock bottom basis of trust and honesty in her relationship with Edward. At the same time, as some of her
highly ambivalent comments about her father and the
particular intensity of her need to confront Edward
reveal, she will take the same tack with the others,
particularly when we see, as in the next scene, that
her father has more defenses than Edward and he has
affected her life even more.

The second phase of the play, Wyatt's appearance,
stands out in striking contrast to the first because,
while father and daughter both come on strong and in
some sense perform, they have very different purposes.
Admittedly, the contrast might be more dramatic were
Wyatt to appear immediately after Frederica and Edward
leave as they do (to go for a swim as a sign of their
truce). Instead, there follows a brief episode that
mainly involves the other members of the family commenting on Frederica's behavior and on what Wyatt will
likely say. Yet this episode reveals that Frederica's
family, especially her brother-in-law Robert, the
school teacher who considers himself a great student of
human nature, don't understand her very well. As far
as they are concerned, she puts people on the defensive
merely to protect herself. From all the evidence of
the preceding scene, such comments not only represent
a great exaggeration but make clearer why Frederica's
position is so painful since those close to her don't
understand her. On the other hand, while waiting for
Wyatt to appear, the family recount many familiar ploys
and, in doing so, reveal how uncritically they accept
him. In turn, such acceptance makes it easier, as the

rest of the act will disclose, for him to go on posing as he has and more difficult for Frederica to have to deal with such behavior because it bothers her so much.

However, the real focus of the rest of Act I is on Wyatt himself. From the time he appears and coyly asks, "what's that you were saying about me?" to the moment some thirty minutes later when he sits down to rest, he puts on a dazzling performance that fools everybody, possibly even himself.

His very first speech clearly reveals how readily he takes over the conversation and how quickly he casts himself in roles:

> WYATT: What's that? What are you saying? You can't be talking about me. Gosh, I'm in a soak from all this sun! What a <u>day</u> it is! Think of all those people freezing in the Home Counties, hoping the rails and points won't ice up again! Ice and floods to <u>come</u>, I dare say. And everybody'll be so astonished. As usual. I <u>have</u> had a time. Spoke to such a nice <u>lot</u> of people. Charming lot in the shops, and I went to that smashing little market. Got a splen-did new hat. Do you like it?

Here Wyatt casts himself deprecatingly but smugly in the role of the fatuous old tourist who likes everyone but does all the right things. To say the least, he is poles apart from Frederica with her slashing but candid attacks on doctors and other targets, herself included. Moreover, in being so talkative, Wyatt has thrown out many leads for others to pick up and which he can then seize upon to mold the conversation as he wishes. Needless to say, this very willingness to cast himself in such a role keeps others at a distance since they are relating to him primarily through his persona.

At the same time, Wyatt dominates the conversation even when he doesn't appear to be. He does this by moving so quickly from one topic to another that his family begins to ask him questions to slow him down. In turn, he can then stop at any point and start on a new track or go on as before. Whichever way, Wyatt remains in command. Even as the others try to slow him down by interrupting, Wyatt uses this itself as a springboard for another foray. When, for example, Robin tells him that she just came back from putting her mother-in-law on the plane after her annual visit and had to take a drink to recuperate, Wyatt first expresses interest in the latter as a contemporary with whom he can share common memories. But then, immediately, he expresses concern that he might trouble his daughters by his visits. When, of course, they say no, he is encouraged to talk more openly about himself as some one who finds it increasingly difficult to share his memories. Naturally, some one asks him which memories, and he then proceeds to reminisce about his days in public school and in World War I. Although he is open, he expresses opinions that in a different way are just as patronizing as those he expressed when he first appeared on the scene. The reason is that he makes his audience feel that they are being let in on something special.

Still another way he dominates is to seize upon an interruption to express patronizing phrases he has regularly used and which the others accept. Then, in turn, he uses them as a springboard for candid comments which seem to bring him closer to his family but also distance him all the more. At one point, he seizes upon a remark that Evangie makes to the effect that people should go on loving regardless of what will happen as undeniably true since she is, as he has said many times before, "the bright one." Then to corroborate this assertion, he points out in contrast that he certainly couldn't claim that he treated his wife in such a manner as Evangie described. When some one protests that this isn't so, he confronts them all with a remarkably candid reminiscence about how he really felt at his wife's funeral:

> WYATT: . . . Your mother was a bit like that and I never realized it till she was dead. I must have enjoyed a few brandies since that funeral. Awful thing to say, but I think that was almost the most enjoyable day of my life. When those ropes slid down into that grave, I had to lower my head right down so that no one could see my face...I must be very unfeeling indeed, I mean not to feel anything but, no, not relief, merriment, that's the word for it, merriment at my own wife's funeral! Even good old Cranmer's words didn't affect me. Well, of course, none of you really remember her. Except Robin, I suppose?

That Wyatt should act in this way suggests that he need

not pose at all since he isn't afraid of revealing what could have been a painful experience for him. Still, by being indiscreet so unexpectedly, Wyatt can forestall any criticism of his behavior, especially since he gets his daughters to admit that they don't remember their mother much. Yet Wyatt doesn't recognize-- or chooses not to--that if his daughters don't remember their mother very much they might have a greater need to feel close to him. As a result, in confiding to his daughters, Wyatt is really distancing himself from them and so protecting himself, at least for the time being.

Not only is Wyatt able to dominate his family, but he also seems able to deal with what could be a real threat from the outside, namely the appearance of another equally celebrated writer, Lamb. Again Wyatt admits what others might dare not acknowledge, namely how disquieting such a meeting can be because it can make a person conscious of his limitations. Yet, despite these anxieties (which Wyatt elaborates on at considerable length to his family), when Lamb appears, Wyatt clearly overshadows him. The reason is that the latter does little more than acknowledge what Wyatt has recalled to the others, namely that they did meet once before. Moreover, since the earlier meeting was really embarrassing for Wyatt, Lamb might well have been able to make Wyatt feel uncomfortable. However, Wyatt simply doesn't give Lamb such an opportunity. He does so by posing a stock rhetorical question: "why do we writers endure the ordeal of writing," and then proceeds to answer it in personal terms:

> WYATT: . . . I never bothered with my children. Some people would say I was selfish and maybe it's so but I've always been fascinated by myself long after everyone else was bored to death with me.

His answer is devastating. In the first place, Lamb as a homosexual with no family of his own can neither answer in kind nor take issue with Wyatt. In the second place, Wyatt is hurting his family even more than in his account of his merriment during his wife's burial since he is openly acknowledging how much he neglected them. Besides, Lamb's presence seems to forestall any response. This seems all the more evident when, after Lamb unobtrusively leaves and Harry, whom Wyatt has never previously met, appears, Wyatt greets the latter as though he were an old friend. Clearly his greeting is patronizing and hypocritical. Nor does Harry object;

he merely acknowledges it with, "We try to do our best."

From all I've been describing, Wyatt's behavior so far appears to be a tour de force so that we could expect the scene to end for him on a note of triumph. But, instead, Wyatt sits down and admits how tired he is and how much he misses England:

> WYATT: Yes. I know what you mean, old thing.
> I wonder where Frederica's got to...I miss
> the cold and the damp and the colours that
> change all the winter and then...I miss
> it...I wish I didn't...

At this moment he clearly seems to have let down his guard--although just for an instant. Yet it is possible in retrospect to feel that the considerable skill he displayed in forestalling criticism may suggest that his candor was also a defense against feelings of self doubt and concern for his family that he couldn't as yet acknowledge.

iii

Whereas Act I, as indicated, ends poignantly, Act II, which begins after the Brigadier's special high tea lunch, seems warm and friendly. Understandably, the conversation seems discursive and varies in tone as it would on such occasions. Yet throughout it all, Frederica dominates mainly because she cares about all of them.

Accordingly, she begins with a stock question, "What do you remember about the place where you were born?" In reply, she gets stock answers about colonial life that could almost come out of Kipling, such as references to the Casino Palace, Port Said, or a cricket match. However, the memories become more concrete and intimate:

> FREDERICA: Mummy as Lydia Languish in The
> Rivals.
> WYATT: Daddy on the prompt book.
> EVANGIE: Field batteries, elephant batteries!
> I never understood them going into tor-
> ches...The Newcastle Mounted Rifles.
> FREDERICA: Inspected by grandfather. Men do
> inspect.
> ROBERT: England Inspects...

EVANGIE: Frederica on grandmother's pony.
FREDERICA: In a white party frock.

Unwittingly, Wyatt points out the real significance of
these memories when he remarks, "I'm surprised you
remember so much. I don't. You were all such
children.." In turn, Frederica's comment, "Ah--home
to England.." shows that the family are recalling
memories of home and affection they really value. That
Wyatt recognizes her drift is shown by his defensive
reply, "...I took it for granted then. Busy being a
writer. God, Lamb, why do we do it?" But, significantly, this time he doesn't go on to answer the question or let Lamb do so.

Nevertheless, at this point Frederica doesn't challenge him possibly because the memories have made her
feel part of the island. "The sky is so clear," she
muses, "the trees seem darker than they are..What was
it like before?" From her tone, it is apparent that
she clearly hopes for some response that would reinforce her memory of a happy past. But, instead, Lamb
in one of the most articulate and chilling speeches in
the play clearly disappoints her:

LAMB: The police band played the dreadful
national anthem, all deliciously out of
tune; you couldn't believe it, the comedy
and pain of it. I think someone actually
recorded it as a collector's item. Some
relief, I suppose. A bit of apprehension
but not over much. The climate was the
same, the people were the same, we were
the same. Except...You see...There was
despair in a lot of hearts. Even in those
who...who...oh, who...

The crucial sentence is, "The climate was the same, the
people were the same. Except...you see...There was
despair in a lot of hearts..." Since Lamb furnishes
so many details, his reply seems to deny the value of
what Frederica is doing. But not necessarily so, for
the real point may be that too much of the life in
the past consisted of empty routines rather than
experiences in which people acknowledged real feelings.
Or it may be that because private and public life
consisted of so much role playing and ritual it was
difficult, if not impossible, for people to be open
and honest. Yet the desire was present. This yearning becomes more apparent when Lamb, who is not
given to displays of feeling, admits apologetically

how much he and the other will miss the family when
they return to England:

> LAMB: It's just that we shall miss you. But I
>   shouldn't have really said so.
> FREDERICA: Why not? You <u>thought</u> it.
> LAMB: Do <u>you</u> say everything you think?
> FREDERICA: No. People think I do. Sometimes I
>   think I do.
> LAMB: Robin will miss you.
> ROBERT: Sisters are strange things.
> FREDERICA: We all travesty ourselves. It
>   seems unavoidable. Totally...

On the one hand, Frederica, in reply, emphasizes that
people should speak as they feel, even though admittedly
this can be difficult. On the other, she seems to be
implying that somehow much of the time they don't and
consequently fail to do justice to themselves. Perhaps
even more than that, they really harm themselves and
deny some real ideal of self worth they may aspire to.

Significantly, no one elaborates on what she has
said for she may be touching a sensitive nerve.
Instead, Wyatt, with great amusement, calls everyone's
attention to a series of programs on BBC about social
planning that they are missing because they aren't home.
That everyone, including Frederica, joins in to lampoon
the report (which may be a very earnest Labour Party
Manifesto) ironically reinforces her comment already
quoted, "We all travesty ourselves." I say this since,
judging from quotations they cite from the Manifesto,
it is such an easy target to ridicule.

Nevertheless, the fact that Frederica joins in
doesn't invalidate what she is attempting, namely to
stop the travesty. Rather it shows how difficult such
an effort will be and how much patience and persistence
it will require. Appropriately, Frederica doesn't
begin with a direct attack on her father but actually
uses a comment that Robert makes about one of Wyatt's
assertions, "Mustn't be patronizing" to get things
going. She does so by acknowledging that she herself
is always being patronizing. When Robert insists that
this is all right because she really is very intelligent
and therefore can feel superior (which, of course, shows
how patronizing <u>he</u> is), Frederica retaliates with her
father's most patronizing comment. "Oh no. I'm not.
Evangie's the bright one." This comment draws Evangie
in because the latter feels compelled to admit that,
while she doesn't believe her father's assertion, she

175

doesn't want anyone to challenge it. The reason is that then they might be inclined to argue with her own assessment of herself as a "voracious intellectual." Although Evangie believes that she is such a person, it becomes evident from the way she responds to Frederica's questions that she isn't prepared to accept the consequences of being such a person and wishes that others would spare her having to feel this way. Significantly, Wyatt avoids getting involved in this discussion.

Having taken the first step, Frederica then takes another, which really seems to show cruelty on her part but, in reality, doesn't. After Evangie leaves for a swim, Frederica bluntly asks all of those present, "You all think I'm a shit?" In doing so, she would seem to be embarrassing them. Yet she is permitting them to put the onus on her if they wish. At the same time, she is also making it difficult for them to ignore what has happened. Nevertheless, the only one who dares respond is Lamb who tells her, "You are a clown with all the privileges and penalties. You say what is obvious but not necessarily true or the whole truth." While Lamb may seem to be acknowledging how difficult it is to discover the truth, it becomes clear, when Frederica challenges them, that his real purpose, as he admits, was to prevent her from attacking him. Having made this clear, he shifts ground. Yet even by saying this much, he has made it possible for others to respond more openly. But instead, Wyatt tries to cover everything up: first by changing the subject again; and second, trying to excuse all of them by a seemingly honest, but really patronizing comment, "Why are we all so cruel to one another?"

Since Frederica has had some impact on Evangie and Lamb and her father has apparently thrown up his usual defense, Frederica feels it necessary to take a third step. She does so by replying to her father in the same way the others do, namely to agree with him. In turn, he answers, as he always has in comparable situations, that he really is cruel. However, this time something different occurs. Both Robert and Frederica agree with him. Such agreement by Robert enables Frederica to confront her father and the others more openly than she has before. "Frankly," she replies, "But no one thinks you're a shit. They think you're lovable."

At first, Frederica's comment seems to backfire. Not only does it provoke another argument with Lamb who insists that she should show some concern for her father's feelings, but Wyatt himself repeats his most patronizing comment of all, "Evangie was always the bright one." Yet immediately afterwards he does something quite different: he admits that he shouldn't have said it. Moreover, when Frederica agrees that he shouldn't have, he not only admits her assertion but acknowledges how nauseating such a comment is. True, in doing this, he may be defusing opposition since Frederica never made such an assertion. However, he goes on to make a more damaging admission, " . . . Actually, I don't quite know how to make it ring true. Or indeed anything...". For the first time, he recognizes that he may be the victim of his own posing, and that it is difficult to change. Yet instead of exploring what he can do to change, he shifts to a safe subject, moon landings, about which he and the others can joke.

As for Frederica's argument with Lamb, it represents possibly more of an advance because she shows herself to be more accepting of his feelings. When she demands of him why she shouldn't begrudge her father for having some concern for himself, Lamb simply replies, "Because I feel it." Considering how Frederica has criticized Lamb previously, we might expect her to go after him. But she merely answers, "There. That's all" and backs off, perhaps because she can't face opposition. What seems more likely, though, is that she respects Lamb for reacting spontaneously rather than being glib.

Nevertheless, the rest of the scene before Mrs. James appears shows that Frederica still has a long way to go. The family seize upon Wyatt's comment about moon landings and play out a skit about whom they would send to the moon. As for Wyatt, the earlier reminiscences about his daughters' lives years ago do affect him enough that he tells the Brigadier about them when the latter (who had been inside all the time) finally appears. On the other hand, Wyatt says nothing about the strong family affection these reminiscences revealed which could cause him to question more of his behavior as a father.

iv

With the arrival of Mrs. James, the next major episode of the play begins. It is appropriate to use the word begins because, at least so far as some of Wyatt's comments are concerned, we seem to be back in Act I, if not even further than that. The reason is that, as will be evident, Wyatt initially treats Mrs. James more patronizingly than he has anyone else to date. That one of the crucial episodes of the play should involve a character who just appears once and almost as a walk on may suggest that Osborne has to contrive something at this point. But since, as was just evident in the preceding scene, Frederica, for all of her persistence and concern, was only beginning to get her father to act more honestly, something else has to happen to make more of an impact on Wyatt. That the person who makes that impact should be a member of a race whom the British have exploited forcefully shows the consequences of treating people as inferiors. Moreover, that it takes an outsider to make more of an impact emphasizes more strongly how restricted the English are by their role playing, or, to paraphrase Frederica once more, 'their travestying themselves.'

Without greatly oversimplifying the details of this lively, free wheeling encounter, it is possible to divide it into three phases. In the first, as already suggested, Wyatt shows that he can be even more patronizing than he has to date. That he acts in this way has been prepared for because, when earlier he complained about having to be interviewed, Mary suggested that he can just repeat what he has already said many times over since no one on the island would know the difference. His first comment, in answer to Mrs. James' request that he say something to test the tape recording equipment, reveals just how denigrating he can be:

> I don't really know why you should want to talk to me at all. I've got no interesting views or opinions about anything. Never have done. I don't believe in much, never have done, never been inspired by anything. I'm simply over-talkative, vain, corpulent, and a bit of a played out hulk, as I think most of the world knows and I'm surprised the news hasn't even reached this delightful island of yours.

Compared to this performance, his garrulous comments about the island in Act I seem almost gracious. Yet, whereas the family (except for Frederica) might have condoned such fulsome hypocrisy, Mrs. James openly confronts him with, "Isn't it a bit early to start being patronizing?" Even Frederica might not have gone this far. Nevertheless, Wyatt brazenly denies her charge, "I am never patronizing. I am in no position to be so. And never have been..." Then, despite Mrs. James' threat to end the interview if he goes on in this way, he does just that. In answer to a question as to what

he thinks of man, Wyatt replies, "As a defect striving
for excellence." When Mrs. James challenges him with,
"Do you really think that?" he frankly acknowledges,
"No, but presumably you want me to say something, however dull." But then, perhaps to show Mrs. James that
he can think otherwise, he continues, "However, I do
think that there is a disastrously false and very
modern idea that you can be absolutely honest." This
answer, while more direct, is still subtly patronizing
by its overstatement. Spurred on, Wyatt continues in
this vein, which represents the second phase. In this,
instead of parrying Mrs. James' questions, Wyatt
answers them brazenly and, within some limits, honestly.
He freely admits how much he dislikes critics, how glad
he is that he no longer concerns himself with women and
love, and how prone he is to adopt a public pose, as he
says, "Because it makes life slightly more tolerable.
The same applies to public life..." After his cliché
mongering during the rest of the play, such unabashed
cynicism seems refreshing. We might almost think that
the real Wyatt or a real Wyatt is emerging. However,
when we look more carefully, we see that this "real
Wyatt" is affirming at a gut level what previously he
had stated through the persona of the garrulous old
colonial. For example, when Mrs. James asks him what
he thinks about the island and the people he has met,
he remarks, "All the good things seem to be legacies of
the British, Spanish . . . and that the people [as
already indicated] seem to be a very unappealing mixture
of <u>hysteria</u> and <u>lethargy</u>, <u>brutality</u> and <u>sentimentality</u>."
Then a few minutes later, when he tells Mrs. James how
he feels about the English class structure, he shows
what an unregenerate snob he can be:

> I'm very fond of it [class structure]. It pro-
> vides a great deal of entertainment, fun, and
> speculation for people who have nothing better
> to do. Like many of the upper class, I've liked
> the sound of broken glass.

After comments such as this, it might seem very difficult for the interview to go further or unnecessary
either since Wyatt has made clear where he stands. But
it does go in to a third phase in which Mrs. James asks
even more provocative, open-ended questions and Wyatt
recognizes more pointedly how complex such answers can
be. It does so not just because Mrs. James continues
asking questions, but because Wyatt at the same time
that he continues to say what he feels seems to approach
being self-aware and able to be more detached about
himself. For example, when Mrs. James asks him what he

179

thinks about the family, Wyatt seems more aware than
previously of how his daughters might feel:

> I don't believe in its continuance, if that's
> what you mean. I do think it had its pleasures
> while it lasted and I was fortunate enough to
> have enjoyed and suffered them. I had a
> father whom I loved and now I have daughters
> whom I love, no doubt largely selfishly. But
> I wouldn't call it a write-off either for them
> or for me. Or indeed their mother. Like the
> passing of empires and pride of tongues.

If Wyatt remains a snob and an imperialist, still he is
becoming a more discriminating and cautious one. Perhaps because he does seem more self-critical, Mrs. James
goes on to ask an even more basic question, namely,
what he thinks about sin, virtue, and, finally, death.
For each of these he has an answer:

> MRS. JAMES: What do you think of as real sin?
> WYATT: The incapacity for proper despair.
>   About talking about loss of faith as if it
>   were some briefcase you've left behind you
>   on the tube.
> MRS. JAMES: What do you look on as virtue then?
> WYATT: True innocence.
> MRS. JAMES: Lastly, Mr. Gillman, what do you
>   dread most at this stage of your life?
> WYATT: Not death. But ludicrous death. And I
>   also feel it in the air.

Although he is too glib and epigrammatic for comfort,
Wyatt does distil some penetrating feelings that represent a far cry from what he passed off at the beginning
of the interview, not to mention what he has been
parroting to his family during earlier episodes of the
play.

   If Wyatt's responses during the interview weren't
disquieting enough for Frederica, since they brought
out more explicitly the worst in him and yet something
far better, his reaction to what happens next, the
unexpected appearance of two American tourists, surely
is. The tourists (who are members of a Folk Dance
Group visiting the island for a day) wander in because
they mistake the villa for a gift shop down the road.
Although they do apologize for their mistake, they
express amazement that anyone could possibly live on
the island. Admittedly, Frederica, who deals with
them, makes no bones about what she thinks of them.

But she has reason to do so since their reactions, even
if unintentional, are insensitive and, in their own
way, patronizing. Nevertheless, after the couple
leaves, Harry immediately rebukes Frederica (despite
her assertion that these people aren't as harmless as
Harry insists). To prevent the argument from going
further, Wyatt intercedes. But what he says, "I thought
they were a couple of old dears" only infuriates
Frederica because, as she lets her father know immediately, "You pretended that you did. Like you pretended to so much always." Of course she is right, as we
have seen so many times during the play. Moreover,
just as in the past, Robin intercedes on behalf of her
father by telling Frederica that she can't treat Wyatt
like this. For Wyatt and Robin to react as they do is
to ignore not only the interview but much of what
occurred earlier in Act II. This means that for the
fourth time the play almost seems to be starting over
because no one has apparently learned anything or dares
react differently. For these reasons, Frederica now
launches her strongest and most sustained attack on
her father:

> Why should I? [stop treating him like this] (To
> WYATT.) The trouble with you is that you've
> always been allowed to get away with it. Yes,
> I mean get away with it. Like some of us can't.
> You get away with it all. Bad manners. Lazi-
> ness. Cowardice. Lateness. Hurtful indiscre-
> tion. And we're all supposed to be stunned by
> the humour and eccentricity of it. (Pause)

That her allegations are accurate is clear enough from
the many examples I've been citing. Moreover, considering how much more she could have said, her
remarks seem restrained (although they also indicate
that she, too, is inhibited by the very social forms
she is attacking since she does sound proper). Nevertheless, by being restrained and proper, Frederica is
making it easier for her father to challenge her if he
wishes. Yet, even more important, her reaction crystal-
lizes what her father's varied responses to Mrs. James
revealed. On the one hand, she is angry that for all
these years her father has been so hypocritical, indifferent, and even cruel. On the other, she is pleading
that he really knows better, as some of his comments
have shown. But more than anything else, she is showing how much she cares for him, possibly more than she
even realizes or did until this moment, and how disappointed she is with what he has done with his life.

At first glance, Wyatt's response seems to justify, if not reinforce, her disappointment and anger.

> I _am_ a clown. People laugh at me in the street when they see me. But, as you say, it's my own fault. (WYATT gets to his feet.) Think I need a bit of a walk after that lunch with the Brigadier.

The reason is that he is neither challenging any of her allegations nor even admitting, as he did previously, that he continues to be patronizing and therefore still is getting away with it. Moreover, in saying, "I am a clown. People laugh at me in the streets..." he is pleading guilty to a charge that she didn't make (this isn't quite the same thing as responding to her comments about "the humour and eccentricity" of what he does). Therefore, Wyatt again seems to be defusing opposition, particularly when he resorts to one of his stock ploys to escape, that of the invalid who needs a rest.

But it is also possible to interpret what he says and does differently. In calling himself a clown, especially after he has proudly told Mrs. James at one point that he is "what my daughter Frederica says she is, just a lot of hot shit, if you'll pardon the expression, blood, vanity, and a certain prowess" he is really passing a heavy judgment on himself--perhaps heavier than is fair. Yet in doing so and acknowledging that it is his fault, Wyatt is showing Frederica that he accepts responsibility for what he has done and cares how she feels about him and how this affects her. If in leaving he is sparing himself another attack and depriving her from responding, he is also showing how insecure he is. As the stage directions reveal, he makes a sad exit: "They all watch him go off in the direction of the beach."

At the end of the episode, Wyatt and Frederica, although apart, are much closer than they have been previously. Yet it is also clear that they might have been still closer and that perhaps only now is each aware of how much he has wished for this.

v

The fifth and last phase of the action (II, ii) centers on Jed's outburst, which (as indicated) is the most dramatic and explosive moment in the play. However, before this comes a brief encounter between

Frederica and Christopher, her father's secretary, who has left his wife and family to devote his services to Wyatt. In part, the encounter does prepare for Jed's appearance since Frederica keeps asking why some one doesn't stop Jed from being so insulting since apparently he has been down at the beach for a long time talking up a storm. But, in part, the encounter reveals Frederica's continuing concern about her father ("Why does he pretend to be deaf and listen to Jed") and for Christopher himself, although this interest may not seem apparent inasmuch as she seems to pry into his life by demanding why he chucked everything to be Wyatt's secretary. Nevertheless, in doing so, she is also alleviating his anxiety that he may be a homosexual. Rather, she reassures him, he is "Just potty like the rest of us." At the same time, she shows that she won't let herself be a burden to others by rejecting Christopher's interest in her because she is in pain. "There's no future in me," she insists, "Not for anyone. One day it'll be just out. Tell me more about your wife?"

Although some preparation has been made (as indicated) for Jed's appearance, still his tirade, when it comes, is so extreme that it seems almost unbelievable. In what is unquestionably the most abrasive and insulting language that any Osborne character has employed to date, Jed heaps scorn upon the English because of their colossal provinciality and the cruelty they have wreaked upon the natives:

> JED: . . . You know what I think of you? What
> we think of you? What we think of you?
> Fuck all your shit--that's what we think.
> One person, not like any one of you here,
> even if he's the God-damnest cretin, I'd
> make him God, yes, man, rather than you.
> You hear? Hear me. Listen to me if you
> can hear anything but the sound of your
> own selves and present. I'm not interested
> in your arguments, not that they are, of
> your so-called memories and all that
> pathetic shit. The only thing that matters,
> man, is blood, man. Blood...You know what
> that means? No, no, you surely as to hell
> don't. No, no, when you pigs, you pigs go,
> it ain't going to be no fucking Fourth of
> July. All I see, and I laugh when I see
> it, man, I laugh, is you pigs barbecued,
> barbecued in your own shit. We're, yes,
> we're going to take over and don't you begin

to forget it. Man, I feel real sorry for
you lot. No, I don't...You got it coming.
And you have soon. Think of the theatre of
the mind, baby, old moulding babies, except
you won't. We count and we do, not like you,
we really, really do...Why, we fall about
laughing at you people, not people, you're
not people, you pigs. We are people. We
are. But not you. You don't understand
and why should you because, believe me,
babies, old failing babies, words, yes I
mean words, even what I'm saying to you now,
is going to be the first to go. Go, baby,
Go. You can't even make love. Do you understand one word, those old words you love so
much, what I mean? No. And you won't. If
it ain't written down, you don't believe
it...There's only one word left and you
know what that is. It's fuck, man. Fuck...
That's the last of the English for you
babies. Or maybe shit. Because that's what
we're going to do on you. Shit. That's
what you'll all go down in. One blissful,
God like shit. You think we're mother-
fucking, stinking, yelling, shouting shits.
Well that's what we are, babies. And
there's nothing, not nothing you or anybody
else can do about it. Jesus is sort of
shit. But you're not even shit. We think,
we fuck and we shit and that's what we do
and you're on the great gasping end of it.
Because you're pigs. Just take one little
look at yourselves. You're pigs, babies.
Pigs. And we're gonna shit you out of this
world, babies. Right out of this mother-
fucking world. You know what? I just had
an idea. Like that old prick writer there.
Colonialism is the fornication of the twentieth century. You can't be young...So all
you'd better do, all you will do, is die,
die, baby. And pretty soon. Just real soon.
Like tomorrow. Or even tonight.

Clearly, much of what Jed pours out represents a gross
and vicious exaggeration. However insensitive and cold
Wyatt is, neither he nor the others are personally
responsible for the evils of imperialism. Moreover,
however decadent English upper class society may be, it
is difficult to believe that it can be any worse than
that which Jed and his like could bring into existence.
Nevertheless, making all such allowances, at a gut

level Jed is articulating some of the major criticisms of English society that Frederica and Mrs. James have implied or pointed out. That Jed has hit home is evident by the profound impact he has on one character, namely Wyatt. That in itself makes all the difference since after all Wyatt could continue to pretend to be deaf:

> I was never a young man. I think I always felt old. I was always wrinkled somehow. More than I am now. Well, nearly. Now I am sort of old. No, old. But something always kept telling me that I was young. Very young. But of course I never was. Something started without me. Too slow. Never got off the old ground. Never got off the ground. Wasn't sure about the ground at all. Never capable of inspecting it. Or, anyway, closely. Not closely...Not closely...I think I ought to go to bed.

Undeniably, Wyatt sees himself differently from the man who admitted that he adopted poses, knew all about the islanders, and had firm opinions about art, literary criticism, religion, the family, sin, and death. Even when he admitted, "I am a clown," he didn't ask himself why he behaved as he did. But here he does that carefully and yet modestly because he sees how profoundly uncertain he has been all his life. That he was never a young man may mean that he never felt hopeful, passionate, or open to experiences. This perhaps explains why something started without him--that, despite the appearance of a fascinating, varied life, something was missing. What this something was perhaps becomes evident from "never got off the old ground," namely that he never broke away from the ritual, accepted attitudes, and forms of behavior of his snobbish society (that itself would use such an expression as "the old ground").

Although Wyatt doesn't say so explicitly, he may be questioning the value of his literary work as well since one characteristic of a good novelist is that he understands those areas of life he portrays in his work. And to have to do so under the force of an attack that comes from someone who stands for everything that Wyatt abhors and who, moreover, is so hateful and destructive accentuates Wyatt's embarrassment, if not shame.

On the other hand, Wyatt offers no apologies for what he has done with his life. Nor does he recognize that he has exploited imperialism and class differences and let them victimize him.

That immediately afterwards a group of anonymous,
armed islanders appear and shoot Wyatt down when he
tries to run away would seem to undercut the impact of
Wyatt's painful self discovery. As Edward says to Jed
right after the shooting, "There's an old English
saying. Don't suppose you've heard it? 'My God,
they've shot the fox.'" Such a death, to paraphrase
Wyatt's own comment to Mrs. James, does seem ludi-
crous, for it seems to show the futility of trying to
come to terms with oneself and his society since
immediately afterwards the only result is violent death.
But, if anything, the circumstances of the death and
Edward's comments reinforce the value of Wyatt's poignant self awareness. Yet they also make clear its
limits and the need for something more. That the
natives do arrive armed underlines all the more the
need to inspect the ground a lot more closely than the
English have, for a lot more has started than they
realize. Yet all Edward perceives is that in killing
Wyatt the natives have made an awful gaffe. He doesn't
recognize the human tragedy of Wyatt's loss, especially
since the latter came to view his own life much more
critically than he ever did before. Yet Edward also
doesn't understand what impelled the natives to act as
they did nor how contemptuous of the English Jed really
is (as his reply to Edward's proverb about the Fox,
"So what is it?" reveals). Nor does he realize that,
if Wyatt had stood his ground rather than tried to
escape, the natives might not have shot him since they
hadn't opened fire on the rest and yet easily could.
At the end Wyatt has come a long way, and yet finally
he does still try to escape as he did all his life
rather than try to overcome his limitations.

That Wyatt does try to get away at the end, that
Frederica can only stand by, and that the basic social
structure and family relationships remain relatively
unchanged, certainly makes the ending seem bleak. On
the other hand, that Frederica tries so hard and yet
encounters so much resistance shows how powerful and
destructive a social system and personal relationships
grounded in condescension, dishonesty, and fear of
acknowledging one's self doubts can be. Consequently,
the need for change becomes all the more urgent as the
violence that erupts at the end makes clear. Moreover,
that Frederica has persisted as she has with so little
feedback and affection all these years and that finally
she and her father do begin to show more openly how
much they care for one another represents some hope.

XII

A SENSE OF DETACHMENT

Onto a bare, open stage (except for a projection screen at the back, and a barrel organ and an upright piano downstage) come six actors carrying chairs. They sit themselves down, engage in some spirited back biting at each others' (and the audience's) expense, and begin what presumably is the business at hand, to present a play or revue. One of the actors is a proper, no nonsense upper middle class person (in his mid-forties) who is called the Chairman because on this occasion (as on many others) he is elected to take charge; a second is a slightly younger man of the same social class, but more free wheeling in his manner, called the Chap, whose main topic of conversation is his experience with women about which he is both apologetic and boastful. The third is a young, attractive, witty, and outspoken Irish girl with feminist, anti-establishment, and anti-English views. The fourth is a vigorous and outspoken, but also gracious, Old Woman, who likes to think of herself as sympathetic to young people's attitudes and behavior. As for the fifth, he is an eighty year old man, called the Grandfather, who is also vigorous and outspoken but much more traditional in his views than the others mentioned so far. And the last is a man in his seventies, the father of the Chap, who in spirit is the oldest of all because, as he sadly admits, he seems so lost in the world of the 1930's that there is some question as to whether in reality he is still alive.

Although the Chairman insists that there is a play to be put on, the characters keep strenuously resisting the effort. Instead, they make various false starts which usually involve satire on some of the formlessness and stock situations of popular television and audience confrontation theatre. Their banter and delay, in turn, cause two plants in the audience, called the Box Man and the Interrupter, who represent the Middle and Low-brow tastes of the audience before whom the group are appearing (as did Archie in The Entertainer) to begin protesting. In turn, these protests cause the actors, especially the Young Girl and the Older Woman, to counterattack. Unabashed, the plants resume their attack, as do the actors. True, at one point, the Chairman does announce what the play is to be about, "To stylize, or give some sort of life to, the various personalities--female I mean--who thread their

way through one man's particular experience." But this
presentation never does get underway as the confrontation between actors and audience becomes more abrasive
and apparently disorganized. While it appears that
nothing really is happening, except to enable all
involved to fight off boredom, such confrontation does
enable the actors to shake things up and to create a
more open and accepting audience. When one character
suggests that they should establish order out of chaos,
the Chap retorts that the converse is nearer the truth;
they should be making chaos out of order. And, like
the Marx Brothers but in a more tentative way, this is
just what they do through their resistance to getting
started, their digressions, and their attacks on
tastes of both themselves and the audience. As they
do, the mood of all becomes more mellow, and the Act
ends with all of them singing their version of an old
folk song, "Widdicombe Fair." However, instead of
doing it straight, they substitute for the names of
the local rural people involved those of Osborne's contemporaries: Harold Pinter, Samuel Beckett, Arnold
Wesker, and David Storey. In doing so, the actors
are suggesting that, like the playwrights mentioned,
they are just out to entertain. Conversely, this is
just what the former are doing so they need not be too
uppity about it. If all have made 'chaos' out of
"Widdicombe Fair," they have also established a model
for recreating order--or more proper feedback--and
that is through song, which is just what occurs in
Act II.

For example, early in the Act, the Father comes
out (afterwards joined by the Chap), sits down by the
piano, and begins playing a popular love song. Their
singing causes others, including the plants, to join
in and present excerpts from a wide variety of sources,
ranging from Renaissance poetry to contemporary pop
art songs. Then the Chap (presumably in accordance
with the Chairman's announcement in Act I to give
some sort of life to the various personalities who
'thread their way through a man's experience') begins
telling about the numerous women he has known. This is
the equivalent to the "identity" crisis we find in the
other Osborne plays and the chief source of the Chap's
insecurities and need for love. His assuming this
role, as though appearing on a TV talk show, causes
others to assume comparable roles, such as that of a
theatre critic on a talk show and to interrupt. Then
suddenly the actors drop their role playing and begin
quoting and singing to each other more excerpts about
love as well as related subjects. After this, the Chap

interrupts to resume his account of his love life, aided by the Young Girl who keeps prodding him caustically for being so facetious. In the meantime, the Older Woman, stimulated by the Chap's account, reveals that she has just received in the mail some information that fascinates her and which she begins reading, namely advertising accounts of some hard core pornography films. From this point on, the counterpointing expands as the Older Woman, urged on by the delighted Interrupter, as well as other actors, keeps reading these excerpts which become more obscene; the Chap recounts more of his love life (which contains as many failures as conquests); while all the other actors keep singing and quoting more excerpts, principally from love poems and songs. In the process, the Older Woman (who is also undergoing a crisis of sorts in adjusting to her changing life style) and the Chap clash. They do so because she feels he has too romantic a notion of womanhood and too little appreciation of the harsh realities of women's lives (as revealed particularly in the ordeal of menstruation). In turn, he feels she denies too much of the romantic idealism and overlooks the annoyance that menstruation creates for men. Although these differences become more acute, both the Older Woman and the Chap become more aware of each other and come closer together, with the result that the Chap brings on a portable lecture platform that each character might use to present his views in more depth. To start things off, the Chap gets up and assumes the part of a last ditch British patriot outraged by the violence occurring in Northern Ireland. Presumably he does this to needle the Young Girl into responding. He succeeds, for in no uncertain terms she gets up and lets everyone know in the bluntest way that the British must get out of Northern Ireland. Although no one agrees, they all listen. Then, at the Chap's urging, the Old Woman comes in and spells out in even more blunt detail that has a sharp feminist thrust her objections to the Chap's romanticism. She begins by warming up, "If men had to undergo what they so cheerfully call the curse, they would long ago have invented some alteration." After a confrontation with one of the plants, she concludes with this harsh warning:

> . . . We women can be put down, that is the
> expression, by the flimsiest physical or intel-
> lectual failing. We have been eternally aban-
> doned from the Old Testament onwards. All I
> say now is that we may all probably totally
> abandon you . . . Men, I mean.

Having finished and having made clear how she plans to cope with her personal frustrations, she invites the Chap who applauds (though he also disagrees strongly), to help her down. After he does this, he ascends and delivers his sermon (which turns out to be the longest speech in the entire play, and one I want to comment on in more detail shortly) in which he exalts his romantic view of women and love that underlies his whole life. His speech makes such an impression on the Girl that, despite her earlier hostility, she embraces him. Encouraged by her response, he lets her know frankly and crudely how much he wants her right here and now. While very sympathetic, she points out, as he has to agree, that in public is hardly the place. But still she likes the idea and likes him. Hearing this open admission, the Chairman feels that it is time to wind things down. To expedite matters, he invites all to join in singing once more, "Widdicombe Fair," but to do it straight. Having gotten everyone to sing, the the Chairman turns to the audience to make sure they leave, "And may the Good Lord bless you and keep you," he remarks, "Or God rot you." He succeeds as the play ends with the Stage Manager and an assistant coming on and sweeping the place out.

Just from this somewhat extended analysis of A Sense of Detachment, it would seem unlikely that this could be one of Osborne's major works. Since the play uses two dimensional stock type characters who speak mainly through excerpts from others, how could it present articulate, aware, and individualized characters, the hallmark of Osborne at his best? Yet, curiously enough, this isn't the most significant reason for the play's limitations. If anything, it is the converse-- namely that the one occasion (the Chap's sermon) when a character speaks at great length, articulately, and in his own voice, represents what is possibly the play's most embarrassing moment. I say this because, in the first place, the Chap's efforts to justify his career as a lover seem exaggerated beyond the particular experiences he has been recalling. For example, he describes one such memory in these words:

> CHAP: Then there was a younger, blonde fat one,
> but I don't remember her name. But I do
> think she was more sort of humiliating than
> the rest. Then there was my Auntie Viv.
> She had very dark, curly hair.
> FATHER: I used to call her the Gypsy Queen.
> CHAP: That's right. But she had a funny way
> with handling the children. And I remem-

ber she said to me, 'Don't lift your
trousers'--we used to wear what were called
'short trousers' then--when you go to the
toilet'.

Here a somewhat embarrassed and self conscious man
recalls a humiliating experience with some restraint.
However, in the pulpit the Chap describes some of his
experiences with women in these words:

CHAP: . . . Being in love. Desolation in the
sea of hope itself. Sentimental? False?
Infantile? Possibly. And infantile
because my memories of the phenomenon, if
there be such a one, is or ever will be,
start so young. From three, yes, I know it
was three, even till the only twenty-one,
there were so many girls, girl-women, women
of all ages, I loved. Very few of them were
in love with me, alas. Being in love blun-
ders all negotiations and certainly differ-
entials. I have been sometimes indecently
moved to tears and if there were a court of
justice in these things, I would have been
dealt with summarily as a persistent offen-
der, asking for innumerable, nameless and
unspeakable offences to be taken into
account. However, if I have been such a
villain in this manor of feelings, I have
tried to be as clever as I know how. Knowing, as we all know, that there is no such
thing. . .

Here he becomes sentimental and pompous, a very different attitude from that of the excerpt. Nor is his tone
even consistent. On the one hand, a phrase such as "if
I have been such a villain in this manor of feelings"
seems formal and stilted, on the other, "avoid soft
risks and go only for the big stuff" sounds like the
words of a macho character in a Hollywood movie. Moreover, when the Chap tries to become more philosophical,
as in his efforts to apotheosize women, he really sounds
facetious and overly serious, like an adolescent trying
too hard to impress:

CHAP: The naked male may be powerful, even beautiful, but self-defining like a jet aircraft
in flight. Seldom is it more than technology made Flesh, Female, in this sense,
is Art. The Male is Critic. Or, so it
seems to me at this moment. Female is Art,

191

secretive even when it conceals nothing.
Revealing all, it is no sphinx for nothing,
it contains and sustains life itself,
taming random seed and even time. Making
mystery of woman, the liberationists would
say, is to belittle her in a glib religious
conspiracy of fake mystery. . . . I believe
in Woman, whatever that may be, just as I
believe in God, their inventor, they are my
creators, and they will continue to exist.
During most of my life. What made me think
of it? Watching a couple in a street late
at night in a provincial town. Being in
love, how many times and over such a period.
Being in Love! What anathema to the Sexual
Militant, the wicked interest on free capi-
tal. Anathema because it involves waste,
exploitation of resources, sacrifice,
unplanned expenditure, both sides sitting
down together in unequal desolation. This
is the market place I have known and wan-
dered in almost as long as I indecently
remember or came to forget . . .

In reading this long speech, it is difficult not to
feel that it represents a last ditch effort by a
beleaguered male chauvinist who feels threatened by
changes in women's roles, possibly as a result of
Women's Liberation and/or his own insecurities. I make
this observation because at one point he describes
Women's Liberation advocates as "Those long-shore bul-
lies with bale hooks in bras and trousers seamed with
slogans and demands." Were the dramatic context to
support this interpretation of a beleaguered sexist
trying desperately to protect himself, then the very
excesses I've emphasized might be dramatically appropriate. But since the Young Girl, to whom the sermon
is mainly addressed and is the person who could represent such a threat, doesn't sense any of these feelings
in his remarks and instead, as indicated, accepts him
joyously, we obviously can't press such an interpretation.

For all the reasons I've been citing, the speech
clearly represents turgid dramatic prose that could
almost be enough to turn a person totally against the
play. But to do this is to be unfair to much of the
rest because when the play stays more within its own
bounds (as I've described them), it does project some
authentic feelings and attitudes that pervade
Osborne's earlier plays but in a different key.

To begin with, much of the confrontation format of
the play, in which from the beginning actors challenge
one another as well as the plants (and vice versa),
creates a mood of tolerance and acceptance of differences. In this regard the Young Girl plays an important
role because from the moment she comes on stage she
challenges and, if need be, shocks people out of their
complacency (or detachment) so that they become more
open and ultimately more accepting. While she is
abrasive, she doesn't keep hammering away. Besides,
she can be supportive, as she is when she listens to
the Chap's stories about all the women in his life.
Even in her sermon about the need for the English to get
out of Ireland (where she could put everyone down
without much risk of confrontation), she uses short,
incisive thrusts which enable the others to answer her
line by line:

> GIRL: You all know what I think--
> BOX MAN: I should say we do, we've heard it
> enough times.
> GIRL: Well, it needs repeating to get into con-
> crete skulls like yours. Get out of Ire-
> land!
> BOX MAN: Get out of England!
> GIRL: Don't think I won't!
> BOX MAN: Good!
> GIRL: You've oppressed us for three centuries.
> BOX MAN: What about it? Bloody idle lot.
> Think you're all poets and dreamers, I
> know. Shall I tell you something, mate?
> The only thing that ever came out of Ire-
> land--
> GIRL: I know, is horses and writers.
> BOX MAN: And who said that?
> GIRL: A lot of Horse Protestants. And I'll bet
> you didn't know who said that . . .

While she clearly expresses more hostility to her audience than does the Chap, she gives them more freedom to
express their feelings.

Even the plants, who clearly disapprove of much that
the actors are saying and can be rude, still help create
a mood of acceptance and tolerance. They do so because
they actually welcome confrontation and admit their own
preferences without embarrassment. For example, at one
point in Act I, one of the plants, called the Box Man,
who is an avid sports fan and a great beer drinker,
vigorously protests because the actors aren't satisfying
his tastes. As a result, he starts an argument with the

Young Girl and Chap, both of whom really insult him and give him grounds for answering them in kind, particularly when the Chairman makes matters worse by trying to get rid of him. But, instead, the Box Man remains good natured about what goes on:

> BOX MAN: . . . When I think of what people like us, people like us who do a real job of work, not like you, you've never done a job of work...
> GIRL: Piss off!
> BOX MAN: Pay for their seats with their hard-earned money, and don't you use that filthy language at me.
> GIRL: Why not?
> BOX MAN: Because you're an educated woman, and you ought to bleeding well know better.
> GIRL: Well, I'm not educated and I don't know any better.
> CHAIRMAN (to Box Man): I think you've made your point, sir.
> BOX MAN: Sing us a song! Oh Christ, I've got to go back to that stinking hellhole again! (He blunders out.)

What is more, in Act II he and the other Interrupter join in with the actors by quoting their own excerpts from poems and songs. On the other hand, the Interrupters still find things to complain about and not always good naturedly. Yet the fact that they do actually makes their acceptance of the actors' different life styles and tastes more credible. In addition, the Interrupters often differ with each other. At one point, when the Father begins singing a sentimental song and the Grandfather and Older Woman begin dancing, one of the Interrupters complains, "How sentimental." Instead of supporting him, the other replies from the back of the theatre, "Give the old bag a break, or I'll come down and give you a right duffing up." One thing that examples such as those I've just cited do is to make all involved accept quarreling within limits as a given.

In the second place, the apparent formlessness of the play, creating chaos out of order in Act I, and then order of a sort out of that chaos in II, becomes another effective means of bringing characters closer together. As a result, it makes more credible their affirmations about the value of love and, to a lesser extent, sexuality. I would have to say that of the two Acts, the second is more effective and interesting because the first does set up some easy targets of the mass media to exploit, and it provides an easy technique of attack, that of interruption itself. About all I would say is that Osborne doesn't overdo the attack by interruption.

However, Act II uses something very simple, which actually began in I, spontaneous breaking into song as a basis for introducing, expanding, and varying its presentation of the richness and diversity of loving. Yet it manages through ironic deflation, or to use a word from the title, detachment, to keep this from becoming too easy and therefore unrealistic.

The act begins with the Interrupters complaining to the Stage Manager that they haven't gotten their money's worth--a complaint that could become tedious. Nevertheless, it doesn't because the Interrupters fortunately have drunk enough beer that they don't feel too unhappy, with the result that they express their complaint in a song "Why Are We Waiting." When the Stage Manager objects, they protest more loudly but also admit that they really don't like violence so that they have no objection to the actors coming on. And this, as indicated, is just what they do, as the Father comes out and starts playing the piano, followed by his son, the Chap, coming out a moment or so later and joining him in a popular song. That the song they choose is a love song isn't shocking since this is what most such popular songs really are about. But before the two get carried away, the Young Girl comes on and makes a flippant comment about the "I" in the song who fell in love. Then, because of the Girl's comment, the Chap, in defense of his father, addresses himself to her. But the way he does so, singing a verse of a love song, also expresses conciliation and enables the two to begin responding to each other--a form of feedback. Appropriately, when a moment later one of the Interrupters objects to the song, she sides with the Chap. At this point, the Chairman comes in and begins putting down the complaints of the Interrupters. Encouraged by this, the Chap, accompanied by his Father, begins singing some lines from Robert Burns, "Oh my love is like a red, red rose." Simultaneously, he expands the range by inviting the audience to join in. However, one of the Interrupters objects with, "We don't want any of that modern rubbish," and the Young Girl ridicules what the Chairman sang with this comment, "Oh, My God, His love." While the ridicule seems to be threatening the song, it also gives it some credibility since she is listening. Possibly encour-

195

aged by that, the Grandfather interjects this quotation, "Every one suddenly burst out singing," which
gives momentum to the Chairman to continue quoting
more from Burns. Yet at the same time everyone
doesn't join in the act because the Chairman also uses
this as an opportunity to even up a score with the
Young Girl (who had earlier ridiculed one of his comments about the Scotch) by remarking: "I do hope
you're not going to be cheap and obvious about the
Scots."

At this point the ironic deflation could dominate
what goes on. However, this doesn't happen because
the Girl answers with, "I couldn't be bothered" and to
show this (since a record happens to be playing) begins
dancing with the Chap, another instance in which they
are coming together. Yet it is also clear that they
still remain apart because she comments, "You're not
very good are you?" as he readily agrees. At this
impasse, the Grandfather steps in and sings some
verses from "Rock of Ages." Why he sings these rather
than a love song, I don't know, except that this seems
more in character for him. While his doing so creates
a different mood, it also provides another opportunity
for the Chap and the Young Girl to agree on something,
the Grandfather's performance, and this time not at
either's expense. To his remark, "Very good," she
answers with, "Of course, he's good."

Just from the way I've described this sequence with
which Act II begins, it is obvious how easily singing
love songs comes about yet without becoming overdone as
is often the case at comparable moments in many other
revues. From this careful, controlled beginning, the
movement I've described continues with characters
playing off exchanges to each other but with the Girl
and the Chap beginning to pay more attention to each
other, even at times picking up on verses the other has
sung or quoted earlier. As a result they do begin to
show some feeling for each other, although not necessarily justifying her saying after the Chap's sermon,
"I've waited for you all my life."

In the third place, the order and range of contrasts, provided mainly by the excerpts from poems
and songs and those from the pornography films and
images flashed on the projection screen at the back
of the stage, reveal how moving and diversified love
and sex can be. A very good example is a sequence
which begins with the Older Woman reading some brief
excerpts about the pornography films as a prelude to

the more detailed ones she reads later. Among others, these refer to sex in prison and in girl scout camps. These accounts so interest one of the Interrupters that he offers the actors ale, which they accept. Then suddenly the lights dim and the projection screen shows film clips of a column of British soldiers marching. This linking of the pornography excerpts and the films, together with the patriotic responses they generate, creates the impression that both at least are recognizable forms of British behavior that audiences should recognize. Then, after the lights come back on, the Chairman gets up and recites lines from Burns' "The Cotter's Saturday Night" which reinforce the theme of being honest with oneself and therefore accepting many different kinds of behavior. In turn, the Chap responds with these lines from another poem, very different in tone, but also a prayer of sorts: "Oh England, full of sin but most of sloth/ Spit out thy phlegm and fill thy breast with glory." We could regard this excerpt as a reminder of how many different ways in which the English might perceive their behavior or an encouragement to aspire to something nobler than pornography or patriotism. Whichever the case, the Young Girl seems inspired to quote some lines from a moving love poem: "Love is a circle that does restless move/ In the same sweet eternity of love" and the Chap to respond comparably with lines that emphasize another aspect of love: "I do love I know not what/ Sometimes this and sometimes that. . "

Just at this point, when we might expect many more verses about love, the mood switches dramatically as the Grandfather quotes lines from a John Bettjemann poem that emphasizes how depressing is the life of an old person awaiting death:

> When I'm sweating a lot
> From the strain on a last bit of lung
> And lust has gone out
> Leaving only the things
> More worthless than ever,
> seem all the songs I have sung . . .

These lines would seem to contradict the happy assertions about love that were just made, particularly since they inspire the Chairman to quote some additional ones from the same work:

> But oh, ambitious heart, had such a proof forth
>   drawn
> A company of friends, a conscience set at ease

> It had but made us pine the more.   The
>   abstract joy
> The half read wisdom of demonic images,
> Suffice the ageing man as once the growing boy.

On the other hand, both the Grandfather and the Chairman's excerpts emphasize the value of people caring
for one another and coping with painful realities.   If
anything, the very sombreness of the contrast accentuates the need for love.

I've explored the foregoing sequence in some detail
because it illustrates the particular kind of diversity
and vigor achieved through such a considerable range of
contrasts, especially in love, and how these reinforce
each other as they permit people to express their affection for one another.   What is even more important is
that the spontaneous playing to each other through
excerpts and adapting techniques from the talk show
and the church sermon enable characters to admit some
of their insecurities and receive helpful feedback that
enables them to accept themselves more readily.   Moreover, when we view the play in relation to earlier
Osborne plays, it is apparent how some conflicts have
become muted.   If parents and children express less profound and moving affection for one another than they do
in The Entertainer, they also accept one another more
easily.   If the characters are vulnerable in a less
interesting way (the Old Woman possibly excepted), they
deal with such problems more easily and hopefully, if
on a more shallow level.

Admittedly, the Chap's peroration almost wrecks the
play.   But I don't think that it does.   What remains
is interesting because it does point to some possible
easing of the concerns that have been tormenting
Osborne's characters in just about all his previous
plays.

Whatever the case, undeniably this play isn't, as
some reviews insist, the expression of a bored, cro-
chety playwright vainly in search of a subject and just
lashing out in all directions.[65]   It is alive and in
its way on target--or targets.

XIII

WATCH IT COME DOWN

i

Whatever else it may be about, <u>Watch It Come Down</u> has a lot to say about how much people need each other for love, understanding, and reinforcement of self worth, particularly in a society where narrow self interest and lack of community are all too prevalent. It does so by revealing extremes of reaction that possibly no other Osborne work expresses, or at least does so in such an apparently outlandish and bizarre manner.

While the play has other plot ramifications, it centers on the confused efforts of an early fortyish couple, film director, Ben Prosser, and his novelist second wife, Sally, aided by their friends in the commune Ben has established, to try to find some way to deal with their painful and debilitating marriage that is virtually destroying both of them. Starting the commune, by converting an old country railway station into a comfortable ranch house, was itself an effort to shore up the marriage by creating an extended family through which Sally and Ben and the four others living with them could deal with their undeniable dependency needs. These others included Shirley, Sally's sister, a painter, whom Ben invited because he somehow thought her presence might provide an entree to Sally since as sisters they would presumably have something in common. That Ben should invite Shirley, a woman who has little sense of how people relate to each other and tries to remain dissociated from personal relationships, shows how confused Ben must have been--and may still be. Yet the fact that Shirley accepted shows that, without realizing it, she clearly needs people but can't acknowledge this. The second is Raymond, a young, far from handsome, working class homosexual, whom Ben has invited ostensibly to keep Sally company and to be cook and general handyman. Although Ben doesn't realize it, he has also invited Raymond because he could then feel some sexual superiority to the latter--an indication of his own insecurity as his relationship with Sally and the jealousy he comes to feel towards Raymond clearly shows. Raymond, for his part, has accepted because he, like Shirley, has almost no sense of himself as a distinct person so that

he lets Sally instruct him in what to do. Yet he is
honest enough to acknowledge how much he needs people
and likes to have someone to take care of.

The third, and a considerably more important member,
is Glen, an old, celebrated biographer, social histor-
ian, and upper class homosexual who, as we can surmise
from corroborative biographical details in the play,
seems modelled on Lytton Strachey.[66] Ben invited Glen
partly to get ego support to counteract the devastating
attacks Sally makes on his self worth and partly
because, as he says at one point, he loves Glen. In
turn, the latter seems puzzled as to just why he has
come, especially when he had such a good life in London.
But the fact that he asks the question indicates that
he also might have some dependency needs but which he
couldn't dare acknowledge publicly. He is, it turns
out, terminally ill and is trying to complete a book
which spells out his convictions as to why Western
European culture since the Renaissance has declined.
Although Glen hopes that the book will help reverse
this trend, he knows that it won't, and he is trying
to reconcile himself to this bitter disappointment.

The fourth and most important member is Jo, a thirty
year old young woman with a very strong interest in the
arts. From comparable corroborative biographical
details, we can surmise that she is modelled on Dora
Carrington, a young woman who was so very much in love
with Strachey that in despair, after his death, she
took her own life.[67] However, Jo's real talent, and
the main reason for her presence, though only Glen will
admit it to begin with, is her remarkable openness and
empathy for others. Or, as Glen remarks, "her magic
and her misfortune." These enable her to love just
about everyone and in a way appropriate to each; as she
says at one point, "the same only different." While
she understands these qualities in herself, she also
undervalues them and her own need for love. Only Glen
realizes that she needs, as he says, real love.
Although Jo loves Ben and Sally, it is Glen she loves
and respects the most and around whom she centers her
life. In turn, he appreciates and accepts her as no one
else does. At the same time, she is poignantly aware
of his imminent death and the impact it can have on her.

In an effort to do something about their marriage,
Sally (with Ben's complicity) arranges to have Raymond
spread a rumor among the others that they are separating. In this way she hopes that possibly the reactions
of the others somehow will cause something to happen

that they themselves can't bring about, caught up as they are in the dynamics of their relationship which feeds on negative reinforcement and makes them afraid to take responsibility for their actions. In addition, as Sally facetiously remarks, at least the rumor will do something to relieve the boredom of her life. Not surprisingly, nothing comes of Raymond's efforts. Yet the cumulative pressures that have been building during many years--their mutual sexual frustration, their feelings of personal inadequacy which their very relationship accentuates, and their strong need for love and self acceptance--become so great that the marriage literally breaks down in a gruelling fist fight. Nor is this the end because then the characters have to begin living with the feelings they have released.

At the same time the lives of Jo and Glen, though strikingly different but which counterpoint those of Sally and Ben because they embody more love and trust, take an even more tragic turn. Despite the fact that Glen completes his book, he does die. As a result, Jo finds that life without him is unbearably painful and confusing to endure, especially when both Sally and Ben, in different ways, turn to her for love and support. Consequently, like Dora Carrington (although under different circumstances and with different implications) she takes her own life.

If all of the foregoing confusion and pain aren't enough, I should add that Marion, Ben's ex-wife, whom in desperation he has asked to come down when the quarreling with Sally escalates, tries unsuccessfully to get him to leave with her. At the same time the neighbors in the area feel so threatened by the different life style of those in the commune that they open fire on it and kill Ben when he angrily rushes out to protest what they are doing.

Like West of Suez, Watch It Come Down shows individuals and their society living under such tension that ultimately violence erupts and wreaks havoc. However, in the latter play not only is the tension greater but the disruption as well. After all, at the end of West of Suez family stability and personal relationships still retain much of their force. In contrast, here they become a shambles as characters acknowledge openly some of the most intense feelings of self degradation, an almost unbearable yearning for love, and yet a capacity to see humor in some of the most despairing moments.

For such reasons, as I want to make evident through a discussion of selected episodes in each act, Watch It Come Down has a curious resilience and leavening impact. For if characters can show such extreme insecurities and yet try to cope with them, then just possibly hope for something better and a greater potential for endurance may emerge.

ii

Just as thematically Watch It Come Down has a lot in common with West of Suez and yet differs, or, as Jo says about loving, " . . . the same only different," the same is true structurally. Both plays contain considerable violence, use self consciously theatrical (or melodramatic) elements in some of their episodes and action, and employ a great range of contrasts between and within incidents. Yet significant differences also exist.

In the first place, in Watch It Come Down the violence is more extensive and pervasive. Not only does it occur at the end of both acts as the neighbors first kill Ben's dog and then, as indicated, open fire on the commune itself, but it informs many of the episodes, particularly at a verbal level whenever Sally and Ben meet up with each other. As Michael Billington justly remarked in his review of the play in The Guardian, these people have a talent for digging their teeth into each other's necks.[68]

In the second place, whereas the theatricality in West of Suez is largely confined to the end, in Watch It Come Down it occurs from the very beginning to suggest how unbelievable everything is and yet how real it is because of the desperate needs and terrible conflicts that can no longer be contained, each of which leads to some extreme reaction. Yet these extremes, although they may appear outlandish out of context, are credible because whatever anyone does, whether inside the commune or outside, strongly affects the others. To paraphrase one of Newton's laws of motion, for every extreme action in one direction, there is an equal and opposite extreme reaction in another. For example, the play begins with a long, highly concentrated and acrimonious exposition in which Sally is telling Raymond, while they are awaiting Ben's return from London (where he had one of his infrequent lunches with his eleven year old daughter from his first marriage), how crazy Ben must have been to set up this commune since it clearly isn't working out

at all. With devastating wit, she proceeds to ridicule
Ben's efforts:

> SALLY: . . . You're here because he's doing me a
> favour having someone to talk to and he can
> feel generous and big too because he knows
> you don't go for girls. Also, he doesn't
> really like you. He only likes old-style,
> exotic or bitchy, brainy poufs. Shirley
> he allows to do her old painting here--
> which he more or less openly despises even
> to her--because he still has a daft, mysti-
> cal itch that she might be the enigmatic
> tally to me. He doesn't really believe it,
> but it helps to flesh out a pretty dull
> scenario. If he did get to bed with her,
> he'd find acres of hand-picked, morning
> fresh peas under that mattress! . . .

Nor does she spare herself:

> SALLY: . . . What am I doing in a bloody rail-
> way station! A caravan would be better.
> Intimate community living. Nothing to do.
> Except bottle fruit and make vile wine,
> like Jo, and try and explain ourselves to
> odd journalists from comfortable houses in
> Islington or Wembley why we're as barmy as
> they think we are. 'The Prossers, tired
> of the rat race'--I wasn't tired, I was
> still in my stride--'decided to change
> their life style, get away from it all as
> so many of us would like but lack their
> initiative.' Initiative! We could have
> had a Palladian gem for the graft we bled
> out to bolshy, careless, barricade-minded
> builders for this railway folk-weavers'
> folly. No one to see...I almost wish Will
> Hay would walk in with Graham Moffat under
> his arm. Except that Ben would go into
> some mad, menopausal ecstasy and then I'd
> have to leave. I wish the trains did still
> come through. I could throw ham rolls at
> the passengers.

Then, after Raymond informs her that one train a week
still comes through on the adjoining tracks, there is a
sudden noise and the train itself makes its appearance.
While Sally doesn't, as she threatens to, throw out ham
rolls to the passengers, she does call out to them, "Get
out someone. Even if you're a ghost. Ben'll be home

soon." Almost immediately afterwards in what seems an
even more bizarre action, Raymond casually asks Sally,
"Would you like me to tell the others first?" To this
Sally replies, "What about us separating? Ben and me?"
Despite the fact that Raymond gets Sally to admit that
the separation is only a possibility, she insists on
his spreading the rumor and gleefully begins imagining
how their friends will react. Then, before she scarcely
finishes, Ben himself appears on the scene. Yet Sally
says nothing to him about this scheme but shifts gears
again and acts out the part of the loving wife faith-
fully greeting her husband, home from a long gruelling
day at the office. Ben, in turn, acts out another,
that of the misunderstood, harassed husband who is
ready to go through hell for the nth time. But since
neither of these ploys works, they begin, as they have
apparently for years, quarrelling. Although Raymond
does spread the rumor, not only does nothing come of
the scheme, but, except for a question Glen asks about
it just before his death, no one even refers to it.

   Just from my account, it seems apparent how bewil-
dering, inconsistent, and overdone much of this
sequence seems to be. It is no wonder that some of
the critics pounced on this episode. Alan Brien in
his review pointed out that, as exposition, this
episode was long, awkward, difficult to follow, and
symptomatic of a self destructiveness that permeates
the play. Besides, having the train come on as it does
seems so contrived as to be unbelievable.[69] So far as
the separation rumor is concerned, Robert Cushman felt
that Osborne introduced it to defend himself against
the charge that he didn't rely much on plot sequence
any more but left the flow of events come from, as it
does in Inadmissible Evidence, and to a large extent
The Hotel in Amsterdam, the main character's inner
feelings as they surfaced. But then having used the
separation device, Osborne found it cumbersome and so
abandoned it.[70]

   However, if we look at the scene in more detail, it
is just possible that these apparent gaffes may really
dramatize the characters' dilemma. The discrepancy
between Sally's long harangue and her brief announcement of the separation scheme does show how bored Sally
is, how much of her energy she dissipates, and how recklessly she acts. Moreover, the way she facetiously dismisses Raymond's objections that what she is doing isn't
true, "Who knows? It might (be true). It almost is.
Perhaps it will be. Perhaps they'll jolly it along.
Should be interesting their concern I mean," shows how

mixed up she is. Not only does she want others to
assume responsibility for what she does, but she herself
then wants to pass judgement on the way they do so!
Yet her acting in this way may show that she is both
defending herself against feelings she can't admit into
consciousness and yet is trying, by means of the crazy
separation scheme, to do something about them. In comparison to Frederica who is trying to change her relationship, first with her husband and then her father,
Sally seems irresponsible. Yet the fact that she will
go to such lengths and joke about what she is doing
also suggests a possible openness that Frederica may
not possess. As for the appearance of the train, it is
unreal, but Sally herself perceives it in this way as
her jokes indicate. Consequently, this episode shows
that Sally's life, as she herself recognizes, does seem
like something out of melodrama--but one which she
helps fashion. That nothing comes of the whole scheme
may show bad plotting on Osborne's part, but also that
real life pressures are stronger than the fictions
Sally creates.

In the third place, in relation to West of Suez, the
contrasts in this play are more extreme and yet in some
ways more complex. To begin with, right after Ben's
return from London, he and Sally have, as indicated, a
bitter quarrel because each constructs elaborate
defenses to protect himself and punish the other rather
than admit the need for love and attention, and in that
of Ben for feedback to raise his self esteem. Appropriately, the scene ends with Sally bursting into tears
because she wasn't honest with herself or Ben. He, in
turn, stands idly by while Raymond takes over, because
he is too embarrassed to express concern, as well as
afraid that Sally might reject him.

Clearly the scene shows a real breakdown in striking
contrast to Sally's fiction.

Then right after this comes a very short scene
between Jo and Glen in which almost the only words
spoken are by Jo, "You are really so gentle." Yet such
restraint accentuates the great contrast between the
two relationships since it shows that openness and concern can exist. Still, the restraint may also suggest
how tentative these feelings may be, for immediately
afterwards comes a longer, much more acrimonious scene
in which Raymond, under orders from Sally, appears to
tell Glen the rumor about the separation. Here,
instead of being gentle and trusting, Glen shows himself to be bitchy as he questions Raymond's motives and

snobbish as he condescendingly tells Raymond how unrecep-
tive the world is likely to be to his book. Nor does
Raymond treat Glen with kid gloves. "You're an old,
old before your time pouf pig," he replies, "stewing
about in past glories and handing down all these in
lofty 100-page indexes." For a moment we almost seem
back in the earlier scene with Sally and Ben. However,
as the scene goes on, each admits his hostility to the
other, and Glen apologizes to Raymond for treating him
so badly. Still, the scene doesn't end harmoniously
because Glen can't resist getting in one more final dig
at Raymond, "You were only doing your job. Bearing your
errand. Perhaps it's because I find you so ineffably
unattractive. It's a fault we all share, I'm afraid."

While this scene may appear to contradict the preceding one, so far as Glen is concerned, actually it
reinforces the value of openness, honesty, and concern
for others. Yet it escalates the difficulties involved
in realizing these. I would also add that Glen's
lament "I find you so ineffably unattractive" and the
lecture he gives Raymond about the poor reception
likely to be afforded his book emphasize a motif that
recurs throughout the play, the strength of disappointment but the efforts to cope with it.

iii

As forceful evidence of the increasing difficulties
involved in being honest, open, and loving, comes a
still longer and more acrimonious scene between Sally
and Ben. This centers on Sally's reaction to a gift
which Ben brought her from London, a fine dress he took
great pains in selecting. He did so to gain her
approval and perhaps try to alleviate his guilt feelings
(since, as we discover later, he had had sex with his
ex-wife while visiting his daughter in London). In
contrast to their earlier scene, this one begins more
cordially, especially on Sally's part, since she still
feels apologetic about what happened in their last
encounter. Consequently, she painstakingly compliments
Ben for his taste and apologizes for her behavior in
the earlier scene.

But rather than give her the feedback she hopes for,
Ben rejects the apology and goes on to justify his own
behavior because he feels so guilty and insecure. In
turn, Sally begins taunting him for his guilt feelings
and for excessive concern for others' reactions since
he states that people will think it odd for him to give
her a gift if they are separating. Nor does she stop

here but begins to attack him viciously for what she
regards as more disgusting feelings--his fear of
facing middle age (or what she calls the "male men-o-
pause.") Through such attacks, she may be showing her
sexual frustration. Yet at the same time she is
clearly aggravating his obvious insecurities, as shown
by the way he tries to put her down sexually and to
belittle her writing. Increasingly, each is degrading
the other's self worth and revealing his own anxieties
and desire for love and attention. Yet each is making
it harder to receive any such feedback. The more Ben
shows how much he wants Sally's approval, the more
rejecting she becomes and the more suspicious of his
motives. When, for example, he finally says he is
sorry, she replies, "No you're not. You just lost."
Then when he tries to touch her, she launches what is
possibly the cruelest attack to date. "You've begun
to smell...Physically I can smell you in bed. And now
in here..." Yet for this very reason his need for some
feedback increases as he begs her to wear the dress at
dinner that evening. Instead, Sally becomes more
rejecting by turning to Raymond and inviting him to go
out for dinner with her and to do so wearing the dress.
Yet Sally doesn't stop for then she proposes to Raymond
that they take Ben's dog out for a walk since clearly,
as she insists, Ben himself doesn't pay any attention
to it.

On the other hand, Ben doesn't remain idle. While
Sally goes upstairs to prepare to take the dog out, Ben
calls up his ex-wife and asks her to come down because
his life is so unbearable. However, Sally, overhearing
the conversation, seizes the phone and brutally seconds
the invitation. "Do come down," she insists, "if your
runty little legs will stand. Bring the brat. No one
will harm her. Certainly not me. I wouldn't touch her.
And, oh yes, fuck him if you like. In my bed. I doubt
if I shall be here to watch the spectacle. But there
will be others. Goodbye..." In turn, Ben tears up the
dress and throws the remains on the railroad track,
while Sally, not to be outdone, reminds him, as she and
Raymond walk out with the dog, that as yet he doesn't
own this part of the property.

To allocate blame for what happened is pointless
since each clearly hurts the other a great deal. Still
it is difficult not to feel that Sally keeps raising the
ante more because at each stage, when she clearly has
hurt Ben, something impels her to go on. Yet in rejecting him sexually as she is, she is also rejecting herself, for she clearly likes the dress and yet makes it

impossible for herself to accept it. Moreover, while she is punishing Ben by taking the dog out for a walk, she is also, without realizing it, expressing concern for something that belongs to Ben. On the other hand, while Ben seems to be trying to preserve peace by buying the dress, his behavior towards his ex-wife shows, as Ben freely confesses, that he isn't really being honest with Sally. In addition, Ben shows how much his sense of his own worth still depends upon Sally's treatment of him and yet how unaware he is of that. At one point, when Sally compliments him for his good taste, Ben expresses amazement, "Oh I thought you said my taste in all things was execrable." The way he says this suggests that he has almost automatically accepted her view of him as a part of his self image. Sally, in her reply, accentuates these feelings. "You're making it up. In women perhaps. Anyway I wouldn't use a pompous word like execrable. You sound pretty funny saying it. More like Glen." Unfortunately, some grounds for this inferiority do exist since Ben has not lived up to the expectations aroused by his earlier work for which he won several Oscars as most promising young director. Admittedly, he may have been overrated to start with; still, granting that, there is strong evidence that living all these years with Sally has hurt him creatively but that as yet he only vaguely surmises this or can't dare face what this means.

However we regard the episode, it shows brilliantly how one apparently small action, the presentation of a gift, can bring out so many conflicting and hurtful feelings that have been building up in both Sally and Ben for years.

Following Sally's departure comes another long episode, dominated more by Jo, which is very different in tone since it is a "love in." Yet is also shows how insecure people are, how the lives of all the characters are united, and how even more hostility emerges than in the preceding episode. It consists of four parts, separate but related, all of them building on one another.

The first, which is totally different from the bruising quarrel between Sally and Ben, shows Jo taking care of Glen. It is a very tender scene in which each again is honest and solicitous about the other. Whereas previously Jo merely told Glen how gentle he was, here she shows, in striking contrast to Sally's hostility to Ben, how much he means to her.

JO;   I do. I do. You are what I care for. The
       thing that's left. Not fleeing away. I
       read your letters. You are in my brain,
       not just my heart. Even in my bed with
       others. I need your rebuke. Your smile
       when I'm naughty or stupid and misunder-
       standing. You've lit my silly schoolgirl
       life. You've brought me up. Slapped life
       into me. Don't let me get old. Not when
       you are still so young. I'm sorry. I
       can't bear to be alone. For I will be.
       The rest means so little, without you. My
       reading and silly letters and walks with
       you and rides and my awful home-weave
       cooking...

But, as much as she appreciates Glen, she is also
expressing considerable pain as she becomes increasingly aware of her impending loss. Although Glen reassures
her that his heart is with her, he doesn't assuage any
of her obvious self doubts or fears of loneliness.
Then, if Jo's pain isn't great enough, she has to excuse
herself to phone the doctor because she sees clearly
that, precisely because Glen seems more responsive, he
really is getting worse. Nor does she get much help
from Ben whom she encounters when she uses the phone.
It is true that he does express concern, but it is
apparent, as Jo clearly senses, that he is depressed
about what has just happened with Sally. Therefore
instinctively in this, the second incident in the episode, she begins to try to give him the love and sense
of self esteem he so badly needs. That she herself also
needs these accentuates the poignancy of Jo's dilemma
and yet shows even more her empathy and generosity.
She reveals her empathy immediately by what seems like
a casual question; how was lunch with his daughter.
Yet it was this same question, expressed somewhat
differently by Sally, that halped generate much of the
hostility in the first quarrel scene. In contrast,
something in Jo's voice tone encourages Ben to reveal
what he couldn't dare admit to Sally, how inadequate
he feels as a father. In reply, Jo lets him know she
loves him, something he desperately wants to hear and
in just the right way. As she clearly understands, he
has so little belief in his own goodness that, like a
child, he needs some source of warmth and trust outside
himself. This is what she expresses through what
otherwise seems like nonsense. "I love you," she insists, "because I am love for you. I am your child,
your protector. Oh, doesn't it sound twee..I am the
seed in your earth. I shine on upon you and you are

there always..." That she does understand his need
becomes even clearer when he confesses to her something he regards as even more shameful, his behavior at
lunch with his daughter:

> BEN: May I? There's no one...I'll cut it right
> down. I was sitting in the restaurant with
> my daughter. She refused a cushion for her
> chair like she used to have. Very politely.
> I looked at her. She looked at me. I
> talked about the restaurant, the waiter,
> the food, who went there, what dishes
> there were. She ordered promptly, cour-
> teously. She tackled her spaghetti, her
> steak, her ice cream, her coke. We said
> less and less. I wanted her to go. She
> wanted to go. To be with her friends, her
> mother, I don't know who. I drank an
> extra half litre of wine. I ordered the
> wine. Got the bill in a hurry. I looked
> at her and, well, yes the awful, the thing
> is I cried all over the tablecloth. In
> front of her. She watched my jowls move.
> I looked away. But I couldn't. Through
> the marble and columns and the rest of the
> silencing restaurant and waiters scrupu-
> lously not watching. I couldn't even get
> out 'Let's go.' Then, suddenly, she leapt
> off her too low chair and put her arms
> round me. And she cried. Like a 'B'
> movie. She took my hand and we walked out
> past all the rows of tables. I left her
> at home and we neither of us said a word;
> just held hands; no, she knew the way
> home. Isn't that despicable? How could I
> face her? That's why I rang...I dare say...

Here we see even more obviously a side of Ben he
wouldn't dare show Sally. Yet it never dawns on Ben
that he could feel some pride in being so open in his
feelings and having a daughter who exhibits such poise
and understanding.

In turn, Ben's openness, as well as his obvious need
for greater self acceptance, encourages Jo to confess
how painful openness such as hers can be. She does
this so that Ben will begin trusting himself more and
discovering grounds for faith. Yet she is also trying
to do the same for herself and possibly the others (who
have joined her in a celebration honoring Glen for

completing his book). This tribute to love, which
begins the third incident in this episode, is moving
and yet disquieting:

JO: Shirley, Glen's finished his book. I love
      him. I can't bear to go into his room. I
      love Ben, no, you think I'm lightminded, a
      lot of people do. Like they think about
      you. I think and welcome you within all I
      know up to this now, this moment, with my
      heart full and my brain clear and empty.
      Forgive me for what I am not. But I am--I
      am a loving creature...I'm frail and I break
      but bear with me...It's hard to love, isn't
      it? It's like religion without pain, I
      mean it's not religion without pain. It's
      not flowers and light and fellowship. It's
      cruel and we inhabit each other's dark
      places. Let's drink to that. It's not
      much worse than the rest. The time is
      short and all our heads are sore and our
      hearts sick oh, into the world, this cen-
      tury we've been born into and made and
      been made by. Release us from ourselves
      and give us each our other. There: I've
      said, I've invented a grace, not very
      gracefully. Oh, Glen, bless you, the life
      you've given me, at least, and you Ben,
      for the work and pain you long to exorcise,
      and you Shirley for being such a butt with
      such human grace. Damn it, I didn't mean
      to cry. How indecent.

While many Osborne characters have spoken eloquently
about love, it is questionable if any of them, even
Jimmy Porter when he warned Helena about how difficult
loving could be, articulates so pointedly how demanding
it can be. Love can inspire a person to want to go
beyond himself and merge with another. Yet as a result
the lover may demand so much more of himself to give to
that other that he may jeopardize his own self worth.
Equally important, when Jo remarks, "It's cruel [love]
and we inhabit each other's dark places...", she recognizes that the very closeness to the loved one can cause
the other to feel so acutely the latter's fears, doubts,
and hostilities.

Although Jo ends with a grace, it is, as she herself
is aware, a tentative, even precarious, one because she
has such self doubts. This may explain why, instead of
feeling consoled, the others become depressed and des-

cribe the pain they feel in living in the twentieth century. Ben, in particular, seems most distressed
because he feels that the present world seems to have
lost the grace and romantic idealism he associates
(rightly or wrongly) with the Edwardians. At this
point the scene becomes poignant because the characters
keep insisting how heartbroken they feel about living
in the twentieth century, and yet at the same time they
embrace each other for security. The climax comes when
Ben personalizes the desolation he feels all around him:

> Oh, it will totter on. Glen will write
> about the twentieth century and the people
> who lived it. Shirley will paint and barri
> cade. Jo will take lovers. I will grow old
> in films...Oh God...this is a loveless
> place.

If Osborne means us to take this speech straight, it
seems excessive. On the other hand, there is some evidence from the text that the episode may show what can
happen when people become too uncritically subjective.
I mention in particular a stage direction which describes Glen's reaction as he watches Jo and Ben
embracing, "He watches with exquisite desolation."
From this perspective the characters, in letting their
hair down in this manner, may be insulating themselves
so much from the outside world that they are viewing it
too much as a projection of their own torment.

Yet it is true that what happens immediately afterwards, in the fourth contrasting incident in this
episode, may seem to confirm Ben's description of
"this is a loveless place." For just as he finishes
his lament, Sally suddenly appears in the doorway
holding the dog, dead, in her arms and describes how
the neighbors shot it merely because it happened to
break from its leash.

Nevertheless, what happens in the rest of this
brief but powerful scene does show the danger that
results from projecting one's own torments onto
others and absolving oneself from projecting anything.
I say this because Sally, while at first angry at the
neighbors, ignores the fact that she bears some responsibility for what happened (since she took the dog out
to get back at Ben) and instead blames all of the
others as she hurls the dog at him. "Here she is,"
she insists, "your, Your dog." Then, after Ben tries
to put his arm around her, she hits him and they begin
fighting. Although utterly different in tone, the

laments about the decay of romantic idealism in the twentieth century and Sally's denunciation of the others and her subsequent plea "Do something, someone. Let something happen," show how distorted feelings can become when people recklessly project their insecurities onto one another. "I haven't," she replies in answer to Ben's accusation that she has killed everything, "But I would. And somebody else will." That she is right becomes clear when immediately afterwards they go on hitting each other while the rest merely watch them.

Finally, at the end of Act I, Sally and Ben, as well as Jo in her bitter sweet awareness of how openness to love accentuates one's vulnerability, are much closer to confronting some of their deepest feelings than they were at the beginning of the play. In particular, Sally and Ben realize how destructive their relationship has been and how much they hate each other. To have reached this point has been difficult and costly, but at least it represents a profound release and a significant first step. But, as Act II reveals, very real problems remain since Sally and Ben, and to a lesser extent Jo, have to live more openly with feelings that now have become a more active part of their consciousness. And that, to paraphrase Frost's poem, "The Road Not Taken," "can make all the difference."

iv

After the touching and yet painful love scene or "love in," in Act I that occurs following the second quarrel between Sally and Ben, it would be difficult to imagine anything comparable. Yet Act II begins with just such a scene, one involving Sally and Jo right after the bruising quarrel with which Act I ends. It begins in a low key way with each trying to console the other. Jo does so by letting Sally know that she loves both Sally and Ben and therefore, whatever happens, this will remain; Sally does so by asking Jo if she loves Glen, not because she has doubts but rather to reassure Jo that she is aware of this love. Very quickly, however, the scene becomes more passionate and articulate. First Jo, in reply to Sally, describes how much she loves Glen and how this love affects her. Then Sally, encouraged by Jo and obviously aroused by her feelings, implores Jo to love her. When Jo readily agrees, Sally is equally articulate, but in a different way as she reveals just how much she loves Jo. At the same time she admits how unfair such a plea is because of Glen's imminent death and how short lived such a love is likely to be. Yet they should not

213

be deterred because these very difficulties underline
how much each needs and deserves love.

That Jo should express her feelings as she does is
clear enough for they accentuate those she expressed in
the "love in" scene. But that Sally, considering all
the hostility she expressed to Ben, should feel love
may seem difficult to believe. Yet underlying much of
that hostility was considerable disappointment in what
had happened to their relationship, as well as a left
handed acknowledgement of her dependence on him. Even
more to the point, while Sally threw the dog at Ben,
before that she clearly showed how much she cared for
it:

> They shot her. She was on heat and we stupidly
> let her fly off miles away. We saw them from
> the top of the hill, helpless. They tied, yes
> tied her to a tree and set all the male dogs on
> her. And then they shot her...In front of us.

However, what is difficult to assess is the impact
and implications of the scene. The reason is that the
very qualities that seem most evident in their expression of love as shown in the following speeches (the
first by Jo, the other two by Sally), namely their
openness and self awareness, produce markedly different
impressions:

> JO: I love his old clothes. His letters and
> his bad drawings. His restless indolence.
> His sickly athleticism. His tolerance and
> forbearing. Oh, I'm going on as if he's
> dead. But he's breathing heavily in my
> heart, more than he ever did. Oh, Glen,
> my brilliant, kindly, silly Glen. You
> listened to my chirruping and ate my home-
> made jam which you didn't like. Your
> frail, fastidious, greedy body, loving,
> full of lust and circumspection...He was
> ashamed of his boys, you know. No, not
> ashamed of them but himself, his own odd
> body and over-turning mind. . .

> SALLY: Yes. I want to kiss you. On the mouth.
> My tongue between your bright teeth. I
> want to hold you in my arms a whole night
> with our bodies like twin fortresses, lap
> in lap. I want to see you wake up and look
> down at me and get me awake...May I kiss

you?

> SALLY: Jo. Oh, Jo, joke, Sally of OUR alley.
> I love you in a hundred ways and I won't
> look up one anthology to tell you how.
> Strange. I wanted to love my sister. But
> I didn't. Ben wanted to love his sister--
> like an extra wife to carry the burden. But
> she died. And left him with me. Oh, and
> Marion. His father. His mother. And his
> daughter. Thank heavens we'll have no
> children, Jo. Jo and Sally--our own off-
> spring. Hold me again. No man's held me
> like that since I can't remember. (<u>Door
> bell rings</u>.)

That Jo can describe so pointedly how close she
feels to Glen and how well she understands him indicates not only the depth of her feeling but also for
how long a time she has thought about him. That she
can also admit how even closer she wishes to be to
him reveals how open she can be. And that she realizes
how much being with him helps her accept herself more
readily shows how much she understands herself.

Comparably, the way Sally describes Jo's physical
appearance and her yearning for her indicates how much
she values Jo. Perhaps even more, these very same
details show how unashamed she is that she should care
for Jo as she does since this disclosure must come as a
great surprise to her after all the years she has spent
with men. Moreover, as her witty, self disparaging
comments reveal, at each moment she is trying to
remind herself that she must remain realistic about
what can happen and yet refuse to deny what is taking
place right now.

For all of these reasons, it is difficult not to
feel considerable exhilaration, even joy, in this
scene. In particular, I would emphasize that Sally,
after feeling so frustrated and hateful, can care
openly and realize that she has been yearning for love
for years, rather than want to go on hating Ben.
Besides, in passages I haven't quoted she admits that
she has treated Ben unfairly by letting him believe that
he was a homosexual (or was bisexual) when he really
wasn't and that he needed her as much as he thought he
did. As for Jo, her speech and behavior only confirm
all the more her remarkable sensitivity to others. Not
only does she show how well she understands Glen, but
her willingness to let Sally make love to her reveals

how clearly she recognizes the latter's needs.

Yet, on the other hand, the episode is painful. At the very moment Sally is loving Jo, she is also realizing that possibly she can't love men anymore, and that for years she has been frustrated or disappointed in not being able to love her sister. For Jo the pain seems even greater. Although she is most alive and most herself when she is with Glen, she still ends up asking, "He did love me, didn't he?" Her doubts exist not because Glen doesn't love her but because, like all the others, he undervalues himself and so underestimated how much his reassurance could mean. She, in turn, as has been evident all along, undervalues herself even more. But, what is most painful of all, and yet understandable, is that, while Sally clearly is being more honest with herself than she has been before, she still doesn't recognize her own strong dependency needs. This is shown by the way she quickly turns to Jo who obviously wouldn't refuse her. Besides, the way Sally admits that "Strange. I wanted to love my sister and didn't...," and then brusquely analyzes Ben's behavior towards his sister smacks of the intellectuality that Sally revealed in her long opening speech in Act I. Not only do such reactions show that Sally still has only a limited awareness of her own behavior, but they also show, as will become evident in the next scene I want to consider, that unwittingly she adds to the burdens Jo faces when Glen dies.

The scene I refer to is a very brief episode that occurs after Jo learns that Glen is very near death and has just seen him for the last time. At first glance it seems disjunct and clumsy, not at all what we would expect such a scene to be when it turns out, as this one does, to have such tragic consequences. However, that is just the point of the scene: how confusing are Jo's reactions and how difficult are her choices. The scene begins with a heated discussion between Ben, Shirley, and Sally about how to spend the time waiting for Glen's death. Finally, Sally decides that she and Shirley should go for a walk while Ben is to remain behind, if, as Sally facetiously remarks, he can do so. Then just at this moment, Jo appears in the doorway and simply announces, "He did love me. His eyes are so blue, and he held my hand so tight it hurt."

It is true that Sally shows some concern by asking Jo to join her in her walk, but she doesn't press matters when Jo indicates that she prefers to wait outside until the doctor comes. However, immediately afterwards, Sally and Ben begin arguing once again, hastening Sally's departure. Then all that takes place before Jo goes outside is this brief episode with Ben:

> BEN: Just wait. It's ridiculous to say it. But wait. Get drunk. Sleep. It will pass. I want you...I shouldn't have said that.
> JO: Why not? If you mean it. Glen would be pleased. Oh, Glen.
> BEN: There...
> JO: Glen come back. I can't live--with all this. Who can? You couldn't even. Do we give up...
> (She disengages herself from BEN.)
> Sorry. I'll sit in the sun till the doctor comes back.
> BEN: Be careful.
> JO: Of what?
> BEN: Oh, pedestrian traffic.

When we realize that this is clearly the moment at which Jo chooses to take her life, we could feel that this episode is too sketchy. Such an impression becomes stronger particularly if we compare the scene to the original on which Osborne has drawn, the relationship between Lytton Strachey and Dora Carrington. After Strachey died, Carrington, as her diaries reveal, spent a month examining her feelings in great detail as she realized how much of her life centered on Strachey. She thought carefully about suicide, read parts of Hume's treatise on the subject, and then decided that living without Strachey was so unbearable that she chose to take her life. Although her first attempt failed, she succeeded the second time.[71]

By comparison, Osborne's version seems threadbare and unsatisfying, especially since Jo says so little and does so almost incoherently. However, when we look at the whole scene in context, actually it presents a painful dilemma that Jo faces head on. Just when she finally has become convinced that Glen loves her, she has to bear his loss. At just the same time she has to endure renewed arguments between Sally and Ben. When, in addition Ben ignores, or at least greatly underestimates, the force of the plea she expresses in these words, "Glen come back. I can't live with all this. Who can. You couldn't even. Do we give up?" her dilemma becomes even greater.

217

In this full context the confusion and clumsiness express honest reactions: Jo's concern for others' feelings; her plea for help; and yet her friends' failure to respond adequately because, although they care for her, they need her and can't cope with their own ambivalent feelings towards each other. Under the circumstances, it is difficult not to conclude that Jo really wanted to live, but only if she could preserve the integrity of her love for Glen. However, she couldn't do so because of the demands that Sally and Ben were making on her.

Just as Jo's death differs from that of Dora Carington, so does Glen's, as presented in the next scene, differ from that of Lytton Strachey as described in Holroyd's biography. Each man did have a long terminal illness and each died in the country attended by the woman he loved and who loved him. However, Strachey, while not exactly dying in state, was, as Holroyd points out, surrounded by many more friends-- and right up to the end.[72] In contrast, Glen dies with just Raymond present and in a scene that has much of the acrimony of their confrontation in Act I. Raymond hasn't come to pay his last respects to Glen but simply to update the separation rumor of Act I--as though he has to tidy everything up. When Glen discovers that the separation was a hoax, he angrily denounces it as a "vivisection on friendship." On the other hand, he admits how much he admires Sally because on her own she really made something of her life. In response to Raymond's begrudging and self concerned comment, "Well it's all over bar the shouting isn't it? I don't mean you with, well, respect. But what's left in it for any of us?" Glen sardonically answers, "Well, if this is terminal care, I can't say I think much of it."[73] Then finally, when Raymond solicitously remarks that the doctor will be coming shortly, Glen dismisses this by inquiring about Jo. When he is reassured that she is sunning herself outside and that Raymond will stay with him until the doctor comes, Glen then tells Raymond of two road signs he saw while coming down from London that again reveal much of the dissatisfaction, as well as concern, with contemporary life he expressed in Act I:

> GLEN: One was a little triangle of green with a hedge and a bench. And a sign read: "This is a temporary open space"...
> RAYMOND: Oh yes?
> GLEN: And the other was a site of rubble near the Crystal Palace I think, perched high up

over London, where the bank managers and cashiers fled at the beginning of our-- our--of our century. It said 'Blenkinsop-- Demolitionists. We <u>do</u> it. You <u>watch</u> it. <u>Come Down</u>.' (He rec<u>ed</u>es from consc<u>i</u>ousness and RAYMOND reads a magazine with his cof- fee at the bedside.) . . .

What do we make of this scene? Clearly it doesn't present the heroic death of a great man or conversely, the despair of some one watching in "exquisite desola- tion." Rather, it shows a willingness to admit disappointment yet not be defeated by it. However else we interpret this scene, it represents a considerable change from the bitchiness Glen showed in his first encounter with Raymond. Yet common to both is an ironic self honesty and an adaptability to change. For the full significance of this we need only compare him to Wyatt who used posing to resist change and to deceive himself to the end. The fact that, while Glen is breathing his last, Raymond merely sits and (as the stage directions reveal) reads a newspaper may seem like the height of insensitivity. Yet it also shows a mutual need. Raymond could have left after updating the separation rumor, and Glen could have insisted on dying in isolation.

v

Following this brief episode, comes a much longer one that is different in tone. I refer to a scene in which Marion, Ben's first wife, comes down to see Ben in response to the desperate phone call he made to her at the height of his second quarrel with Sally. Although Marion has come in answer to a plea for help, it quickly turns out that she has plans of her own, namely to try to get Ben to leave Sally and come back to Lon- don with her.

In contrast to the sardonic realism and understate- ment of the preceding scene, parts of this seem like something out of soap opera. Marion turns out to be a snobbish, fashionably dressed, and highly conservative woman who has simplistic ideas (derived from the media) about what people in a commune must be like. "And I don't care," she comments about what she expects to find here, "about broken bottles and the flick knives." Moreover, when later in the scene she reminds Ben of some of the happiest moments of their marriage, she sounds even more like a character from one of the day time serials. "We had our moments, oh, who cares, our

moments of happiness. Months of happiness. Penniless
and odd but relaxing, forgetful happiness." Even Ben
himself uses comparable language in describing their
unhappy times (though admittedly with more self awareness), "I know, it's true. You read about it in the
papers. 'A Wife's Problems'! How I won through. Why
did he want so desperately to be alone. Stupid nit.
We did love each other. Dearly. But it was all risk,
risk, damned risk. Gambling Russian roulette."

However, when we look at the scene in more detail,
we could derive some different impressions that give
the scene more complexity and poignancy. Granted that
Marion at times comes on as indicated, she also turns
out to be someone who clearly knows Ben and can, as
this plea clearly shows, admit her own isolation and
despair.

> MARION: Ben, I know you. Do believe me. You
> wake up. You know how. Not 'about' any-
> thing. It's just black and fearsome and
> impossible to get up. Sweat and loathing.
> All too early. You can't read or concen-
> trate or remember. You sleep endlessly
> between good or bad times. It's all the
> same. We've become islands at the edges
> of the bed. You're on your own. I'm on
> my own. Now, for years. Oh, Ben, it's
> been a glass steel wall. Both observing
> the child and her us. We do--did nothing
> with her--or her with us. I tried keep-
> ing her out of the bedroom, for my sake as
> much as yours. We never did things at
> the same time of day. We couldn't. I
> followed you like a dog when I knew you
> wanted to be left alone. You wanted to
> sleep in front of the television.

Furthermore, she goes on to promise that she'll be completely open with him, which is very important since in
retrospect, their main problem, as she points out, was
that they didn't trust each other. At the same time
Ben's own reactions would seem to indicate how much more
open he can be with Marion than with Sally. For example, when the former asks about Glen, he can reveal his
anxieties about having homosexual tendencies (which he
couldn't disclose to Sally precisely because she kept
accusing him of displaying these), his fears of being a
renegade father, and most painfully of all, his feeling
that, "...And in spite of fearing both of it. I am
neither loved nor loving."

For his part, Ben doesn't deny any of Marion's arguments and obviously appreciates her understanding of his low self worth. Moreover, the one objection that Ben offers for not leaving with Marion, when she implores him to, would seem to constitute all the more reason for his wanting to leave. All he can say is, "You see the more pain I FEEL, the more resentment comes out of her." What is more, as some parts of the very last episode will reveal, Ben derives considerable pleasure from attacking Sally. Therefore, the point of the episode with Marion might be to show how little, if anything, Ben has learned from what has happened to him to date in the play and how far he remains from being able to be honest with himself.

Yet, when we look at these details in a fuller context, this view may be too one-sided. While Marion acknowledges that they should have trusted each other, she also urges Ben to come before " . . . she [Sally] starts smashing the place up. And I get scared and run. And you give up . . . " Such a reaction hardly reveals courage. It is true that, before this, Ben, as indicated, did reveal how unloved he felt. Yet Marion's response to this simply was "Ben, let's go, I've the car outside. We can do it." This too, leaves something to be desired. Besides, later in the episode, when Ben did, as indicated, personalize his resentment about Sally in such a way as to show how profoundly Sally affected his feelings about himself, Marion didn't even respond.

In other words, the saddest truth of all may be that Ben really is confused and justifiably so. While living with Sally is hell, returning to Marion may also be disastrous since she is simplistic and too fearful of what may happen. Even more to the point, however much Ben personalizes all of Sally's reactions to his behavior, he has reason because of the cruel and rejecting manner in which she has treated him for so many years. Therefore, for Marion to expect that Ben could simply dissociate himself from such a relationship on the spot is to fail to understand the depths of his feelings--as perhaps she did originally. Under the circumstances, Ben's answer to her plea to leave, "Give me time, Marion darling," may not be a cop out but a realistic assessment of where he stands at present, however painful such a position may be. In particular, he seems to be experiencing at a gut level something that he has only vaguely surmised for years, namely how profoundly Sally has affected his sense of his self worth.

If the incident with Marion has elements of the day-time serials, the very last episode in which Jo throws herself under a train, the neighbors (as indicated) without any apparent provocation open fire on the commune and fatally injure Ben, and Dr. Ashton, the local physician, when he belatedly arrives on the scene, concentrates all his energies on blaming the <u>victims</u> for what has happened, would seem like a caricature of a Mel Brooks movie. As such, the incident may at first glance again seem to indicate that things have gotten worse rather than better.

To begin with, much of the time Ben and Sally quarrel and, if anything, more violently than ever at least so far as Ben is concerned. He excoriates Sally for being ignorant and insists that she has feelings only for dogs. Besides, Bill still can't be honest with Sally for instead of answering her question as to whether he and Marion had sex together (which they did in London), he sanctimoniously reminds her that Glen is dying. Sally, for her part, seems to treat Doctor Ashton in much the same manner as she does Ben by snobbishly putting him down for his philistine tastes. Finally, even the very last comments of Sally and Ben to each other might seem to show how little they know about each other and themselves. Just before dying, Ben remarks to Raymond, "Come and look after your Sally... Look after her Raymond. I know I can rely on you... even when I'm bleeding to death..." Here again Ben treats Raymond condescendingly as he has throughout the play, and again, as in his behavior all during the "love in" scene, Ben seems to be indulging himself. As for Sally, in saying to Ben, "Oh Ben, don't go. Don't leave me. We all, the few of us need one another," she seems to be ignoring or repudiating much of what she told Jo about how badly suited she and Ben were for each other and how tired she is of the bodies of men, not to mention all of their quarreling throughout the play.

However, when we look more closely at some of these details (and others I haven't mentioned) it is possible to see that some change has occurred. For example, Ben in quarreling more aggressively with Sally is acknowledging more openly how much hostility he still feels. Granted that his attacking her for being ignorant is unfair, yet he is showing, though he doesn't realize it openly, a reason why he feels unloved, namely how inferior he feels to Sally. Admittedly, he is also unfair in telling her that she only has feelings for dogs, yet his doing so reveals his jealousy and his awareness that she can care for someone else.

In short, without quite realizing it, Ben is coming to accept the fact that Sally doesn't need him. That he acknowledges this to Raymond with (as indicated) some condescension doesn't invalidate his admission but in a way strengthens it since Ben is trying to accept something that clearly pains him. As for his histrionic assertion, "even when I'm bleeding to death," it also has Mel Brooks overtones. However, such overtones express Ben's effort to look at himself with some detachment and even humor, something he hasn't done before.

As even stronger evidence that Ben isn't wallowing in self pity, I would emphasize just how he did get killed. When the neighbors (or their gunmen) not only open fire on those inside the commune but shoot up Jo's body (which Ben went out and brought in), he becomes so angry that he rushes out and curses them for what they did. (Needless to say, had he remained inside he would have been safe.) When we consider that earlier in the play Ben simply lamented how brutal life had become, we see that his rushing out represents quite a change.

As for Sally, in pointing out to Ben in their argument that it was his dog, she may be coming closer to admitting to herself that she does care for him in some way. Moreover, when Ben escalates the argument, she backs away and simply says, "If only you knew..." I take this to mean that if he understood her better he would realize why she feels as she does. Earlier in the play she would not have shown this much awareness. Yet she doesn't go on to explain how she feels either because she still can't or is too proud to do so. Therefore, in begging Ben not to leave because, "We all, the few of us, need each other," Sally may be beginning to see how dependent she was on Ben and how much she valued him. But most of all, she is accepting herself as someone who is different from her neighbors and at the same time, like Jimmy in his bears and squirrels reprise with Alison, she is acknowledging her defensiveness.

However, in contrast to Jimmy, Sally, as her argument with Dr. Ashton reveals, also shows herself secure and realistic enough to confront those who contribute to her defensiveness and at the same time recognize theirs as well. Granted that she scores some easy points off Dr. Ashton by making elitist cultural references (about Glen's fame) he can't be expected

to know, still she is right in challenging him. After
all, the most Dr. Ashton can say, when he sees three
bodies lying there before him, is, "You've brought
this on yourselves, you know." Yet Sally in her reply
takes his feelings seriously, "I dare say," she answers,
"if it's any comfort to you." To realize how differently Sally is acting, we need only remember her
reaction to the shooting of the dog. "Do something
somebody," she implored, "Let something happen."
Clearly, she is doing something by dealing openly with
Doctor Ashton and preparing to live on her own and as
some one very different from the neighbors. Sally has
all the more need to prepare herself for this experience because, as his last speech reveals, Doctor Ashton doesn't recognize that she has tried to find some
common ground with him. "Well," he answers, "you
people do lead odd sorts of lives don't you." In self
defense she comes back with, "Yes we do, Doctor Ashton.
We do. Most of us. You must be glad."

Admittedly, Watch It Come Down has some limitations.
In the first place, the outside world to which the
characters refer in many speeches seems vague because
it isn't altogether clear just what has happened in the
twentieth century to justify why the characters feel as
much pain as they insist that they do. In the second
place, some of the time Glen remains too much like a
choral figure rather than a dramatic character--and, I
would add, too much of a donn-ish one at that. In the
third place, we know much less about the main characters than their counterparts in other Osborne plays.
Granted that in part this results because Sally and
Ben, in particular, are portrayed as people who have
been unhappy for so long that they can't get beyond
their immediate present. Still, we might expect that
in quarreling they might refer more than they do to
some details from their past.

On the other hand, this is a far better play than
most of the reviews acknowledged, many of which emphasized only the hatred and anger. Clearly these are
there, but they also represent frustrations of what is
just as strong, if not stronger, the power of love. To
a remarkable extent, the play documents Katherine Ann
Porter's assertion, "Love must be learned again and
again. There is no end to it . . . Hate needs no
instruction."[74] For, in trying to admit to themselves
some of their deepest needs, Sally and Ben are revealing how easily hatred comes but how difficult it is to
love, especially when people have so low a sense of

self worth as all the characters, including Glenn, do.
At the same time loving has to be learned even for
someone like Jo who seems to understand it so well
because she is so open to being hurt, particularly when
the others make unfair demands upon her. Besides, the
fact that people such as Sally and Ben, who are far
from admirable, do become more honest, open, and trusting holds out some hope, for, if they can do it, others
who feel less hatred and frustration than they do and
are, to begin with, more open and self aware, might go
much further.

XIV

TOWARDS A CONCLUSION

To venture a conclusion about the achievement of a living writer who is still in his prime and has remained consistently productive, as Osborne has, seems premature, all the more so when that writer himself doesn't anticipate any diminution in his energies, as the last sentence of Osborne's statement on his fiftieth birthday makes evident, "Politicians of fifty are in their prime," he remarked, "So are people in my trade."[75]

Still the fact that Osborne has remained so productive means that he already has a considerable achievement that will endure regardless of what shape the rest of his life will take. On the other hand, to say this isn't to deny that there are reservations I would express about his work to date. In the first place, while Osborne reveals great talent in portraying the anguish and insecurities that love relationships can generate, he doesn't have a lot to say about happiness in love. Or, when he does, it tends at least recently to be near sentimental or facile. Besides the turgidity of the Chap's peroration to womanhood, to which I've already alluded in some detail, there is an episode in one of his most recent plays, The End of Me Old Cigar, that involves a very straight middle aged couple, both of them married, who meet in a high class house of prostitution and fall in love during the night they spend with each other. That two such people could fall in love under such circumstances is somewhat questionable. However, a more serious problem is that they do it with too much ease. Even in Shakespeare's romantic comedies, love at first sight presents considerable difficulty and even doubt. Moreover, the couple reveal a certain amount of sexual chauvinism that seems to diminish their relationship's value. Possibly Osborne is still so much aware of the pain of loving that he is just groping towards something more light-hearted, or he is going too far too quickly in that direction.

In the second place, while many of Osborne's lesser characters, such as Alison, Billy Rice, Phoebe, Hans Luther, the generals in A Patriot for Me, Tizon and Gerardo in A Bond Honoured, Annie in The Hotel in Amsterdam, and Lamb and Mrs. James in West of Suez, are interesting and sharply delineated, they aren't nearly as well realized as are the main characters in these respective plays. This is not to mention how shallow are the minor characters, such as Murray, Pauline

227

(Pamela's half sister), and even her mother in Time Present, or possibly even to a degree Frank and Jean, the two of Archie's children who do appear in The Entertainer. I don't mean to imply that this limitation automatically diminishes the stature or force of the main character, although this comes close to happening in Time Present, or that all of the characters in a play have to be realized to the same degree. Rather it is that the scope of the play becomes somewhat narrower, although exactly how much is debatable.

In the third place, Osborne, although consistently productive, simply hasn't maintained the level of his work from 1956-1971, since only two of the plays I've focussed on, A Sense of Detachment and Watch It Come Down, have been written after this time. What is more, even in the period from 1956-1971, there are two other plays I haven't mentioned, namely Under Plain Cover and A Subject of Scandal and Concern, that represent a considerable achievement, although not comparable to those works I have discussed.

The first, which resembles a revue in its use of skits, portrays a young married couple who have a great time acting out a lot of their sexual fantasies or fetishes. They do so by making up skits involving various sexual role relations, not unlike those in Genet's The Maids and The Balcony. However, they do so in a more low keyed manner and with more enjoyment. Unfortunately, the play takes a sudden tragic turn that changes its tone and thrust in too one sided a manner. This occurs when a newspaper reporter, on the alert for a scandal that would excite readers, discovers that the couple, unknown to each other, are really brother and sister. From this point on, the play like another early Osborne work I haven't explored, a political satire entitled The World of Paul Slickey, becomes a vehicle for a strident and clumsy attack by Osborne on unscrupulous newspaper editors who care more about expanding their circulation than they do the lives of people they expose to generate reader interest.

The other is his first television play, which centers on the career of George Holyoake, an actual historical figure, who was the last person in England to be convicted of blasphemy. A quiet, modest man for whom public speaking was very painful, Holyoake, nevertheless, took it upon himself in his spare time to appear before small groups to express his opposition to the Poor Laws. He did so, not because he was a passionate reformer, but because he felt as a concerned citizen that some one had to sensitize people to the issues involved. At one such meeting, in answer to a question as to what steps should be taken to help the poor, Holyoake suggested that one thing would be for the clergy to cut their salaries voluntarily, to call attention to the great inequities existing between rich and poor in England. Holyoake singled out the clergy because he felt that, although grossly underpaid themselves, they were the group that by virtue of their choice of profession should want to set an example to the rest of society. In presenting his proposal, Holyoake made it clear that he was speaking only for himself and wasn't attacking religion. Nor did his audience feel that he was since no one challenged him or seemed upset afterwards. However, a few days later a local newspaper, looking for some way to stir up its readers, publicized the remarks and subsequently demanded that Holyoake be prosecuted under the provisions of the almost forgotten statute of blasphemy. Because of the newspaper's strong pressure, local officials ultimately did indict Holyoake. Stunned by the revelation that a so called liberal society could act so intolerantly, Holyoake determined to undertake his own defense to maximize the issues involved or, to use a current phrase, to make his case openly political. Even though doing so made it likely he would get a prison sentence, particularly since the trial judge warned Holyoake that he was putting himself at an unfair disadvantage as a novice in the law, the latter pressed his case. Although convicted, Holyoake also discovered in the process how articulate, independent, principled, and determined a man he really was, a far cry from the diffident, conventional person he (and others) always assumed that he was. Moreover, he realized that under the pressure of the trial, the authorities weren't as fair as they professed because they couldn't brook his opposition. Proud as he was of his real identity, Holyoake found himself paying a considerable price for becoming so strong. His wife, who was a very conventional person and a member of a higher social class than he, found herself uncomfortable and couldn't forgive Holyoake for placing such a burden on her. As for Holyoake himself, he discovered in jail that in his new role he was having difficulty expressing his natural affection for people. At the same time he also realized that his reactions were making the authorities uncomfortable because, much as they wanted to, they couldn't feel kindly towards him since his opposition made them feel threatened. In the end, Holyoake chose to minimize some of his differences with the prison authorities because he realized how much he had to express affection towards others and how much the latter wanted to do so towards him but couldn't. The play arouses interest because of Osborne's complex presentation of Holyoake's dilemma as a man who discovers in a crisis strengths within himself that he never before knew he possessed but which also make him unhappy and misunderstood. Aware of both his strengths and his need for others, Holyoake makes painful choices that enable him to live with himself and his fellow men more harmoniously and for his society to become more resilient and tolerant. To a considerable extent, Holyoake reminds us of Luther (and not surprisingly since the two plays were written at about the same time) since each main character discovers the force of his conscience and what it impels him to do. However, Holyoake feels more acutely the impact of that conscience on others and in turn how that impact affects him.

If we are left with the clear evidence that Osborne's work in his first fifteen years overshadows that of the last ten, still an impressive achievement remains for the entire twenty-five years.

In the first place, during the past ten years even in lesser works I haven't discussed, Osborne has extended in interesting ways some of the concerns that dominate his major plays. The first is The End of Me Old Cigar, a short play to which I've already alluded, for its facile presentation of love at first sight. In actuality, the play centers on the efforts of its main character, Lady Regina a clever, articulate, and aggressive lower middle class woman who has made a great success of an exclusive house of prostitution that caters to well known people in public life, to blackmail the latter into passing feminist legislation in Parliament. Unknown to her clients, Regina with the aid of her lover, a former small time music group manager and gambler, has been televising all her clients' assignations through one way mirrors. Since English women are far from liberated, Regina's aim would seem to be worthwhile and make her seem like an authentic Osborne main character who wants to attack the hypocrisy and corruption of her society. However, on closer examination, we see that Regina differs from the other Osborne characters. She is glib and patronizing as shown in the condescending way she extols the virtues of Mozart to her lover who has never even heard of him (as she obviously knew from the start). Much to

Regina's surprise, her lover, whom she regards as such a dim wit, sells out to a newspaper reporter and makes off with the films and her resources which she shares with him in a joint bank account. If the reversal seems one sided, it does permit Osborne to show us that it is possible to be articulate, passionate, and anti-establishment and yet be just as corrupt as the establishment people themselves. Whatever else the play does, it reveals that Osborne can satirize his own brand of characters.

At first glance, the second example I would emphasize, Osborne's adaptation of Shakespeare's Coriolanus, doesn't seem to represent much of an achievement since he has made few changes in the original.

Osborne has transposed the setting to the present, and he has added a scene at the beginning in which Coriolanus, troubled by all the pressures mounting on him, especially from the volatile political situation, his mother's efforts to realize her ambitions through him, and his own self doubts occurring in a mid-life crisis, wakes up early and ruminates about how to cope with what is occurring. In addition, he has added a speech at the end, just before Aufidius and his followers close in to kill Coriolanus, in which the latter criticizes his rival for being cynical and opportunistic, and he has compressed speeches from the play as well as changed its language into prose. Yet these few alterations produce a very different play. They do so not only because Osborne's version becomes more low keyed, especially through the compression and the switch to prose, but because Osborne's Coriolanus turns out to be much more deliberate, flexible, and self aware than Shakespeare's hero. Yet for these very reasons, given the personalities of those around him, he remains deeply affected by them. For example, when his mother urges him to placate the common people and the Tribunes by using expediency as he does on the battlefield, Coriolanus objects that this doesn't do credit to his principles. Nevertheless, he agrees because he trusts his mother and feels that he can meet the challenge presented by the many divergent pressures operating on him. While he does infuriate the common people by denouncing them and their leaders, the Tribunes, he does so deliberately in order not to compromise his principles. Consequently, he openly indicates how contemptuous he feels of the Tribunes and to a lesser extent the common people because they are opportunistic and almost paranoid in their distrust of him. Later, when he accedes to his mother's plea that he spare Rome, he also does so deliberately. Although his mother doesn't understand how much she has hurt him by her earlier advice, she is helping him. By acceding to her pleas, he acts more in accordance with his principles than would be the case were he to destroy Rome in order to satisfy his wounded pride. Finally, by denouncing Aufidius as he does at far greater length than in Shakespeare and in different terms, Coriolanus understands more deeply what has occurred, and he accepts a much greater share of responsibility than is true in Shakespeare's play. Both Shakespeare and Osborne portray Coriolanus as a spectacular failure, but they do so quite differently. Shakespeare's hero is interesting because so much of the time he remains a churlish, willful, and rash boy dominated by a mother to whom he gives unquestioning, if at times begrudging, love. Osborne's hero is interesting because most of those around him, except possibly his wife, project onto him their notions of what he is to satisfy their needs. While Osborne's Coriolanus realizes that his peers and intimates don't do him justice, he accepts their advice because he overvalues their integrity and possibly underestimates his own needs. Although in both versions Coriolanus ends up alone, Shakespeare's hero only vaguely surmises what has occurred and is far from secure, whereas Osborne's hero is secure enough within himself to understand and accept what has happened.

From all I've been saying, it would appear that A Place Calling Itself Rome (the title of Osborne's play) should receive far more attention than I've given it, perhaps even receiving a separate chapter. Certainly the play, even though as yet unproduced, has a lot to commend it. Yet, curiously, its major limitation really is that Osborne, in transforming it at the same time that he remains so close to it, especially in language and basic scenic structure, is almost presenting two plays concurrently. While this represents a brilliant kind of sleight of hand achievement, it does justice neither to Shakespeare's talents nor Osborne's own.

The third example I would emphasize is Osborne's dramatization of Oscar Wilde's novel, The Picture of Dorian Gray. To an even greater extent than the adaptation of Coriolanus, the play represents less of an original contribution by Osborne. Accordingly, this limits claims we can make for it as a significant work by him. Yet, paradoxically, these very limits enhance both Wilde's book and reveal something important about

Osborne's development.

Except for adding stage directions, changing pronoun references from third to first in some introspective passages in the second half of the novel that Osborne compresses into a soliloquy, leaving the painting in ruins after Dorian stabs it, rather than having it return to its original splendor as it does in the novel, and leaving out the moralizing passages where Dorian belabors the deepening corruption that his outward beauty conceals, Osborne remains faithful to Wilde's work. So far as I can tell, every word of the dialogue is pure Wilde. However, one clear result is that we can experience a great deal of the novel in dramatic terms that possibly heighten Wilde's verbal brilliance. In particular, I would emphasize passages in which Lord Henry's one liners represent a superb combination of perverted idealism, pure wish fulfillment, and dazzling half truths. For these reasons he fascinates and demoralizes Dorian. A second result is that Osborne accentuates and clarifies a major thrust of the book--its portrayal of a corrupt society in which people hold onto values they no longer believe in because they are afraid to search for others. To conceal such apprehensions, as well as provide some stability in their lives and an outlet for their energies, the people in this play express themselves through social conventions and role playing. For example, Basil desperately tries to adhere to the sanctimonious conventions of Victorian propriety because he feels guilty about the egotism and sensual aspects of his own nature which his painting of Dorian revealed to him. Lord Henry, in contrast, brilliantly ridicules these same conventions. He does so partly because he sees through them, but also to conceal from himself many of his own repressed feelings and thereby take responsibility for them. Instead, he advances the value of art for art's sake as a substitute for moral action. It is into a society such as this that Dorian arrives as a naïve, gifted but insecure young man who desperately needs some people he admires to help him literally discover who he is. While both Basil and Lord Henry help Dorian considerably, both also harm him because they try to live vicariously through him and to divert attention away from their own insecurities and fears. Basil at first sets up Dorian as an alter ego for the sensuality he recognizes in his own nature. However, when Dorian then expresses that sensuality and egotism recklessly in his rejection of Sybil Vane, Basil becomes horrified and demands of Dorian that he reject such impulses completely. Lord Henry, while supporting Dorian in these very efforts, can't recognize the changes they bring about in the latter because to do so would force him to confront the nihilism that underlies his own behavior. As a result, Lord Henry rejects Dorian's efforts to describe his real nature to him. Through his involvement with his two friends, Dorian does begin to see himself more clearly and trust some of his feelings, although at first he resists the effort strenuously as his murder of Basil clearly shows. Yet, while becoming more open and honest with himself and ultimately a better person who wants to do good, Dorian also feels a greater need for feedback from Lord Henry in particular. He feels this desire to experience his real self more accurately and understand his society better, especially when he is discovering, as Redl does in A Patriot For Me, how corrupt that society really is. Up to a point, Dorian resembles Redl since he acts out in his own life impulses which his society can't openly accept but which it also can't repress. Furthermore, like Redl, Dorian by his appearance and manners serves as a model for what his society supposedly values. However, Dorian has less of an opportunity to realize himself through achievement, and he experiences in a more disquieting manner the conflicts and fears that undermine his society since he remains even more isolated. Redl can tell Viktor how much he cares for him and even attempt to explain to the generals why their society is so corrupt. However, Lord Henry dismisses as absurd Dorian's efforts to reveal that he is both a murderer and some one who tried to save a woman who loved him from the pain of rejection. In stabbing the picture (which remains in ruins) and turning into an old man, Dorian accepts his nature fully and irrevocably.

What is interesting about Osborne's presentation of Dorian, especially when the latter doesn't moralize sanctimoniously as he does in the novel, is his unremitting effort to get to the bottom of his own feelings and to do so on his own. While Dorian may not be any more alone than Maitland or Leonido, he does have to go further to discover his real self and to come to terms with his society.

The play is a considerable achievement and yet, because it remains so close to the book within the limits that Osborne sets, it can't qualify as a major effort on Osborne's part. Still, his dramatization reveals his deepening exploration of the concerns that dominate his best work.

In the second place, just the twelve plays I've discussed in depth, with the possible exception of Time
Present and A Sense of Detachment, are likely to remain
among the enduring works of modern drama of the past
thirty years. I would exclude Time Present because a
considerable amount of the dialogue seems like "in"
talk of the British theatre that is too narrowly topical to retain interest in subsequent years. While A
Sense of Detachment reveals an original way of becoming
more open and self accepting through feedback from
role playing and improvisation drawn from a wide
variety of sources, it is limited because some of the
immediate situations from which the improvisations
originate are also narrowly topical. Another problem
is that, since the main characters are so clearly
typed, it might be difficult to become very much
involved with them especially when they also might
seem dated to subsequent audiences.

To refine my assessment of Osborne's major work even
more, I would say that Look Back in Anger, The Entertainer, Luther, Inadmissible Evidence, A Patriot For
Me, West of Suez, and possibly The Hotel in Amsterdam
represent significant enduring works in British drama
of all time and modern drama of the past century. I
say this because of the range and diversity of their
themes; the complex and moving portrayal of the main
characters as revealed in the expressiveness and articulateness of their language; the varied dramatic
structures that give the plays their momentum, impact,
and resonance; and the creation--or at least the
evocation--of a distinctive outside world that significantly affects what happens to the main characters
and those around them. It is possible that The Hotel
in Amsterdam may not quite measure up to the others
I've mentioned, mainly because the references to the
London from which the characters have fled are vague
and because most of the secondary characters are flat.
However, Laurie is so open and expressive about his
hangups and so genuinely modest and loyal to those for
whom he cares that he just about compensates for these
or other limitations the play may reveal.

At a somewhat lower level of achievement, I would
place Epitaph for George Dillon, A Bond Honoured, and
Watch It Come Down. In Epitaph for George Dillon
Osborne doesn't consistently sustain George's articulateness that is so effectively rendered in his long
scene with Ruth in Act II. A Bond Honoured, despite
the originality of Osborne's portrayal of Leonido's
deep seated insecurity and the brilliance and

235

evocativeness of its repartee, may, as I indicated in discussion, be just too compressed to do full justice to its material. Yet A Bond Honoured undeniably is a greatly underrated work that should merit better response than its limited production received. As for Watch It Come Down, it, too, is compressed in its delineation of the background lives of its characters; its lesser figures such as Shirley and Raymond don't seem very distinctive; and the outside world about which the characters lament so much in their "love in" in Act I seems, as indicated, too personalized and vague to justify their disappointment. Nevertheless, no other Osborne play presents such quick, sharp, varying but interrelated, contrasts of mood, dialogue, and action that reveal the particular extremes of love and hate that characterize this play.

Finally, to make even more pointed the full range of Osborne's achievement to date, I would relate his work to that of two major modern dramatists to whom he bears the most striking affinities, namely Ibsen and Chekhov, and in his own time that of his contemporary, Harold Pinter, with whom he has the most in common.

Like Osborne's characters, those of Ibsen and Chekhov are articulate or certainly strive to be so, have deep, conflicting feelings about self worth, the desire to love and be loved, and their role in their society through which they try to realize themselves and within which many of them (particularly in Ibsen) feel uncomfortable and of which they can be highly critical.

What differentiates Ibsen from Osborne is that many of the former's characters have a more romantic and grandiose self conception, are more unremittingly driven and restless, and more demanding of others, though not necessarily of themselves. On the other hand, Osborne's characters are more acutely self aware and probably more self honest, more troubled by guilt and self doubt, more modest and down to earth, and more concerned with others and their society in which they would like to feel at peace. If they generally do not aspire as highly as Brand Solness of The Master Builder and Rubek of When We Dead Awaken, they do not, quite literally, fall so precipitously. Quite possibly, Ibsen's most outstanding characters experience their conflicts more explosively and irrevocably in escalating dramatic tensions that have a momentum and finality that Osborne's plays don't attain.

In comparison to those of Osborne, a number of Chekhov's characters question more poignantly the value of their existence and human life itself, seem more profoundly aware of the depths of frustration that result from unfulfilled or disappointed aspirations, and are more consistently involved in a circle of lives to which their own are bound and yet from which they may also feel detached. On the other hand, Osborne's characters pinpoint their conflicts more accurately, struggle harder to cope with them, and are more deeply involved in their society and yet probably more deeply critical of many of its conventions and values. Both writers' characters express themselves with unusual articulateness and a great range of nuance about some of their most minute and intimate feelings. Whether any individual Chekhov character achieves the resonance and sustained impact of Jimmy, Luther, Maitland, or even in different ways Leonido or Laurie may be debatable. On the other hand, none of Osborne's works achieve the range of interplay of so many fully realized and diverse characters that give Chekhov's four major plays their particular orchestrated richness and dissonance of thought and feeling.

When we come closer to home, we find that Osborne's work seems closest to that of Harold Pinter in themes and characterization. To say this doesn't mean that there aren't other important figures in contemporary British drama, for certainly John Arden, Edward Bond, and David Storey have made significant contributions. However, Arden and Bond write from a more openly political, economic, and sociological perspective than does Osborne. As a result, they concentrate more on ideological clashes and less on the dynamics of interpersonal relationships and the complexities of individual characters' self realization. Although David Storey does explore conflicts in interpersonal relations to a considerable degree, he doesn't, except in The Restoration of Arnold Middleton or possibly in In Celebration, explore in depth well developed main characters who profoundly experience their insecurities in efforts towards self realization. Rather in plays such as The Contractor or The Changing Room, whatever complexity in interpersonal relations that exists derives more from the interplay of many characters, virtually none of whom are presented in any great depth or in sustained self confrontation.

Harold Pinter, on the other hand, does explore individual characters in depth and in interpersonal conflicts as he portrays how unhappy, frustrated, and even trapped people can be because they are dominated by, if not atrophied by, earlier experiences that make them feel insecure and distrustful. While Pinter's characters need others for love, feedback, and personal security, they also find it necessary to construct elaborate defenses through which they seek to limit such relationships and to deal with a threatening outside world.

Clearly Pinter, like Osborne, also has a lot to say about vulnerability especially in regard to self worth, love relationships, and involvement in society. In particular, he concerns himself with closed in, distrustful people, deeply hurt by past experiences and relationships with which they have difficulty coming to terms, and even at times discovering, and which make them feel withdrawn, if not alienated, from their society. Although Osborne's characters experience many of these same dilemmas, they generally confront them more knowingly, openly, and hopefully, as well as demand more from themselves and possibly less from others. While both writers portray characters who are uncomfortable in their societies, Osborne's struggle more to resolve their difficulties and to concern themselves with what, if anything, they can do to make conditions any better. To sum up, I would emphasize that Pinter delineates with great evocative poignancy a dramatic world that may be more homogeneous and sharply etched than Osborne's. On the other hand, Osborne's world is larger, more open and hopeful than Pinter's.

FOOTNOTES

1. J. W. Lambert in a review of Watch It Come Down, Drama, No. 121 (Summer 1976), p. 41.

2. Robert Cushman in his review of Watch It Come Down in The Observer Review, 29 Feb. 1976.

3. Although I could cite many such articles or reviews, here are three that make Osborne's characters sound like chronic complainers—and little else: John Simon's review of Luther in The Hudson Review, 16 (1963), 584-585; Philip French's review of Time Present in The New Statesman and Nation, 76 (31 May 1968); and Hilary Spurling's review of the same play in The Spectator, 220 (31 May 1968), 752.

4. Willard Gaylin, Caring (New York: Alfred A. Knopf, 1976), p. 164.

5. Erik Erikson, Childhood and Society (New York: W. W. Norton, 1962), p. 7.

6. Gaylin, op. cit., p. 164.

7. Eric Fromm, The Art of Loving (New York: Harper and Row, 1956), p. 9.

8. R. D. Laing, The Politics of Experience (New York: Pantheon, 1967), p. 10.

9. These include the following: Martin Banham, Osborne (Edinburgh: Oliver and Boyd, 1969); Alan Carter, John Osborne (Edinburgh: Oliver and Boyd, 1969; rev. ed., 1971); Harold Ferrar, John Osborne (New York: Columbia Univ. Press, 1973); Ronald Hayman, John Osborne (London: Heinemann, 1968; rev. ed., 1972); and Simon Trussler, The Plays of John Osborne (London: Victor Gollancz, Ltd., 1969). The revisions consist only of brief, summary discussions of West of Suez, and three of the books—Banham's, Ferrar's, and Hayman's—are intended only as brief introductory studies.

10. Mary Holland, Plays and Players, 19 (Oct. 1971), p. 38.

11. Helen Dawson, The Observer Review, 22 Aug. 1971.

12. Benedict Nightingale, <u>The New Statesman and Nation</u>, 84 (8 Dec. 1972), 875.

13. Michael Billington, <u>The Guardian</u>, 7 Dec. 1972.

14. J. W. Lambert, <u>The Sunday Times</u>, 22 Feb. 1976. However, in a later review, <u>Drama</u>, <u>op. cit.</u>, pp. 40-43, Lambert speaks more favorably of the play.

15. Robert Cushman, <u>The Observer Review</u>, op. cit., 29 Feb. 1976. B. A. Young, <u>The Financial Times</u>, 25 Feb. 1976.

16. Frank Marcus, <u>The Sunday Telegraph</u>, 29 Feb. 1976.

17. John Osborne, <u>A Better Class of Person</u> (London: Faber and Faber, 1981; New York: E. P. Dutton, 1981).

18. John Freeman, edited version of interview in "Face to Face" on BBC, 21 Jan. 1967. In Walter Wager, ed., <u>The Playwrights Speak</u> (New York: Delacorte Press, 1967), p. 98.

19. "They Call It Cricket," in <u>Declaration</u>, ed. Tom Maschler (London: McGibbon and Kee, 1957), p. 84.

20. <u>Ibid</u>.

21. "A Letter to My Fellow Countrymen," <u>Tribune</u>, 13 May 1960. (Reprinted in John Russell Taylor, ed., <u>Look Back in Anger: A Casebook</u>, <u>op. cit</u>., pp. 67-69.)

22. Osborne explains his purpose in an interview with Terry Coleman, <u>The Guardian</u>, 8 Aug. 1971, as well as in that with Freeman, in Wager, <u>op. cit</u>., pp. 107-108. Cf. also Osborne's letter to <u>The Times</u>, London, 3 Sept. 1968, in which he apologizes for having written this piece.

23. John Osborne, "Foreword" to <u>Look Back in Anger</u>, Evans Acting Editions (London, n.d.) p. 3.

24. Interview with Kenneth Tynan, <u>The Observer Review</u>, 7 July 1968.

25. <u>Ibid</u>.

26. Quoted in <u>The Chronicle</u>, Willimantic, Connecticut, 12 Dec. 1979, p. 2.

27. Kenneth Tynan, The Observer Review, 16 Feb. 1958.

28. Simon Trussler, op. cit., p. 38.

29. Ibid., p. 39.

30. Arthur Schlesinger, Jr., "Look Back in Amazement," The New Republic, 137 (23 Dec. 1957), 19-21.

31. John Osborne, op. cit., Evans Acting Edition, p. 4.

32. As Osborne himself points out in ibid., "Only a sensitive, intelligent spirit is capable of playing." This is another way of corroborating the hopefulness that emerges, however tentatively, at the end.

33. In conservation with the author in April 1969 in his office in The Observer Review (London).

34. I base this observation primarily on revivals I saw in 1969 at the Nottingham Theatre and the Tower Theatre in London. In both cases audiences scarcely responded to references to Suez. (I did not see the Max Wall revival in 1974.)

35. "They Call It Cricket," op. cit., p. 69.

36. Erik Erikson, Young Man Luther (New York: W. W. Norton, 1962), p. 74.

37. I am referring to Daniel J. Levinson, The Seasons of a Man's Life (New York: Alfred A. Knopf, 1978), which extends some of Erikson's perceptions.

38. Simon Trussler, op. cit., p. 96.

39. Erik Erikson, Childhood and Society, op. cit., pp. 259-260.

40. This, of course, is just an impression, but it does come from reading selections from Luther's work in at least two collections: Luther, ed. Ian Siggins (New York: Barnes and Noble, 1972), and Reformation Writings of Martin Luther, ed. Bertram Lee Woolf (New York: Philosophical Library, 1953), Vol. I.

41. "Sex and Failure," The Observer Review, 20 Jan. 1957. Reprinted in Gene Feldman and Max Gartenberg, eds., The Beat Generation (New York: Citadel Press, 1958),

p. 317.

42. Simon Trussler, op. cit., p. 136.

43. Robert Asprey, The Panther's Feast (New York: Putnam, 1959) appears to be Osborne's main source.
However, Osborne has made numerous changes. In
Asprey's book Redl was a homosexual as an adolescent and was much less complex, self aware, and
self honest than in the play.

44. Asprey, op. cit., pp. 245-247.

45. Irving Wardle, The Times, London, 1 July 1965.

46. John Osborne, "Prefatory Comment," A Bond Honoured
(London: Faber and Faber, 1965), p. 2.

47. Willis Barnstone, "The Outrageous Saint, by Lope de
Vega," The Tulane Drama Review, 7 (Fall 1962), 58-
108.

48. Willis Barnstone, "Lope's Leonido, An Existential
Hero," The Tulane Drama Review, 7 (Fall 1962), 56.

49. The Times, London, 8 June 1966, summarizes many of
the basically unfavorable reviews.

50. Simon Trussler, op. cit., pp. 152-53.

51. Alan Carter, op. cit., p. 125.

52. Martin Banham, op. cit., p. 77.

53. Mervyn Jones, Tribune, 19 and 26 Aug. 1966.

54. Daniel Rogers, "'Not for Insolence, but seriously,'
John Osborne's Adaptation of La Fianza satisfecha,"
Durham University Journal, N.S., No. 29 (1968),
146-150.

55. Ibid., p. 155.

56. Mervyn Jones, op. cit., Tribune, 26 Aug. 1966.

57. Erik Erikson, op. cit., p. 162.

58. Willis Barnstone, "The Outrageous Saint," op. cit.,
p. 92.

59. Ronald Bryden, The Observer Review, 7 July 1968.

60. Margaret Marshall, _The Nation_, 158 (5 Feb. 1944), 167.

61. Philip French, _The New Statesman and Nation_, 12 July 1968.

62. Cf. John Weightman, _Encounter_, 37 (Nov. 1971), 58.

63. Irving Wardle, _The Times_, London, 18 Aug. 1971.

64. Interview with Kenneth Tynan, _op. cit._, 7 July 1968.

65. Benedict Nightingale, _The New Statesman and Nation_, op. cit., p. 875.

66. Besides the obvious similarities mentioned, there are also specific "in group" references by Sally at the end of the play to people such as Lady Cunard and George ("Dadie") Rylands who were close to Strachey. Apart from Strachey, these references in the play would be pointless. Cf. Michael Holroyd, _Lytton Strachey: A Critical Biography_ (London: Heinemann, 1967), II, 359-60, 444-445, 648-649, and 695.

67. _Ibid._, pp. 704-706.

68. Michael Billington, _The Guardian_, 25 Feb. 1976.

69. Alan Brien, _Plays and Players_, 23 (April 1976), 25.

70. Robert Cushman, _The Observer Review_, _op. cit._, 29 Feb. 1976.

71. Dora de Houghton Carington, _Letters and Extracts from Her Diaries_ (New York: Holt, Rinehart and Winston, 1977), pp. 488-500. Also cf. Michael Holroyd, _op. cit._, II, 708-713.

72. _Ibid._, p. 708.

73. This comment seems to provide additional corroborative evidence that Glen seems modeled on Lytton Strachey, since the latter, as Holroyd tells us, remarked just before dying: "If this is dying, I don't think much of it" (_ibid._, p. 706).

74. Quoted in _Newsletter_, Meeting House Singles, Hartford, Connecticut, March 1979.

75. The Chronicle, Willimantic, Connecticut, op. cit. (12 Dec. 1979), p. 2.

BIBLIOGRAPHY

I. Plays for Stage and Television by John Osborne

A Bond Honoured. London: Faber and Faber, 1966.

The End of Me Old Cigar and Jill and Jack, A Play for Television. London: Faber and Faber, 1975.

The Entertainer. London: Faber and Faber, 1957.

Epitaph for George Dillon (with Anthony Creighton). London: Faber and Faber, 1958.

The Gift of Friendship, A Play for Television. London: Faber and Faber, 1972.

Hedda Gabler (adapted from Henrik Ibsen). London: Faber and Faber, 1972.

Inadmissible Evidence. London: Faber and Faber, 1965.

Look Back in Anger. London: Faber and Faber, 1957; New York: S. G. Phillips, 1957.

Luther. London: Faber and Faber, 1961.

A Patriot for Me. London: Faber and Faber, 1966.

The Picture of Dorian Gray (a dramatization of Oscar Wilde's novel). London: Faber and Faber, 1974.

A Place Calling Itself Rome (a reworking of Shakespeare's Coriolanus). London: Faber and Faber, 1973.

Plays for England: "The Blood of the Bambergs," "Under Plain Cover." London: Faber and Faber, 1963.

The Right Prospectus, A Play for Television. London: Faber and Faber, 1970.

A Sense of Detachment. London: Faber and Faber, 1973.

A Subject of Scandal and Concern, A Play for Television. London: Faber and Faber, 1961.

Time Present and The Hotel in Amsterdam. London: Faber and Faber, 1968.

Very Like a Whale, A Play for Television. London:

Faber and Faber, 1972.

Watch It Come Down. London: Faber and Faber, 1975.

West of Suez. London: Faber and Faber, 1971.

The World of Paul Slickey. London: Faber and Faber, 1959.

You're Not Watching Me Mummy and Try a Little Tenderness, Two Plays for Television. London: Faber and Faber, 1978.

II. Screenplays by John Osborne

"The Charge of the Light Brigade," 1962. Screenplay by John Osborne and Charles Wood. Directed by Tony Richardson. A Woodfall Production.

"The Entertainer," 1960. Screenplay by John Osborne and Nigel Kneale. Directed by Tony Richardson. A Woodfall Production.

"Inadmissible Evidence," 1968. Screenplay by John Osborne. Directed by Anthony Page. A Woodfall Production.

"Look Back in Anger," 1959. Screenplay by Nigel Kneale, with additional dialogue by John Osborne. Directed by Tony Richardson. A Woodfall Production.

"Tom Jones," 1962. Screenplay by John Osborne. Directed by Tony Richardson. A Woodfall Production. Published: London: Faber and Faber, 1964.

III. Miscellaneous Prose by John Osborne

"The American Theatre." In Encore, 6 (March-April 1959), 17-21.

"Berliner Ensemble." The Times, London, 15 Sept. 1963, p. 13.

A Better Class of Person. London: Faber and Faber, 1981; New York: E. P. Dutton, 1981.

"Come On In: The Revolution Is Just Beginning." Tribune, 27 March 1959.

"The Entertainer." In Writer's Theatre. Ed. Keith
  Waterhouse and Willis Hall. London: Heineman,
  1967, p. 51.

"Dr. Agostinho Neto." The Times, London, 7 Oct. 1961,
  p. 13. (Letter to the editor signed by others.)

"The Epistle to the Philistines." Tribune, 13 May
  1960, p. 9. Reprinted in Look Back in Anger: A
  Casebook. Ed. John Russell Taylor. London:
  Macmillan, 1968, pp. 62-63.

"Foreword to Look Back in Anger." In Look Back in
  Anger, Evans Acting Editions. London, n.d., pp.
  2-4.

"Intellectuals and Just Causes: A Symposium."
  Encounter, 29 (September 1967), 3-4.

"Introduction." In International Theatre Annual, Number Two. Ed. Harold Hobson. London: Calder,
  1957, pp. 9-10.

"Letter to the Editor." The Spectator, 198 (12 April
  1957), 486.

"A Letter to My Fellow Countrymen." Tribune, 13 May
  1960. Reprinted in Look Back in Anger: A Casebook.
  Ed. John Russell Taylor. London: Macmillan, 1968,
  pp. 67-69.

"On Critics and Criticism." The Sunday Telegraph,
  August 1966, p. 6.

"On the Thesis Business and the Seekers After the Bare
  Approximate." The Times, London, 14 Oct. 1967,
  p. 20c.

"The Pioneer at the Royal Court: George Devine." The
  Observer Review, 23 Jan. 1966.

"Playwrights and South Africa." The Times, London,
  16 May 1968, p. 13e.

"Revolt in Cuba." The Times, London, 19 Apr. 1961.
  (Letter to the editor signed by others.)

"Sex and Failure." The Observer Review, 20 Jan. 1957.
  Reprinted in The Beat Generation. Ed. Gene Feldman
  and Max Gartenberg. New York: Citadel Press, 1958,

pp. 316-319.

"That Awful Museum." *Twentieth Century*, 99 (Feb. 1961),
212-216. Reprinted in *Look Back in Anger: A Casebook*. Ed. John Russell Taylor. London: Macmillan,
1968, pp. 63-67.

"They Call It Cricket." In *Declaration*. Ed. Tom
Maschler. London: McGibbon and Kee, 1957, pp. 61-84.

"Threat to a Theatre for Nottingham." *The Times*, London,
4 June 1960, p. 7. (Letter to editor also signed by
others.)

"Transatlantic Air Race." *The Times*, London, 12 May
1969, p. 11.

"Trial of Two Rolling Stones: Informing the Police."
The Times, London, 14 July 1957, p. 11.

"A Weakness for Causes." *Time*, 90 (8 Sept. 1967), 45.
(Contains a quotation by Osborne criticizing people
who write letters on behalf of political causes.)

"A Working Man." *The Times*, London, 2 Sept. 1968, p. 7d.

"The Writer and His Age." *London Magazine*, 41 (May
1957), 47-49. Reprinted in *Look Back in Anger: A
Casebook*. Ed. John Russell Taylor. London: Macmillan, 1968, pp. 59-62.

IV. Interviews with John Osborne

Alvarez, A. "Osborne and the Boys at the Ball." *The
New York Times*, 28 Sept. 1969, Theatre and the Arts,
p. 1.

"Close Up." *The Observer Review*, 24 Nov. 1971..

Coleman, Terry. *The Guardian*, London, 8 Aug. 1971.

Dunn, Christine. *The Daily Mail*, 21 May 1976, p. 1.

Freeman, John. Edited version of interview in "Face to
Face" on BBC, 21 Jan. 1967. In *The Playwrights
Speak*. Ed. Walter Wager. New York: Delacorte Press,
1967, pp. 90-109.

Hancock, Robert. "Anger." *The Spectator*, 198 (5 Apr.

1957), 438-439.

"Interview with Osborne." The Guardian, London, 2 Aug. 1971.

Tynan, Kenneth. The Observer Review, 30 June and 7 July 1968.

Wyatt, Woodrow. Distinguished for Talent. London: Hutchinson, 1958, pp. 116-122. (Interview with Osborne.)

V. Articles and Books on John Osborne, Modern Drama, and Background Material

Allsop, Kenneth. The Angry Decade. London: Peter Owen, 1958, pp. 96-132.

Anderson, Michael. Anger and Detachment: A Study of Arden, Osborne, and Pinter. London: Pitman, 1976.

Asprey, Robert. The Panther's Feast. New York: Putnam, 1959.

Banham, Martin. Osborne. Edinburgh: Oliver & Boyd, 1969.

Barnstone, Willis. "Lope's Leonido, An Existential Hero." The Tulane Drama Review, 7 (Fall 1962), 56-58.

_____. "Lope de Vega's Don Leonido: A Prototype of the Traditional Don Juan." Comparative Literature Studies, 2 (1965), 101-117.

_____, trans. "The Outrageous Saint by Lope de Vega." The Tulane Drama Review, 7 (Fall 1962), 58-108.

Bierhaus, E. G., Jr. "No World of Its Own: Look Back in Anger Twenty Years Later." Modern Drama, 19 (1976), 47-55.

Brown, John Russell. Theatre Language: A Study of Arden, Osborne, Pinter, and Wesker. New York: Taplinger, 1972.

_____, ed. Modern British Dramatists. Englewood Cliffs, N.J.: Prentice-Hall, 1968.

Brown, John Russell and Bernard Harris, eds. Contemporary Theatre. London: Edward J. Arnold, 1962.

Calvocoressi, Peter. The British Experience, 1945-76. New York: Pantheon, 1978.

Carington, Dora de Houghton. Letters and Extracts from Her Diaries. New York: Holt, Rinehart and Winston, 1977.

Carter, Alan. John Osborne. Edinburgh: Oliver & Boyd, 1969; 2nd ed., rev., 1971.

Denty, Vera D. "The Psychology of Martin Luther." Catholic World, 194 (Nov. 1961), 99-105.

Dyson, A. E. "Look Back in Anger." Critical Quarterly, 1 (Winter 1959), 318-326. Reprinted in Modern British Dramatists. Ed. John Russell Brown. Englewood Cliffs, N.J.: Prentice-Hall, 1968, pp. 47-58.

Erikson, Erik. Childhood and Society. New York: W. W. Norton, 1962.

_____. Identity and the Life Cycle. New York: W. W. Norton, 1979.

_____. Identity, Youth and Crisis. New York: W. W. Norton, 1968.

_____. Young Man Luther. New York: W. W. Norton, 1962.

_____, ed. Adulthood (essays). New York: W. W. Norton, 1978.

Evans, Gareth L. The Language of Modern Drama. London: J. M. Dent, 1977, pp. 102-113.

Faber, M. A. "The Character of Jimmy Porter: An Approach to Look Back in Anger." Modern Drama, 13 (May 1970), 67-77.

Ferrar, Harold. John Osborne. New York: Columbia Univ. Press, 1973, 48 p.

Fraser, G. S. The Modern Writer and His World. Harmondsworth: Penguin, 1964.

Fromm, Eric. The Art of Loving. New York: Harper and Row, 1956.

Gascoigne, Bamber. Twentieth Century Drama. London:
  Hutchinson, 1962.

Gaylin, Willard. Caring. New York: Alfred A. Knopf,
  1976.

_____. Feelings: Our Vital Signs. New York:
  Ballantine, 1979.

Hayman, Ronald. Contemporary Playwrights: John
  Osborne. London: Heinemann, 1968; rev. ed., 1972.

Holroyd, Michael. Lytton Strachey, A Critical Biography. 2 vols. London: Heinemann, 1967.

Hunter, G. K. "The World of John Osborne." Critical
  Quarterly, 3 (Spring 1961), 76-81.

Huss, Roy. "John Osborne's Backward Halfway Look."
  Modern Drama, 6 (May 1963), 20-25.

Kennedy, Andrew. "Old and New in London Drama."
  Modern Drama, 41 (Feb. 1969), 437-446.

_____. Six Dramatists in Search of a Language.
  Cambridge: Cambridge Univ. Press, 1975, pp. 192-213.

Kerensky, Oleg. The New British Drama: Fourteen Playwrights since Arden, Pinter, and Osborne. London:
  Hamish Hamilton, 1977.

Kitchin, Laurence. Mid Century Drama. London: Faber
  and Faber, 1960.

Laing, R. D. The Politics of Experience. New York:
  Pantheon, 1967.

Levinson, Daniel J., The Seasons of a Man's Life. New
  York: Alfred A. Knopf, 1978.

Lewis, Allan. The Contemporary Theatre. New York:
  Crown Publishers, 1971, pp. 315-335.

Luther. Ed. Ian Siggins. New York: Barnes & Noble,
  1972.

Mander, John. The Writer and Commitment. London:
  Secker and Warburg, 1961, pp. 179-211. Reprinted in
  Look Back in Anger: A Casebook. Ed. John Russell
  Taylor. London: Macmillan, 1968, pp. 143-150.

Marowitz, Charles. "The Ascension of John Osborne."
Tulane Drama Review, 7 (Winter 1962), 175-179.
Reprinted in Modern British Dramatists. Ed. John
Russell Brown. Englewood Cliffs, N.J.: Prentice-
Hall, 1968, pp. 117-122.

_____, Tom Milne, and Owen Hale, eds. The Encore
Reader: A Chronicle of the New Drama. London:
Methuen, 1965.

_____ and Simon Trussler, eds. Theatre at Work.
London: Methuen & Co., Ltd., 1967.

Marshall, Margaret. "Review of The Cherry Orchard."
The Nation, 158 (5 Feb. 1944), 167.

Maschler, Tom, ed. Declaration. London: McGibbon
and Kee, 1957.

Milne, Tom. "The Hidden Face of Violence." Encore,
7 (1960), 14-20.

Nicoll, Allardyce. "Somewhat in a New Direction."
Contemporary Theatre, 20, 77-95.

Northouse, Cameron and Thomas P. Walsh, eds. John
Osborne: A Reference Guide. Boston: G. K. Hall,
1974.

Reformation Writings of Martin Luther, ed. Bertram
Lee Woolf. New York: Philosophical Library, 1953,
Vol. I.

Rogers, Daniel. "'Not for insolence, but seriously,'
John Osborne's Adaptation of La Fianza satisfecha."
Durham University Journal, N.S., 29 (1968), 146-
170.

Rupp, E. Gordon. "John Osborne and the Historical
Luther." Expository Times, 73 (1962), 147-151.

_____. "Luther and Mr. Osborne." Cambridge
Quarterly, 1 (1965-1966), 28-42.

Seymour, Alan. "Maturing Vision." London Magazine,
5 (October 1965), 75-79.

_____. "Osborne, V.C." London Magazine, 5
(May 1965), 69-74.

Shakespeare, William. The Tragedy of Coriolanus. Ed. Harry Levin. Baltimore: Penguin Books, 1956.

Sheehy, Gail. Passages. New York: E. P. Dutton, 1976.

Taylor, John Russell. The Angry Theatre: New British Drama. New York: Hill & Wang, 1969. Revision of Anger and After. London: Methuen, 1962.

_____. The Second Wave: British Drama for the Seventies. New York: Hill & Wang, 1971.

_____, ed. Look Back in Anger: A Casebook. London: Macmillan, 1968.

The Times, London, 21 July 1977. (Article on survey about attitudes towards poverty in European Community.)

Townshend, Peter. Poverty in the United Kingdom. Berkeley: Univ. of California Press, 1979.

Trilling, Ossia. "The Young British Drama." Modern Drama, 2 (Sept. 1960), 168-177.

Trussler, Simon. The Plays of John Osborne. London: Victor Gollancz, Ltd., 1969.

Wager, Walter, ed. The Playwrights Speak. New York: Delacorte Press, 1967.

Wellworth, George A. The Theatre of Protest and Paradox. New York: New York Univ. Press, 1964, pp. 221-234. Reprinted in Look Back in Anger: A Casebook. Ed. John Russell Taylor. London: Macmillan, 1968, pp. 117-129.

Wilde, Oscar. The Picture of Dorian Gray. Introduction by Isobel Murray. London, New York: Oxford Univ. Press, 1974.

Worth, Katherine. "The Angry Young Man: John Osborne." In William A. Armstrong, ed. Experimental Drama. London: G. Bell, 1963, pp. 147-168. Also reprinted in Look Back in Anger: A Casebook. Ed. John Russell Taylor. London: Macmillan, 1968, pp. 101-117.

253

VI. Selected Reviews of Productions of
Plays by John Osborne

Epitaph for George Dillon

The Beckenham Advertiser. 6 June 1958.

Brustein, Robert. The Hudson Review, 12 (1959-60),
98-100.

The Daily Post, Liverpool. 15 February 1958.

Hatch, Robert. The Nation, 187 (22 Nov. 1958), 394-
395.

Hewes, Henry. The Saturday Review of Literature, 41
(22 Nov. 1958), 24-25.

McCarthy, Mary. "Odd Man In." The Partisan Review,
26 (Winter 1959), 100-106.

Tynan, Kenneth. The Observer Review. 16 Feb. 1958,
p. 12.

The Western Independent. 16 Feb. 1958.

Look Back in Anger

Ackeroyd, Graham. The New Statesman and Nation, 53
(26 Jan. 1957), 100.

Atkinson, Brooks. The New York Times, 2 Oct. 1957,
p. 28:2.

_____. The New York Times, 13 Oct. 1957, II, p.
1:1.

Beavan, John. Twentieth Century, 160 (July 1956),
72-74.

Clurman, Harold. The Nation, 185 (9 Oct. 1957), 272.

Corina, Leslie. The New Republic, 138 (10 Feb. 1958),
22. (Comment on Schlesinger and review.)

Coveny, Michael. Plays and Players, 20 (Feb. 1973),
39-40.

Gorer, Geofrey. _The New Statesman and Nation_, 53 (4 May 1957), 568.

Hartley, Anthony. _The Spectator_, 196 (18 May 1956), 688.

Hobson, Harold. _The Sunday Times_, 3 March 1968.

Kroll, Jack. _Newsweek_, 96 (14 July 1980), 83-84.

Mannes, Marya. _The Reporter_, 17 (14 Nov. 1957), 38-39.

Marriott, R. B. _The Stage_, 31 March 1968.

Millgate, Michael. _The New Republic_, 137 (9 Sept. 16-17.

The New Statesman and Nation, 53 (26 Jan. 1957), 100. (Letter)

Raymond, John. _The New Statesman and Nation_, 53 (19 Jan. 1957), 66-67.

Robson, Michael. _The Eastern Daily Press_, 27 Mar. 1957.

Schlesinger, Arthur, Jr. "Look Back in Amazement." _The New Republic_, 137 (23 Dec. 1957), 19-21.

Seymour, Anthony. _The Yorkshire Post_, 31 Oct. 1968.

Sutherland, Jack. _The Birmingham Post_, 31 Mar. 1968.

Tynan, Kenneth. _The Observer Review_, 3 May 1956, p. 8. Reprinted in _Look Back in Anger: A Casebook_. Ed. John Russell Raylor. London: Macmillan, 1968.

Worsley, T. C. _The New Statesman and Nation_, 56 (19 May 1956), 566.

Young, B. A. _The Financial Times_, 30 Oct. 1968.

The Entertainer

Brien, Alan. _The Spectator_, 200 (21 Feb. 1958), 232.

Clurman, Harold. _The Nation_, 186 (1 Mar. 1958), 192.

Cushman, Robert. _The Observer Review_, 11 Jan. 1975.

Findlater, Richard. <u>Tribune</u>, 19 Apr. 1957.

Gibbs, Wolcott. <u>The New Yorker</u>, 34 (22 Feb. 1958), 60-63.

Granger, Derek. <u>The Financial Times</u>, 11 Apr. 1957.

Hamilton, Iaian. <u>The Times Educational Supplement</u>, 26 Apr. 1957.

Hewes, Henry. <u>The Saturday Review of Literature</u>, 40 (11 May 1957), 26.

_____. <u>The Saturday Review of Literature</u>, 41 (1 Mar. 1958), 24.

Hobson, Harold. <u>The Sunday Times</u>, 15 Sept. 1957.

Hollis, Christopher. <u>The Spectator</u>, 199 (18 Oct. 1957), 504-505.

Mannes, Marya. <u>The Reporter</u>, 18 (20 Mar. 1958), 39-40.

Marcus, Frank. <u>The Sunday Telegraph</u>, 18 Dec. 1974.

Panter-Downes, Mollie. <u>The New Yorker</u>, 33 (28 Sept. 1957), 140-141.

Raymond, John. <u>The New Statesman and Nation</u>, 54 (12 Oct. 1957), 464.

<u>The Spectator</u>, 199 (25 Oct.-29 Nov. 1957), 544, 576, 605, 688, 746. (Comments)

Tynan, Kenneth. <u>The Observer Review</u>, 4 Apr. 1957.

Wardle, Irving. <u>The Times</u>, London, 3 Dec. 1974.

Watt, David. <u>The Spectator</u>, 198 (19 Apr. 1957), 517.

Worsley, T. C. <u>The New Statesman and Nation</u>, 52 (26 Jan. 1957), 97-98.

_____. <u>The New Statesman and Nation</u>, 53 (20 Apr. 1957), 512.

_____. <u>The New Statesman and Nation</u>, 54 (21 Sept. 1957), 343.

Clurman, Harold. The Nation, 193 (19 Oct. 1963), 244-
    246.

The Daily Mail, 28 July 1961.

The Daily Mirror, 27 July 1961.

Drama, 62 (Fall 1961), 18-19.

Gascoigne, Bamberger. The Spectator, 207 (4 Aug. 1961),
    171.

Gassner, John. Educational Theatre Journal, 12 (Dec.
    1960), 205-208.

Gilman, Richard. The Commonweal, 79 (18 Oct. 1963),
    103-104.

Hamilton, Iaian. The Times Educational Supplement,
    8 Nov. 1961.

Hobson, Harold. The Christian Science Monitor, 15 July
    1961, p. 4.

_____. The Christian Science Monitor, 5 Aug.
    1961, p. 17.

Keown, Eric. Punch, 241 (9 Aug. 1961), 220-222.

Marriott, R. B. The Stage, 3 Aug. 1961.

The Methodist Recorder, 28 Sept. 1961.

Pritchett, V. S. The New Statesman and Nation, 62
    (4 Aug. 1961), 163-164.

Simon, John. The Hudson Review, 16 (1963-64), 584-585.

Small, Christopher. The Glasgow Herald, 22 Aug. 1961.

Smallie, Rev. W. A. The Scotsman, 23 Aug. 1961.

The Stratford Upon Avon Herald, 30 June 1961.

Tynan, Kenneth. The Observer Review, 7 July 1961.

Inadmissible Evidence

Brien, Alan. The Observer Review, 13 March 1964.

_____. The Sunday Telegraph, 13 Sept. 1964.

_____. The Sunday Telegraph, 21 March 1965.

Brustein, Robert. The New Republic, 154 (1 Jan. 1966), 34-35.

Bryden, Ronald. The New Statesman and Nation, 68 (18 Sept. 1964), 410.

Burgess, Anthony. The Spectator, 214 (26 Mar. 1965), 391.

Clurman, Harold. The Nation, 201 (20 Dec. 1965), 508-509.

The Daily Mail, 2 Sept. 1964.

Frost, David. Punch, 247 (16 Sept. 1964).

Hamilton, Iaian. The Times Educational Supplement, 10 Sept. 1964.

_____. The Times Educational Supplement, 16 Jan. 1965.

Hewes, Henry. "Unsentimental Journeys." The Saturday Review of Literature, 48 (29 May 1965), 31.

_____. The Saturday Review of Literature, 48 (18 Dec. 1965), p. 43.

Hobson, Harold. The Christian Science Monitor, 14 Sept. 1964, p. 10.

_____. The Sunday Times, 13 Sept. 1964.

Holland, Mary. The Observer Review, 13 Sept. 1964.

Jones, Mervyn. Tribune, 18 Sept. 1964.

Kerr, Walter. The New York Herald Tribune, 2 Dec. 1965.

Marriott, R. B. The Stage, 25 March 1965.

Rosselli, John. The Guardian, 1 Jan. 1965.

Rutherford, Malcolm. The Spectator, 213 (18 Sept. 1964), 369-370.

The Scotsman, 21 May 1965.

Sheed, Wilfrid. The Commonweal, 83 (24 Dec. 1965), 375.

Shulman, Milton. The Evening Standard, 18 Mar. 1965.

Taubman, Howard. The New York Times, 17 Feb. 1965.

Taylor, John Russell. Encore (Nov.-Dec. 1964), pp. 43-46.

Trussler, Simon. Tribune, 26 March 1965.

Wallace, Philip Hope. The Guardian, 10 Sept. 1964.

Watts, Richard. The New York Post, 1 Dec. 1965.

Young, B. A. The Financial Times, 30 Aug. 1965.

A Patriot For Me

Barnes, Clive. The New York Times, 7 Oct. 1969.

Brien, Alan. The Sunday Telegraph, 4 Apr. 1965.

Bryden, Ronald. The New Statesman and Nation, 70 (9 July 1965), 58.

Clurman, Harold. The Nation, 201 (20 Dec. 1965), 508-509.

_____. The Nation, 209 (27 Oct. 1969), 451-452.

The Coulsdon and Purley Times, 25 Mar. 1965.

Darlington, W. A. The Financial Times, 1 July 1965.

Gilman, Richard. Newsweek, 59 (13 Dec. 1965), 90.

Gross, John. Encounter, 25 (Oct. 1965), 42.

Hewes, Henry. The Saturday Review of Literature, 52 (14 Aug. 1965), 45.

_____. The Saturday Review of Literature, 52 (18 Oct. 1969), 20.

Kretzmer, Herbert. The Daily Express, 1 July 1965, p. 4.

Kroll, Jack. Newsweek, 74 (18 Oct. 1969), 129.

Levin, Bernard. The Daily Mail, 1 July 1965.

McCarthy, Mary. The Observer Review, 4 July 1965, p. 17.

_____. The Observer Review, 25 July 1965, p. 26.

Marriott, R. B. The Stage, 9 July 1965.

Masters, Anthony. Plays and Players, 21 (June 1974), 54. (Revival)

Smith, Warren Sylvester. The Christian Century, 80 (1 Sept. 1965), 1066-1067.

Tynan, Kenneth. The Observer Review, 18 July 1965, p. 261. (A Reply to Mary McCarthy)

Wardle, Irving. The Times, London, 1 July 1965.

A Bond Honoured

Anderson, Lindsay. The Times, London, 24 June 1966, p. 13d.

Betjeman, John. The Times, London, 18 June 1966. (Letter)

Brien, Alan. The Sunday Telegraph, 12 June 1966.

Jones, Mervyn. Tribune, 19, 26 Aug. 1966.

MacFayden, Joanna. The Times, London, 10 June 1966. (Letter)

Marriott, R. B. The Stage, 9 June 1966.

The Times, London, 7 June 1966, p. 149.

_____. London, 8 June 1966.

Wardle, Irving. New Society, 16 June 1966, pp. 22-23.

Weightman, John. *Encounter*, 27 (Aug. 1966), 145-147.

Time Present

The British Weekly, 27 June 1968.

The Cambridge News, 9 Aug. 1968.

The Daily Telegraph, 26 May 1968.

The Dorking Advocate, 19 July 1968.

Hamilton, Iaian. *The Times Educational Supplement*, 14 June 1968.

Hobson, Harold. *The Sunday Times*, 21 July 1968.

Hurren, Kenneth. *What's On*, 19 July 1968.

Jebb, Julian. *The Financial Times*, 8 Aug. 1968.

Kingsten, Jeremy. *Punch*, 254 (5 June 1968), 825.

Lawson, Nigel. *The Spectator*, 221 (19 July 1968), 97-98.

Lewis, Peter. *The Daily Mail*, 12 July 1968.

Spurling, Hilary. *The Spectator*, 220 (31 May 1968), 752.

The Hotel in Amsterdam

Bryden, Ronald. *The Observer Review*, 7 July 1968.

French, Philip. *The New Statesman and Nation*, 76 (12 July 1968), 59-60.

Hobson, Harold. *The Christian Science Monitor*, 7 Aug. 1968, p. 12.

Kretzmer, Herbert. *The Evening Standard*, 4 July 1968.

London Magazine, 9 (Sept. 1968), 102-106.

Maxwell, Robert. *The Scotsman*, 6 July 1968.

Trewin, J. C. Illustrated London News, 253 (13 July 1968), 41.

Wardle, Irving. The Times, London, 4 July 1968, p. 113.

Wells, John. The Spectator, 221 (12 July 1968), 61-62.

West of Suez

Chapman, Don. The Oxford Mail, 21 Sept. 1971.

Dawson, Helen. The Observer Review, 22 Aug. 1971.

De Jongh, Nicholas. The Times, London, 7 July 1971.

Hillgate, Jason. What's On in London, 27 Oct. 1971.

Hobson, Harold. The Christian Science Monitor, 21 Aug. 1971, p. 7.

_____. The Sunday Times, 10 Oct. 1971.

Holland, Mary. Plays and Players, 19 (Oct. 1971), 38-40.

Kretzmer, Herbert. The Daily Express, 18 Aug. 1971, p. 13.

Lambert, J. W. The Sunday Times, 22 Aug. 1971.

Lewis, Peter. The Daily Mail, 7 Oct. 1971.

Marcus, Frank. The Sunday Telegraph, 10 Oct. 1971.

Time, 98 (30 Aug. 1971).

Walker, John. The Paris Herald Tribune, 21 Aug. 1971.

Wardle, Irving. The Times, London, 18 Aug. 1971, p. 8.

_____. The Times, London, 7 Oct. 1971.

Weightman, John. Encounter, 37 (Nov. 1971), 56-58.

A Sense of Detachment

Arts Commentary. British Broadcasting Company, 8 Dec. 1972.

Billington, Michael. The Guardian, 7 Dec. 1972.

Birnbaum, Jessie. Time, 100 (25 Dec. 1972), 36.

Brustein, Robert. The Observer Review, 17 Dec. 1972, p. 32.

Bryden, Ronald. The Observer Review, 10 Dec. 1972.

_____. Plays and Players, 20 (Feb. 1973), 36-37.

Hobson, Harold. The Sunday Times, 10 Dec. 1972.

_____. The Christian Science Monitor, 15 Dec. 1972.

Lambert, J. W. Drama, 108 (April 1973).

Nightingale, Benedict. The New Statesman and Nation, 84 (8 Dec. 1972), 875.

Peter, John. The Times Educational Supplement, 15 Dec. 1972.

Trussler, Simon. Tribune, 15 Dec. 1972.

Watch It Come Down

Billington, Michael. The Guardian, London, 25 Feb. 1976.

Brien, Alan. Plays and Players, 23 (April 1976), 24-26.

Cushman, Robert. The Observer Review, 29 Feb. 1976.

Ellsom, John. The Listener, 95 (4 Mar. 1976), 279.

Hobson, Harold. The Sunday Times, 29 Feb. 1976.

Lambert, J. W. The Sunday Times, 22 Feb. 1976.

_____. Drama, 121 (Summer 1976), 40-43.

Marcus, Frank. The Sunday Telegraph, 29 Feb. 1976.

Marriott, R. B. The Stage, 29 Feb. 1976.

Shorter, Eric. The Daily Telegraph, 25 Feb. 1976.

Shulman, Milton. The Evening Standard, 27 Feb. 1976.

Wardle, Irving. The Times, London, 25 Feb. 1976.

Young, B. A. The Financial Times, 25 Feb. 1976.

ABOUT THE AUTHOR

Herbert Goldstone is Professor of English at the University of Connecticut where he has taught courses in Drama, Twentieth Century British Literature, and Modern Irish Writers, along with those in Poetry, Black American Writers, and Creative Writing. He has published a critical study of Sean O'Casey entitled In Search of Community: The Achievement of Sean O'Casey (Dublin and Cork: The Mercier Press, 1973). He has also edited A Casebook on The Cherry Orchard; with Irving Cummings, he has done a textbook, Poets and Poems; and with Irving Cummings and Thomas Churchill a textbook on short fiction, Points of Departure.

Mr. Goldstone did his undergraduate work at the University of Chicago and received his Ph.D. from Harvard in 1951.